Between Yafeth and Shem

American University Studies

Series V
Philosophy

Vol. 21

PETER LANG
New York · Bern · Frankfurt am Main · Paris

Ze'ev Levy

Between Yafeth and Shem

On the Relationship between Jewish and General Philosophy

PETER LANG
New York · Bern · Frankfurt am Main · Paris

Library of Congress Cataloging-in-Publication Data

Levy, Zeev.
  Between Yafeth and Shem.

  (American university studies. Series V,
Philosophy ; vol. 21)
  Includes indexes.
  1. Philosophy, Jewish.   2. Philosophy.   I. Title.
II. Series: American university studies.   Series V,
Philosophy ; v. 21.
  B154.L47 1987   181'.06   86-20182
  ISBN 0-8204-0373-3
  ISSN 0739-6392

CIP-Kurztitelaufnahme der Deutschen Bibliothek

Levy, Ze'ev:
Between Yafeth and Shem : on the relationship
between Jewish and general philosophy / Ze'ev
Levy.—New York ; Bern ; Frankfurt am Main ;
Paris : Lang, 1987.
  (American university studies : Ser. 5,
  Philosophy ; Vol. 21)
  ISBN 0-8204-0373-3

NE: American university studies / 05

© Peter Lang Publishing, Inc., New York 1987
All rights reserved.
Reprint or reproduction, even partially, in all forms such as
microfilm, xerography, microfiche, microcard, offset strictly
prohibited.

Printed by Weihert-Druck GmbH, Darmstadt, West Germany

TABLE OF CONTENTS

Foreword

Part One	The Quiddity of Philosophy	1
Ch. 1	Definition of general and Jewish concepts of Philosophy and of Philosophizing	3
Ch. 2	Philosophy and Art; The attitude to the heritage of the past	9
Ch. 3	Philosophy and Science: "Knowledge" in general and Jewish philosophy	13
Ch. 4	"Knowing ignorance" and "Learned ignorance"	17
Ch. 5	Philosophic classification	21
Ch. 6	Philosophy's goal – theory or practice – in general and Jewish thought	25
Ch. 7	The value and usefulness of philosophy	35
Part Two	Philosophy and Religion	41
Ch. 8	Identical in content, different in form?	43
Ch. 9	Knowledge versus encounter	47
Ch. 10	Religion and science	51
Ch. 11	Logical, Aesthetic, Moral and Religious Utterances	57
Ch. 12	The copula in religious language	63
Ch. 13	Faith and Belief	67
Ch. 14	Knowledge versus Faith; Autonomy versus Heteronomy	75
Ch. 15	Philosophy of religion and theology in Jewish and general philosophy	79
Ch. 16	What is Jewish theology?	83

Part Three	What is Jewish Philosophy?	95
Ch. 17	Jewish Philosophy and the Philosophy of Judaism	97
Ch. 18	Is there a Jewish philosophy? A few preliminary assumptions	103
Ch. 19	What is Jewish Philosophy?	107
Ch. 20	An attempt at summary: Jewish philosophy as the philosophy of Judaism	127
Part Four	Fundamental Problems in Jewish Philosophy	133
Ch. 21	Some basic problems in didactics	135
Ch. 22	The sources of inspiration of Jewish philosophy	139
Ch. 23	Is there Jewish philosophy in the Bible?	141
Ch. 24	Medieval and modern influences on Jewish philosophy	147
Ch. 25	Extra-philosophical motives for philosophizing; in Jewish philosophy in particular	151
Ch. 26	Christian Dogma and Judaic Law	159
Ch. 27	The Doctrine of the Two Truths - The version of Sa'adja Gaon	163
Ch. 28	The two meanings of the Torah - Exoteric and Esoteric - Maimonides' version	165
Ch. 29	The difference between the esoteric dimension in Jewish medieval philosophy and that in the philosophy of Spinoza and the modern era	173
Ch. 30	Revelation, prophecy and miracles in Jewish philosophy - tradition versus modernity	179
Ch. 31	Reason and revelation - two faculties of cognition	187
Ch. 32	Revelation in Judaism versus revelation in other religions	191

Part Five	Medieval and modern Jewish philosophy compared - differences and changes	193
Ch. 33	The centrality of medieval Jewish philosophy	195
Ch. 34	Segregation in the Ghetto and cultural-spiritual isolation	197
Ch. 35	From dependence on authority to independent thought	199
Ch. 36	Liberation from submission to religious commandments and Revelation in a new light	201
Ch. 37	New subjects for study: Political science and philosophy of history - their significance for Jewish thought	203
Ch. 38	The shift in content: from election to mission	207
Ch. 39	Change in the conception of Exile	211
Ch. 40	Changes in the Messianic idea	213
Ch. 41	The causes for the decline of the historical approach in philosophy as reflected in Jewish Thought	217
Notes		219
Index of Names		239
Index of Subjects		247

Foreword

This book is not intended to serve as an introduction or guide to Jewish philosophy. Its purpose is to clarify in an ordered manner the system of relations between Jewish and general philosophy. In the process, the claim of Jewish philosophy to the status of an independent discipline within the framework of general philosophy will be considered. This subject is dealt with, in the main, in Section Three of this work.

The first two sections deal for the most part with subjects pertaining to general philosophy, such as the quiddity of philosophy, its function and goals, and the links between philosophy and religion, as revealed in the writings of both Jewish and non-Jewish philosophers. The final two sections are devoted to an inquiry into certain basic problems inhering in Jewish philosophy and into the changes that have taken place in their development over the years, with emphasis on the reciprocal relations between Jewish and general philosophy.

Generally speaking, this study is made from the vantage point of modern, contemporary Jewish and general philosophy. However, it has been impossible to ignore the significance of medieval Jewish philosophy for Jewish thinking over the generations, first and foremost the doctrine of Maimonides. Jewish philosophy was in full flower in the period between the 9th and 15th Centuries. Most of the problems posed by modern Jewish philosophers received their fundamental formulation in that era. Accordingly, the present work deals with the nature of Jewish philosophy systematically rather than from a historical perspective.

Philosophical speculation is inevitably bound up with this work by its very nature. Consequently, the author's attitude adopted toward the matters under discussion, their evaluation and the positions taken with regard to them quite naturally reflect his philosophical preferences, even his personal taste. The author assumes sole responsibility for them.

I owe special thanks to my colleague, Dr. Meir Ayalli, who encouraged me to write this book, and who made significant improvements in the text. His contribution was most important in matters dealing with the Sayings of the Sages, that are scattered throughout the text. Of course, whatever errors remain, if there are such, are my sole responsibility. I also wish to thank Haya Argaman who read the manuscript and offered valuable comments. And finally, I wish to express my thanks to the team of Kibbutz Kfar Blum who prepared the English translation of this book, to the Research Authority of the University of Haifa for its support, and to Heather, Danielle and Angela for their painstaking care in producing the word-processed version of the book.

I wish to dedicate this book to the memory of Professor Moshe Schwarcz, teacher and friend, who regarded the combining of Jewish thought with that of general philosophy and culture as a matter of paramount importance. He saw in it the natural path of the development of philosophical discourse in Israel. His scholarly work, lamentably cut short by his untimely death, gives ample witness of the quality of his thought.

Z.L.
Hama'apil, Spring 1986

PART ONE: THE QUIDDITY OF PHILOSOPHY

CHAPTER ONE
Definition of General and Jewish Concepts of Philosophy and of Philosophizing.*

Philosophy is perhaps the sole discipline among the sciences, where a consideration of its quality and of its nature constitutes a part of its fundamental concerns. According to Plato and Aristotle, it was the Pythagoreans who claimed that Heraclitus, the "gloomy" sage of Ephesus, was the first to employ the term philosopher: "Men that love wisdom must be acquainted with very many things indeed."(1) According to this ancient version, Sophia (Wisdom) is a term that is applicable to God alone. As far as man is concerned, the most that he can aspire to is to be a friend or a lover of wisdom, Philosophia. [In Greek, philos means "love" and sophia means "wisdom."] Thus Plato indicated: "Wise, I may not call them; for that is a great name which belongs to God alone - lovers of wisdom or philosophers is their modest and befitting title."(2) In a similar manner he comments in the Symposium: "No God is a philosopher or seeker after wisdom, for he is wise already."(3) The important Jewish philosopher of the Renaissance, Don Judah Abarbanel, the son of Rabbi Isaac Abarbanel, also commented on the subject in his book, Dialoghi d'Amore (1535), written in the form of a dialogue between a man and a woman, called Philon and Sophia. [Abarbanel wrote the book in 1502; however it was published about thirty years later.]

Thus the very etymology of the word implies its essential aspect of continued striving for wisdom, for knowledge, for truth. This, in contradistinction to the popular perception of the philosopher as the possessor of wisdom. The philosopher merely seeks to "philosophize." This term, which in present-day conversation is often met with derision ("For goodness sake, stop philosophizing"), in its early usage expressed the aim of the philosopher precisely. It was in the latter fashion that the Jewish philosophers of the Middle Ages understood the meaning of the term. The term "philosopher" already appears in the Talmud and is primarily used to denote wise men among the Gentiles, who concerned themselves with theological questions. 'The elders in Rome were asked by philosophers: "If (your God) has no desire for idolatry, why does he not abolish it?"'(4) The Sages tended to call Greek Philosophy "Wisdom," to differentiate it from the "Law", which is reserved for Israel: "Should a person tell you there is wisdom among the nations, do not believe it."(5) The Sages were not too sympathetic to philosophic investigations, as may be gathered from the tale of the "four who entered the Pardess" (v.ff.) The word "philosophize" first appears in Jewish thought in the works of Maimonides:

> My speech in the present Treatise is directed, as I have mentioned, to one who has philosophized and has knowledge of

---

* Matters discussed in this chapter deal only with those subjects that are relevant to this work. They are not meant to be an all-encompassing methodical description of philosophy, nor even an introduction to philosophy.

the true sciences, but believes at the same time in the
matters pertaining to the Law and is perplexed as to their
meaning because of the uncertain terms and the parables.(6)

In a like vein, Shem-Tov Falakeira (who is known for his book <u>Moreh HaMoreh</u>
(1280), a commentary on the works of Maimonides), wrote in his essay <u>Reshit
Hochma</u>: [This essay is not particularly original. For the most part it
contains the thoughts of others, chiefly those of Al-Farabi, whom Maimonides
considered to be the greatest Arab philosopher.]

And this is known as simple wisdom. And the great wisdom is
called philosophical wisdom. Its meaning is the love of the
great wisdom, and who acquires it is known as the
philosopher. He is the lover of the great wisdom and this
wisdom includes all wisdom and all perfection, and is called
the wisdom of wisdoms, the mother of wisdoms, and the skill
of skills.(7)

Falakeira's formulations were undoubtedly influenced by Aristotle's
definition of philosophy as "the queen of sciences." (v.ff.)

The view that philosophy, in essence, is a search for wisdom is to be
found in the works of most philosophers throughout the ages. G.E. Lessing
who, together with Moses Mendelssohn, was one of the foremost proponents of
the 18th century Enlightenment in Germany, wrote: "Were the Lord to give me
the choice of seeking after the truth or the truth itself, I would choose
the search, for only He is worthy of the truth itself."(8) The
existentialist philosopher Soren Kierkegaard adopted this concept, as
evidenced by his quoting the foregoing words of Lessing.(9) Kant, as well,
expressed the same thought, in secular terms, when he wrote at the end of
his <u>Critique of Pure Reason</u>: "Mathematics, therefore, alone of all the
sciences <u>(a priori)</u> arising from reason, can be learned; philosophy can
never be learned, save only in historical fashion; as regards what concerns
reason, we can at most learn to philosophize."(10) Hegel's Dialectic, its
speculative aspect apart, is also based on the idea of search and approach.
The history of philosophy reflects the process of the concretization of the
spiritual idea, which becomes increasingly knowledgeable. According to
Hegel, reason reigns supreme in History, including the History of
Philosophy, even though the great historical personages were unaware of its
content and purpose. Hegel's view is opposed to that of Aristotle, who
regarded History as Philosophy's foe, because it lacks the rational order of
Nature. Law rules in Nature, according to Aristotle, whereas History is
guided by chance. Hegel rejected this idea. He held that Absolute Truth
does exist, and at every given historical stage the philosopher makes his
contribution toward its achievement. There is a certain parallelism
between Hegel's philosophical position and that of the Biblical concept,
that God reveals Himself in History and that all historical events are
necessary revelations of the Divine Will. Therefore, the Bible is clearly a
history book that seeks to express general assumptions through detailed

descriptions. Greek philosophy argued for chance, whereas the Bible predicates an Omniscient Divinity. Generally, Hegel distinctly preferred Greek philosophy to the Jewish religion, but as to the revelation of the Idea in History he adopted the Jewish view, however reluctantly.

In essence it was our purpose here to emphasize the concept of the <u>approach</u> to the Absolute. In the thinking of the Jewish philosopher Hermann Cohen, the dominant theme is that only the search for truth constitutes the truth <u>per se</u>. Because of this position, Cohen's philosophy has been described as "Pan-Methodism."

It is of value to note that the modern orthodox Jewish philosopher Rabbi Ya'akov Moshe Harlap, a pupil and follower of Rabbi Kook, pursuant to his studies in Maimonides's philosophy, expressed an idea very similar to that of Lessing. "Desire is more purpose than attainment. This is made especially clear from Maimonides's explanation that there is no purpose other than the Holy One - the basis of a goal is only a search for purpose.... We must prefer the search for wisdom to its attainment...."(11)

This view of philosophy as a search for truth but not necessarily its attainment is doubtless valid in its general outline, and expresses man's healthy feeling, that he cannot attain "Absolute Knowledge." [Hegel did not remain faithful to the guideline of his dialectic. He thought that by his philosophy he did attain Absolute Knowledge, and that antecedent philosophies were mere way-stations on the road to the final goal. He believed to have succeeded where his predecessors had failed.] In our times, some of the conclusions about the relations between philosophy and truth, based on this feeling, have created a number of problems. For example, Bertrand Russell thought that, apart from the realm of formal logic, philosophy's task was to ask questions, and not to provide answers. Indeed, he correctly added that the formulation of questions and their proper presentation was no small undertaking.

> Philosophy, if it cannot <u>answer</u> so many questions as we could wish, has at least <u>the power</u> of <u>asking</u> questions which increase the interest of the world, and show the strangeness and wonder lying just below the surface, even in the commonest things of daily life.(12)

In opposition to Russell, there are many philosophers today, who cast doubt on philosophy's ability to formulate questions, that are indeed novel or original. They argue that all the questions that are being asked have already been proposed. All that remains for philosophy or, more properly, for philosophers, to do is to offer better answers than have been heretofore given. Thus R.L. Lotze, as early as the second half of the 19th century, argued that, after 2500 years of development, philosophy can no longer make a contribution of propounding new and original thoughts; therefore, it should restrict itself mainly to aspiring to greater preciseness. This aim, nowadays, is dominant in Analytic and Linguistic Philosophy, principally in the English-speaking world. For example, H. Reichenbach, closely associated with the famous Vienna Circle, in his book, The Rise of Scientific Philosophy (1951), denounced the traditional philosophy for purporting to provide answers based on hasty and naive generalizations, before there was any possibility of giving "correct answers", to wit, "scientific explanations."(13) However, this charge is only partially correct. Even though, from a methodological point of view, philosophy's purpose is to pose questions, it is still impermissible to avoid the search for answers by deferring it to an indefinite future. Even from the point of view of public morality alone, such a deferment is not to be tolerated. It is simply nothing less than refraining from doing one's duty.

The duty of the philosopher, throughout the ages and at present, as well, is to take a stand with reference to the problems with which he deals, including intellectual problems that engage his interest as a philosopher. The Jewish philosopher Franz Rosenzweig expressed this thought well by emphasizing the actual aspect of "the concept of the new philosophy... that makes philosophizing at all possible after Hegel:... in lieu of the old-type philosopher, professional, non-personal, no more than the official spokesman for the History of Philosophy, which is, of course, one-dimensional, there comes a type of philosopher, very personal in his approach, a type possessed of a world view - and even of a point of view - of crucial significance."(14)

Furthermore, without having experienced giving answers that turn out to be wrong, one can never arrive at better ones. This is the method of trial and error. Philosophy, like other theoretical sciences, is based on the assumption that sometimes it is preferable to err after having made investigations, experiments and tentative intellectual assumptions, than to be correct on the basis of faith alone. In consequence, one understands the extreme importance that is assigned to the term "critique" in its philosophical sense. Russell even held that "The essential characteristic of philosophy, which makes it a study distinct from science, is criticism."(15)

This whole complex of problems has far-reaching implications, primarily on the methodological plane and on the present-day philosophy of science. Hence, K. Popper's view of "conjectures" and "refutations", namely, a conjecture must be capable of refutation before it can be considered scientific, and the opposing notion of T. Kuhn as to the causes and structure of scientific revolutions, are both derived, in one way or another, from the critico - methodological concept mentioned above.(16) However, there is no point in expanding on the subject here. It will suffice to cite two examples from the realm that is close to the present study. When Spinoza, in his Theologico-Political Treatise dealt with Biblical criticism based on philosophic criteria, or when he wrote Compendium Grammatices Linguae Hebraeae,(18) he expressed ideas and opinions largely incompatible with the findings of modern, scientific Biblical research or with the criteria of modern linguistics. Yet these two branches of science could not have achieved their present status were it not for Spinoza's pioneering contribution in his time, and were it not for the many other scholars whose works subsequently underwent criticism. It was in this spirit, that Moses Mendelssohn, in taking issue with the philosophical ideas of Thomas Hobbes, wrote: "We forget the painful effort that was needed to clear a trail through the wilderness."(19)

From what has been said up to this point it would follow that philosophic investigation is organically linked with the thinking of the past, as embodied in the classic phrase <u>Philosophia perennis</u> (first used in 1540), namely, that duration and <u>continuity are to be</u> found in philosophy. The philosophical trend here mentioned - Analytic Philosophy in its various versions - leans toward the same conclusion that Spinoza reached in his day: a contempt for the history of philosophy as a factor in present philosophizing. [For instance, Spinoza announced quite arbitrarily that until he gave his attention to political philosophy, "philosophers have never conceived a theory of politics which would be turned to use."(20)]

CHAPTER TWO

PHILOSOPHY AND ART
The Attitude to the Heritage of the Past

In connection with the subject at hand, it is refreshing to note a certain similarity between philosophy and art. For instance, art suffers less from obsolescence than does technology. A flight-engineer is not required to learn the techniques of wagon manufacture. A technician need not be acquainted with the history of technology (although it might be good for him for other reasons). The situation is different in art, both from the aspect of the value of the work of art, and from the aesthetic response of the viewer or reader. Pleasure from viewing a painting by Picasso does not derogate from the pleasure of looking at a Rembrandt. The pleasure to be derived from reading a book by Thomas Mann or Hemingway is no obstacle to our enjoying the works of Homer, Shakespeare, and Goethe. The aesthetic response of the Israeli reader to the works of Bialik, Shlonsky, Amihai and other modern writers of Hebrew is no impediment to his appreciation of the poetry of Judah Halevy, Shlomo Ibn Gabirol and the other bards of the Golden Age of Spain. It is understood, of course, that our concern is not with the taste and preferences of the individual. Possibly this phenomenon is somewhat less striking in the realm of literature and poetry than in that of the plastic arts, since an intellectual effort is required before one can properly understand words that have been written hundreds of years ago, a condition precedent for an aesthetic response. Therefore, it is no accident that non-obsolescence is most prominent in children's literature. Above all, this phenomenon is especially striking in the case of music, where classical and modern creations are both acceptable, and very often performed in a single concert.

Without pursuing a more detailed investigation into the field of aesthetics, we may note that, unlike what occurs in technology, old values in art do not make way for new ones. Indeed, the modern painter will not paint in the same mode as Rembrandt, the modern Hebrew poet will not write as did Judah Halevy, nor will the modern writer of Hebrew attempt to imitate the style of the Bible,(21) but the creations of Homer, Shakespeare, Goethe, Halevy, Rembrandt, Beethoven and the like retain their specific value, with no loss to their aesthetic worth.

The same is true of philosophy. There is no possibility, indeed, there is no point in carrying on a philosophical discourse as did Plato, Spinoza, Hegel, Maimonides, Judah Abarbanel or Krochmal. However, modern philosophy does not cease to take an interest in Ancient and Classical philosophy. The contrary is true. The speculations of the great philosophers of the past continue to shed light on the problems that engage modern philosophy in its varying trends and branches. They have not become obsolete. They do not belong to the History of Philosophy, but to Philosophy, hic et nunc. Since this assumption is of fundamental significance for Jewish philosophy, in which ties to the past constitute a prime function, it might be of value to elaborate somewhat on this theme.

In philosophy, the <u>diachronic dimension</u> (which exists in the flow of time) and the <u>synchronic dimension</u> (which exists at one and the same time) are interlinked. One must not ignore the historical dimension of philosophy, the tracing of the roots and the development of various ideas and concepts; nevertheless, the crucial dimension is the systematic - theoretical one. The history of philosophy is part of philosophy, or, as Hegel put it, philosophy and the history of philosophy are one and the same. Even though Hegel's speculative method was a matter of controversy even in his time, and is more so today, and even though no authority is prepared to accept his radical idealism unqualifiedly, yet the essence and vitality of his methodological conclusions, as implied in identifying philosophy with its history, continue to have force. The constructive foundation of this view is actualized in the term <u>Aufhebung</u>, which Hegel chose because of the three distinct meanings the word has in German: 1) negation, to dispose of; 2) existence, preservation; 3) lifting, raising. This is a key term in understanding Hegel's dialectic view of the subject. In the development of philosophy over the years, every philosopher embodies a certain stage of the idea on its way to the attainment of absolute truth, and thus makes his contribution to the perfection of the idea. Undoubtedly, the kernel must be preserved, but one must discard from the idea the elements that have failed to stand the test of theoretical criticism and have become misleading and superfluous. Of course, it is not sufficient merely to engage in selection, to prune away the dead matter, though it is important in itself, if thereby no new, original speculative contribution has been made. Therefore, in Hegel's view, the essence is to raise the idea to a higher level by virtue of the philosopher's original thinking and to bring it closer to the longed-for truth. This is what Hegel called the concretization of the idea, namely, making it more and more familiar. Our reservation as set forth above, following Rosenzweig's philosophical perspective concerning the Hegelian method of turning the philosopher into a tool at the disposal of the idea at all levels of its development, here receives affirmative meaning, methodologically speaking. "Science is enriched by its innovations, but it also preserves the old, to the extent that the old has been tested and found satisfactory."(22)

Perhaps the most important conclusion to be drawn from Hegel's philosophy is that the truth cannot be reduced to a simple sentence. Every philosophic system is a kind of small brick laid in erecting the structure. True, every philosopher errs in thinking that the whole truth is embodied in his theory, but such error should not result in the total rejection of his view. The truth is a totality to which every philosopher throughout the ages has made an indispensable contribution. The above concept, however, is beset with certain dubious aspects, that arise from the speculative nature of Hegel's theory. Every new level, "higher" than its predecessors, i.e., coming later in time, is more reliable. Even if all the preceding levels were incomplete, they were necessary, and each contributed its share to the final concept of the entire truth. However, it is not our immediate task to evaluate the speculative aspects of the foregoing concept. Certainly, it is not for us to deal with the question as to whether Hegel's presumptuous claim, that his philosophy attains absolute knowledge and puts an absolute end to the dialectic, is compatible with his own scheme of history. However, it was important to stress that the above outlook was based on respect for the early philosophers and their original contributions. Each of them "opens for us a window to the truth."(23)

But, as previously noted, the above mentioned concept was bitterly opposed by a number of philosophers, especially existentialists, among them Franz Rosenzweig. They were not prepared to turn the philosopher into a mere tool of the Idea (v. supra), to a part of a philosophic system, possessed of universal objectivity and independence. Therefore it is necessary that the philosopher be "a man who philosophizes not as a part of the continuum of the history of philosophy, inheriting, as it were, the condition of its problems at the time, but rather 'a man who is dedicated to a search for life.'"(24) The philosophizing man must conquer philosophy,(25) so that it becomes a tool in his hands for achieving his humanity. "We don't want to be philosophers when we are philosophizing, but human beings, and so we must bring our philosophy into the form of humanity."(26)

Incidentally, Hegel's concept also has methodological significance for understanding the relation of the modern Jew to his heritage and tradition. Not every Jew identifies with the path of Orthodoxy, that accepts tradition and the Oral Law as defined by the Shulchan Aruch ["the prepared table", the code of Jewish Law par excellence, written by Joseph Caro, and first printed in Venice in 1565.] - "Follow the example as holy" - with no room for questioning. Nor is the path of the newer trends in Judaism, such as the Conservative and Reform movements, satisfactory, because, by the above-mentioned Hegelian dialectic, they fail to complete the task, since they confine themselves only to two of the three meanings of the Aufhebung: preserving of the traditional contents and commandments, which seem to them valid today, and negating that which they regard as obsolete. In so doing, only the reductionist dimension, and nothing of the broadening, comes into play. Therefore, the major part of the work lies ahead of us, namely, raising the ties to the Jewish heritage to a higher level by devising improved modes of Jewish life rich in contemporary spiritual content. But this is not the place for such an evaluation.

These latter comments, set forth in a schematic fashion, are not meant to be a serious consideration of the religious trends in Judaism. These require a far broader investigation. They are merely meant to furnish a hint of the potential relevance of a philosophic and methodological viewpoint - such as Hegel's in this case - for the specific matters that Jewish philosophy encompasses.

CHAPTER THREE

PHILOSOPHY AND SCIENCE: "KNOWLEDGE" in GENERAL and JEWISH PHILOSOPHY

In the preceding chapter the distinction between technology and its history and philosophy and its history was noted, as was the interesting similarity that exists between art and philosophy and their histories. It is meet to discuss the basic difference between scientific theory and philosophic thinking, as well, despite the clear similarity between them. Originally the Hebrew word "madda" was an expression that bridged the two, as a term that stood for science, knowledge, reason, wisdom: "but hast asked wisdom and knowledge ("madda") for thyself."(27) "Because I endowed you with intellect ("madda") above cattle, beasts and birds."(28)

It was in this sense that medieval Jewish philosophy understood the word. Maimonides assigned the term "Book of Knowledge" to the first section of his Mishne Torah; Judah Halevy wrote, "The essence of success for man is none other than theoretical knowledge."(29) This phenomenon was not limited to the Hebrew language. At least until the days of Hegel, the German word Wissenschaft was understood in a similar manner, namely as "dealing with knowledge." It was only in the 19th century that the present-day meaning came into vogue, especially in the case of the English word "science," (which itself was derived from the Latin scire, "to know"). Science is now taken to refer, in the main, to the disciplines that are known as the "exact sciences, natural sciences," (which began to expand rapidly only after the Renaissance), and, latterly, the "social sciences." [A symptom of this phenomenon is the fact that the Hebrew use of the term "the sciences of the spirit", the German Geisteswissenschaften, and French les sciences humaines find their parallel in the English term humanities, which does not include the word "science", as opposed to "the natural sciences." The use of the word scientist, as well, is of recent origin and has a relatively short history.]

It is imperative to remember that in ancient times and in the Middle Ages "science" had a very different meaning from that in our day. These are two separate concepts despite their common root derivation. The clear differentiation between philosophy and science belongs to the modern era. When the philosopher deals with scientific problems, he does so synoptically; whereas the scientist concerns himself with the particular, the exceptional. The philosopher tends to generalize, refraining from going into detail. The danger inherent in generalization is that human thinking finds it difficult to liberate itself from the "self-evident."

Therefore, despite the historically close relationship between philosophy and the sciences (in the not-so-distant past they were one and the same; more on the subject below), it is impossible to ignore the vital difference between the two in the present. A criterion of truth exists both for scientific theory and philosophic thought. However, when a scientific theory turns out to be false, it loses all value, and is relegated to the archives of the history of science. It has no relevance for present-day science. The theory of phlogiston, for example, that was regarded as valid for more than two hundred years, disappeared, never to return, after A.L.

Lavoisier disproved it at the end of the 18th century. In astronomy, the geocentric theory made way for the heliocentric, which, in turn, has been improved upon since the days of Copernicus. Theoretical science may preserve its status in a limited aspect of reality, as, for example, Newtonian physics, even though its validity for all of reality has been found wanting by the theories of Einstein and of those who followed in his footsteps. Occasionally, two antithetical theories may remain under discussion for a short period, until one emerges as the victor. This is characteristic of "scientific revolutions".(30) However, the overall picture in this matter is completely clear.

Philosophic theory is different. Even if a theory conflicts with, or is regarded with reference to, some other theory, it does not in any way lose its philosophic value and relevance. When a school of philosophy, such as present-day Logical Empiricism, tends to characterize all other philosophical schools of thought as "meaningless" (the term is used in its cognitive sense), these have not disappeared. Logical Empricism has only caused many people to turn from philosophy to science. While the sciences have reaped and are reaping success, philosophy (in the opinion of scientists) has not achieved like esteem. Its answers do not possess the same degree of certainty as do those of science.

Furthermore, it may be assumed that no new texts of early philosophers, such as Plato, will be discovered, even though the eventuality cannot be ruled out. (Just a few years ago a letter of Spinoza's hitherto unknown, came to light.) In a similar way, now and then manuscripts of medieval Jewish writers are discovered and often shed new light on their thought – not to mention the sensational discovery of the Dead Sea Scrolls. But, even barring the possibility that new texts by classical philosophers may turn up, their thought will continue to evoke new interpretations, which often constitute valuable and original contributions to the understanding of the writers' ideas. Not only the new research, but also – and most important – the philosophic discussions about Plato, Aristotle, the Jewish philosophers of the Middle Ages, Descartes, Spinoza, and others are an integral part of modern philosophic activity. [Support for this thesis, among others, was to be found in the 1977 tercentenary of Spinoza's death. It gave powerful impetus to the investigation of the actual significance of various aspects of his philosophy, both by virtue of the numerous national and international conferences that were held and the avalanche of the learned publications that followed in their wake. The same happened in 1982, when the 350th birthday of the great philosopher was commemorated.]

This phenomenon contains an important lesson: in philosophy there is always more than one interpretation. It educates, by its very nature, to modesty and tolerance in intellectual life – to recognizing, in principle, the possibility of differing views and solutions regarding given problems. Let us consider the "Big Three" in medieval Jewish philosophy, Ibn Gabirol, Maimonides and Judah Halevy. They belonged to different schools of thought. The first tended toward Neo-Platonism; the second was an Aristotelian; the third rejected both Plato and Aristotle, and, in fact, had reservations as to the worth of philosophy altogether (even though he himself was an important philosopher). Our philosophic preference may tend toward one of them, but surely we will not discard or reject the other two. It may well be that we will not identify with any of them, yet we are able to appreciate the importance of their contributions to Jewish and general philosophy.

That there exist different and often even contradictory viewpoints, should not bring one to the pessimistic conclusion that: "he that increaseth knowledge increases sorrow."(31) We may well doubt if man's wisdom throughout the past 2500 years of the existence of philosophy has increased any, but there is no doubt that he has increased his knowledge and his understanding, including recognition of the limitations of his knowledge. In the language and in the outlook of the Bible, and, in consequence, in Jewish philosophy of the Middle Ages, the verb "to know" has a unique meaning that contains important philosophical implications. "To know" in Hebrew denotes both spiritual - intellectual and sexual activity, emphasizing the living contact. "And Adam knew Eve his wife."(32) Knowledge is not achieved in solitude.

> The original meaning of the Hebrew verb 'to recognize, to know', in distinction from Western languages, belongs not to the sphere of reflection but to that of contact. The decisive event for 'knowing' in Biblical Hebrew is not that one looks at an object, but that one comes into touch with it. This basic difference is developed in the realm of a relation of the soul to other beings, where the fact of mutuality changes everything. At the center is not a perceiving of one another, but the contact of being, intercourse.(33)

In medieval Jewish philosophy this meaning was attached to the description of man's relation to God. For Maimonides, "loving" God and "knowing" God were synonymous. To the contrary, the Commandment "And thou shalt love thy Lord with all thy heart and all thy soul and all thy might" includes the obligation of knowing the Lord, and so converts philosophy into a religious commandment. What applies to knowledge also applies to learning. One cannot love that which one does not know. In order to gain an understanding of the Deity, one must understand the Universe which He created. Thus, the precondition for knowing the Creator is the understanding of Creation. "The Heavens tell of God's Glory." This view holds for most of the Jewish medieval philosophers until we get to Judah Abarbanel (Leone Ebreo) who begins his book, <u>Dialoghi d'Amore</u>, by entering into a deep philosophic inquiry into the relationship between "desire," "love," and "knowledge." In this entire discourse there is an implication that Judaism, unlike Christianity, has always regarded sex as one more phenomenon of nature. The Sages dealt with sexual relations openly and as a matter of fact, whereas Christianity developed the viewpoint that sex is connected with sin, and incurs guilt. It is certainly not a matter of chance that in some languages the words "innocence" and "virginity" are coupled. The purpose of Judah Abarbanel's book was to elucidate the meaning of Divine Love, but it also includes many investigations and descriptions of love and the sexual life of man and woman. In fact, Part Three of his book (very much longer than the preceding parts)is devoted to the clarification of the meaning of "Divine

Love" in the spirit of "the Knowledge of God." Spinoza's concept "Intellectual Love of God" is derived from Abarbanel. The concept of "cling" in Jewish mysticism reflects, to a large extent, this conceptual tradition.

It is of interest to note that knowledge in Greek philosophy was also bound up with inter-personal contact, and was not understood as the intellectual achievement of the individual. Even its association with sex is not absent. [In Greek the word eran (to love) is derived from the word Horan (to see). Its meaning has been expanded to signify understanding and investigation. (v.ff).]

Socrates compares his philosophical activity to midwifery.(34) Plato emphasizes the maieutic (the midwife-like) character of Socrates in several dialogues, especially in Menon. He seeks, by the artful use of sophisticated questions and answers, to play the widwife in elucidating the truth from the individual whom he has engaged in conversation. From this aspect, the form of the Platonic Dialogue is something more than a literary device. It had a marked influence on the philosophizing of later generations. As is well known, it was a favorite form with the Jewish philosophers, beginning with Judah Halevy and Ibn Gabirol, through Judah Abarbanel, and even Mendelssohn.

CHAPTER FOUR

"KNOWING IGNORANCE" and "LEARNED IGNORANCE"

The main contribution of Socrates in this area is embodied in the concept of "knowing ignorance," which is perhaps the archetype and the paradigm of dialectic thought: knowledge and ignorance bound in mutual embrace. This concept is the direct consequence of his vital contact and conversations with his fellow men, whom he met in the streets of Athens. This is why he declared, as he stood opposite his judges, that he indeed thought himself to be wiser than they. By talking to soldiers, judges, statesmen and others, it became clear to him that they were all of the opinion that they were well versed in their professions, but, since they were unable to answer the questions he set to them, he came to the conclusion that, in fact, they were not. The philosopher is distinguished from the statesmen, poets, artists and others, that is, from all those whom public opinion holds as wise, in that he criticizes both his own ideas and those of others. Here again one encounters the concept of "criticism." The soldier is incapable of defining valor; the judge is unable to define justice, and so on. He, Socrates, at least, is aware that he is ignorant, and, as a result, there exist the challenge and the desire to study and to acquire additional knowledge. The others, because of their false sense of security in their quasi-knowledge, lack motivation and become conservative and dogmatic. [This is a free rendition of the Socratean concept of "consciousness of ignorance." It would be well to read this matter in the original text of Plato's Apology.(35)] Philosophically speaking, this position is vulnerable, because the idea of "knowing ignorance" contains the thought that we have positive knowledge of at least one idea, to wit, that man is incapable of achieving complete knowledge. But this assertion in itself, that the totality cannot be understood, is a metaphysical argument that is not subject to confirmation. What could Socrates base his argument on (which in itself was reasonable and very fetching) concerning man's inevitable ignorance? However, this theoretical obstacle does not in the least diminish the stature of Socrates and Plato as teachers who opposed dogmatism. Even one who does not accept Plato's metaphysical Theory of Forms (Theory of Ideas), or has reservations about some of the totalitarian ideas expressed in The Republic, cannot remain indifferent to his philosophic doctrine. A serious and thorough study of the Platonic Dialogues effects a change in man's approach to intellectual life, and causes him to be more cautious and more critical. That some of the Dialogues, especially the early ones, do not seek to arrive at a clear solution to the philosophical problem under discussion; that even for Socrates victory in a given debate was not always assured; that Plato on occasion leaves to the reader the task of making a decision based on his own judgment - these are matters of great spiritual and pedagogical importance. Both Plato and Aristotle were aware of the problem of aporia, namely the existence of difficult philosophical problems, for which they lacked the appropriate key that would enable them to escape from the complex of contradictions. This concept is an unintended echo of the position adopted by the Jewish Sages. They frequently reached a stalemate in their investigation of problems - not all of which were of a philosophical nature.

In short, they were unable to take a clear-cut stand. (Some hold with one authority, and others with another.)

These matters are of great weight in modern philosophy. Today, more than in the classical period in Greece or in the days of the Sages, there are many problems that still await solution. Thus the concepts of aporia and the stalemate complement the assumptions made at the beginning of this investigation, from an analysis of the source of the term "philosophy." They provide evidence that different opinions and outlooks can dwell alongside each other, without one having the right to claim exclusive ownership of the truth. Awareness of the inherent limitedness of human knowledge ought to educate one to a readiness to listen to the other, to intellectual tolerance, and should urge man on to continue studying and exploring. Philosophy, as opposed to religion (more on this subject below), creates hypotheses, and in this respect, as well, demonstrates its close kinship to the sciences. Philosophy's concern is not with finding the truth, but, as has been stated above, with seeking it. (Cf. Lessing and Hermann Cohen, above.)

Thus the characterizing indicia of philosophy are open-mindedness and the rejection of dogmatism. This does not mean that every philosopher is possessed of these attributes. The main difficulty for the investigator in his scientific and philosophic endeavors lies not in assimilating new ideas, but in his ability to free himself from commonly accepted conventional notions. Thus, the fact that the philosopher and the scientist are thwarted in their search for a reasonable solution of the problem at hand serves to provide them with a motive to maintain their interest, to engage in tireless pursuit, and also to test again accepted truths. This is not a passing need, but an ongoing one. Unlike the words of Ecclesiastes, "he that increaseth knowledge increaseth pain", cited above, the difficulties that challenge man's intelligence should not lead to resignation, but to an awareness that an increase in knowledge leads one ever closer to the truth. In this spirit did the philosopher Nicholas of Cusa, in the transitional period between the medieval era and modern times, convert Socrates' dictum of "knowing ignorance" to "learned ignorance" (the name of his first philosophic work in 1440, Docta Ignorantia.) Socrates stated that he knew that he did not know, whilst Nicholas of Cusa argued that this was not sufficient: Philosophy must know that the very search after truth, which he identified with God, even though human intelligence cannot achieve it, is philosophy's daily bread and essence. Man must not abandon his intellectual effort to approach the truth ever closer. Just as in Socrates, here too one finds at least one piece of a priori knowledge: the existence of truth. Nicholas of Cusa, who was a superb mathematician, illustrated his idea by the example of the polygon and the circle, as illustrated below:

 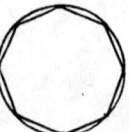

The circle represents the truth, whereas the sides of the polygon are the sides of knowledge, which the human intellect seeks to acquire. Just as the polygon will never coincide with the circle, as every mathematician knows, so will the intellectual knowledge of man never coincide with the truth, which belongs to the Deity, and is identical with Him. However, the greater the number of sides, the greater will be man's knowledge. He will be more learned, and in this fashion will approach nearer to the truth. Furthermore, knowledge is the project of all humans, and does not belong to any single individual. The consolidation of all intellectual achievements furthers man's knowledge.(36)

Three hundred years later the Jewish philosopher Salomon Maimon returned to the example of the polygon and the circle, probably unaware of the work of Nicholas of Cusa. When he dealt with the Ding-an-sich (the "thing-in-itself") of Kant, he spoke of our knowledge as ever approaching the Ding-an-sich, even though its attainment in its totality is forever beyond man's capacity. But our intellect, even though limited, is capable of narrowing the gap between them. In this connection Maimon also used the mathematical example of the polygon approaching the circle, as its sides grow more numerous, "the circle being the thing-in itself with relation to the polygon."(37)

Maimon's and Nicholas of Cusa's outlook is more optimistic than that of the influential German physiologist and philosopher of the preceding century, E. Du Bois-Reymond, who sought to establish the present bounds of our knowledge as the final ones for all future times. In his famous motto "Ignorabimus" ("we shall never know"), he intended to allude essentially to metaphysical problems, such as the quiddity of life, free choice, and so on. However, in addition, he felt that our knowledge of nature is also finite. On the other hand, Maimon and Nicholas never doubted the limitless progress of human knowledge toward the truth, and never set it any a priori boundary.

These hasty remarks concerning the ideas of Socrates, Nicholas of Cusa, Salomon Maimon and Du Bois-Reymond well illustrate the true content of philosophic thought: on the one hand, there is a consciousness of the bounds of human knowledge, for man is finite, but withal there exists a recognition of the infinite capacity of man's spirit to enhance his knowledge.

CHAPTER FIVE

PHILOSOPHIC CLASSIFICATION

Philosophy is made up of several departments or branches. A specific philosopher usually develops a special interest in one or some of these branches, and makes his contribution to their clarification and progress. Some of the fundamental branches in philosophy are: Logic, Epistemology, Ontology, Ethics and Aesthetics. The attitude to the foregoing branches has kept changing throughout the history of philosophy. Aristotle, who laid the ground for the principles of Logic, never regarded it as belonging to philosophy. He regarded it as an instrument (organon) that constituted a condition precedent to philosophic thought. Later, Maimonides expressed a similar opinion. At the beginning of the modern era Francis Bacon attacked deductive logic, namely the process of deriving the particular from the general, which was the Aristotelian legacy. He suggested that it be supplanted by inductive logic, deriving the general from the particular. He gave it the name Novum Organum, a "new instrument." Ontology has also had its ups and downs in the history of philosophy. From the end of the medieval era to the present day it has not been very popular. Aesthetics as a branch of philosophy, as well as the term itself, first saw light in the 17th and 18th centuries. [By the way, Kant still used this word in the first part of his Critique of Pure Reason in an entirely different sense. He used it as an overall term for space and time, as "forms of pure observation."]

In general, the above terms did not always have the same meaning for all philosophers. A prime example is that of epistemology. Philosophy in the English-speaking world, and consequently in Israel as well, regards "epistemology" as denoting an idea that is quite different from the way it is perceived by French philosophy. To this day, in France, epistemology means a critical investigation of principles, hypotheses and conclusions of the various sciences, in order to establish their logical source and to determine their value and their objective validity whereas the Anglo-Saxon term signifies "theory-of-knowledge."

Among the branches of philosophy, metaphysics occupies a unique position. Its meanings are almost as numerous as the number of those who deal with it. Let us enumerate some of the major ones:

1. Originally, metaphysics meant those philosophical problems that Aristotle discussed in his First Philosophy or Theology, and that were later included in the book called Metaphysics, a continuation of his Physics. It discussed such subjects as God, which come after problems of nature. (There is a charming tradition that the book was called Metaphysics because in the famous library in Alexandria it stood behind, or above, the book on Physics. The story is made up of whole cloth.) At any rate, this is the sense of the term in Maimonides' writings too.

2. Metaphysics is a theory about everything that cannot be perceived by the senses.

3. Metaphysics deals with things in themselves, rather than as appearances (Kant and Schopenhauer.)

4. Metaphysics clarifies moral truths, the concept of the "ought," ideals and so on, as an expression of an order of reality that is superior to the order of facts (essentially found in French philosophy).

5. Metaphysics is an intuitive cognizance of the Absolute not achieved by the regular type of theoretical inquiry (Bergson).

6. Metaphysics is the totality of all cognizance, which stems from Pure Reason alone, without dependence on empirical or experimental data (Kant); this definition bears a similarity to the second one above.

Indeed, as has been said, the word has been used very freely as to its connotation. There are those who regard Spinoza's <u>Ethics</u> as constituting his metaphysics rather than his <u>Theologico-Political</u> Treatise which allegedly expressed his political philosophy. Other such distinctions are made, as well.

To the foregoing branches, a number of additional disciplines have been added in the past two hundred years, such as the philosophy of religion, the philosophy of history and political philosophy. In the present century, the philosophy of science and linguistic philosophy have been added to the roster. Two of the branched in the list, metaphysics and ethics, deal with problems that human intelligence sought to deal with through myth and religion before philosophy came into being; whereas logic and epistemology developed within philosophy itself. The differentiation is essentially historical, and is of no significance as far as method is concerned.

From this hasty survey it becomes quite clear that some of the branches of philosophy have great relevance for Jewish philosophy, while others fail to relate to it. Jewish philosophy does not deal particularly with logic, even though traces of that discipline are clearly evident in it. [For instance, the comments of Maimonides on "equivocal terms" and so on (v. ff.), and his small essay on <u>Words of Logic</u>; or the distinction that Judah Abarbanel makes between "love" and "desire" et al.] Nor did Jewish philosophy, generally speaking, deal with aesthetics. Perhaps the interdiction "Thou shalt not make unto thyself any graven image or any likeness of anything"(38) brought about a relative lack of interest in this field, even though its purport was not necessarily directed against art, but rather against idolatry. The sentence that precedes the above reads: "Thou shalt have no other gods before me," and the sentence following is: "Thou shalt not bow thyself down to them, nor serve them; for I, the Lord thy God, am a jealous God ..." The intent, therefore, is clear: a prohibition of worship of idolatrous statues and drawings. Artistic endeavor largely arose out of religious drives, and there were religions that encouraged artistic creations to a great degree. But in the main, artistic endeavor was motivated by extra-religious factors. The Parthenon was not built only as a temple, but as the Greeks themselves averred, as "the glory of the city." Artists whose drawings, statues and music were based on religious motifs, were influenced to no lesser a degree - perhaps even to a greater degree -

by considerations of harmony, of aesthetic completeness. Their creations, more than they were intended to arouse religious uplift, sought to arouse the aesthetic response of the viewer or listener. For this reason not only in Judaism, but also in Christianity, some religious philosophers displayed animosity to art. One need only mention Savonarola, Kierkegaard, and even Tolstoy. They regarded art created for aesthetic purposes as a kind of idolatry. (Kierkegaard characterized an artist who painted a picture of Jesus as a murderer.) However, all the foregoing could not prevent the continuation and flourishing of art. In fact, even in Judaism the interdiction was not maintained very strictly. Yet, as has been mentioned, aesthetic discussions were rare in Jewish philosophy. It should be emphasized that not only Jewish philosophy, but medieval philosophy as a whole, ignored the concept of the beautiful. Aesthetic inquiry, in its strict meaning, first appeared in Judah Abarbanel's Dialoghi d'Amore. From this point of view, it may be said that Abarbanel fulfilled a sort of pioneering function in philosophy, when he called attention to the fundamentals of aesthetics in Plato's philosophy. This was one of the reasons for the remarkable success of his book during the Renaissance. He even pointed out that as a Jew he was turning to the intellectual world of the non-Jew. Moses Mendelssohn in his general philosophic works also gave consideration to problems in aesthetics. But aesthetic deliberation as an inseparable part of Jewish philosophy is only to be found in The Star of Redemption by Franz Rosenzweig. Here myth, language and art constitute the three main criteria by which the matters discussed in the book are measured. Jewish philosophy as a whole focuses its attention primarily on epistemology - reason and revelation as the two faculties of knowing (v. ff.); on ontology - the nature of God, proofs of His existence; and on ethics - man's moral behavior, the reasons for divine commandments, and so on. Of course, metaphysics, whatever its exact definition, was also an inseparable part of Jewish philosophy. All these subjects will be dealt with, at length, in the following chapters. Modern Jewish philosophy pays a good deal of attention to the philosophy of religion and of history, especially in connection with the status and existence of the Jewish people throughout two thousand years of Exile. (On this subject, as well more below.)

CHAPTER SIX

PHILOSOPHY'S GOAL - THEORY or PRACTICE - in GENERAL and JEWISH THOUGHT

The essence of philosophy includes a search for understanding, an enhancement of knowledge, in a word, cognition. But already in the early days of philosophy the question arose: Knowledge for what purpose? "Philosophy" means "the love of wisdom," but as to the purpose of this love there were differences of opinion. In early Greece, philosophy soon split into two major directions:

1. The love of wisdom in the sense of a search for understanding.

2. The love of wisdom in the sense of a search for the good life.

The first approach was concerned with learning about the universe that surrounds us, in knowing the existent. The pre-Socratic philosophers of ancient Ionia began the process, thinkers throughout the ages continued it, and it ends with the several offshoots of Logical Empiricism of our day.

The second approach concentrated upon clarifying man's status in the universe, problems of ethics and the like, and on knowing what should be. Socrates began the pursuit, and it has continued to the present. Many typical representatives of this trend are to be found in the existentialist movement and among those close to it.

The fundamental element of the first goal is reason. By means of it man contemplated the existent, in order to understand it, whereas the basic component of the second goal is the will, that seeks to convert the existent to that-which-will-be. By virtue of his will, man may reform and change the world, in accordance with his capacity or in accordance with what should be.

Not every philosopher must necessarily be classified as belonging to one of these two streams. The division is merely made for schematic and didactic purposes. Many philosophers, perhaps the greatest among them, devoted their philosophic research to problems that touch upon both fields. However, in general it may be said that the foregoing schematic division has left its mark on the history of philosophy throughout the ages. The Neo-Platonist schools, in the general and Jewish philosophy of the Middle Ages, cast their lot with the will, e.g., Shlomo Ibn Gabirol; whereas the Aristotelian schools depended on the intellect. The former displayed greater interest in ethical problems, focusing upon "the good," while the latter centered their inquiry on questions of knowledge, with its focus on "the truth." But, as has been remarked, this is merely a generalization whose function it is to define goals. Aristotle himself, in his Ethics and Politics, devoted penetrating studies to ethical, social and political problems.

In the philosophy of our day, most of the problems that are largely typical of the second goal are concerned with the complex of "relations between science and values," which, in turn, divide up into two areas:

1. The scientific, to wit, the cognitive, status of values.(39)

2. The influence of modern science on human values.

The question concerning the aim of philosophy - is it a search for understanding, i.e., on the theoretical level, or a search for the good life, i.e., on the practical level, inter alia determines not only the nature of the philosophical activity, but also the status and function of the philosopher in society and his attitude to it. Plato differentiated among three types of knowledge:

1. A founding science (like building houses, ships and so on.)

2. An operative science (like politics, law, but also the playing of music.)

3. An observational science (like geometry, astronomy.)

A parallel distinction was made by Aristotle, who discussed three types of activity:

1. Poetics, namely an activity that has a goal, generally of a material nature, that contributes to man's comfort.

2. Praxis, which is also a goal-orientated activity, but is more public in its nature; it contributes to the decorous life of the citizens of the state.

3. Theory, an activity that is substantially set apart from the previous two, because it has no goal. In contradistinction to the other two, it does not seek for a purpose beyond itself. Its purpose lies in the intellectual enjoyment of its very self. Its contribution is to happiness.

We find traces of this distinction between theory and praxis in the Jewish philosophy of the Middle Ages as well. For instance, Judah Halevy writes in the Kuzari:

> When the rational soul turns its attention towards science, its activity is called theoretical reason. If, however, it undertakes to subdue animal instincts, its activity is called guidance, and it assumes the name of practical reason.(40)

Theory, for both Plato and Aristotle, is set apart in that it does not concern itself with the status of the matters that are being observed. By virtue of Theory man succeeds in discovering that which is concealed in things. Observation applies to matters that do not change (or that were thought to be unchanging in those times.) That is what Aristotle termed "Primary Philosophy," while the other two kinds of activity or knowledge apply to matters that change, matters that permit intervention or the making of changes. Therefore knowledge, as regards practice, is a condition precedent, whereas, as regards theory, it is its own purpose. In this fashion Aristotle identifies true happiness with intellectual observation. In the same spirit Maimonides later identified true religion with man's intellectual observation of the Deity, a binding of oneself in love to Him.

However, the emphases that Plato and Aristotle placed on activity and knowledge with reference to values were quite different. According to Plato, knowledge must serve man as a guide to the moral and just life in society and in the State. Since, in the opinion of Socrates and Plato, man commits evil only because of a lack of knowledge, knowledge becomes the foundation of morality. In order that political life be based on morality and justice, it must necessarily be rooted in knowledge. It then follows that the governing of the State should be left to those whose profession is science (knowledge), namely, philosophers. The governing power should not be found in the hands of an aristocracy based on origin or inheritance, nor in the hands of an oligarchy based on wealth and property. Nor is democracy a good form of rule, because it could permit many who are congenitally unfit to participate in the wielding of power. Power should be in the hands of an aristocracy of knowledge, in the hands of men of culture. Plato did not have in mind what are now called technocrats, because they are afflicted by a type of narrowmindedness. At the head of the state there should be men with broad knowledge, capable of encompassing the world and all it contains. The philosopher-king is, in his opinion, the proper solution for society's ills, for realizing its goals, and for governing the ideal state.

Again, as has been previously noted, it is not Plato's political doctrines that are of interest here. Its principles may well arouse sharp criticism and reservations. However, his basic position, that it is the function of the philosopher to acquire wisdom for the good of the public weal, is relevant. Theory is designed to serve Praxis. The most beautiful literary expression of this concept is to be found in the "Parable of the Cave," at the beginning of Book VII of The Republic.(41) The prisoner, representing the philosopher, who escapes from the prison of his underground cave, after reaching the pinnacle of understanding returns to the other prisoners, in order to share with them in the understanding that he has gained and to free them. The pessimistic ending of the allegory, which undoubtedly reflects the trauma he had undergone because of the sad fate of his mentor, Socrates, does not affect his basic position regarding the philosopher as destined for a politico-public mission. As is well known, Plato not only spoke beautifully, but also behaved admirably, when in his old age he did not hesitate to sail three times to Sicily, to establish there, at the request of the ruler of Syracuse, a society based on his ideal model. The failure of the venture, because it was not feasible in the historical circumstances of ancient times, in no way affects the moral lesson of conscience in itself, the readiness to act in order to realize his beliefs.

The influence of the Parable of the Cave on latter general and Jewish philosophy was great. Maimonides, who ordinarily tended to follow Aristotelian philosophy as he learned it from Arab philosophers, explained the Biblical story of Jacob's Ladder in the mode of Plato, to emphasize the social mission of the philosopher.

> For the angels of God are the prophets with reference to whom it is clearly said: And he sent an angel; and an angel of the Lord came up from Gilgal to Bochim (Judges 2:1). How well put is the phrase ascending and descending (Gen. 28:12), in which ascent comes before descent. For after the ascent and the attaining of certain rungs of the ladder that may be known, comes the descent with whatever decree the prophet has been informed of - with a view of governing and teaching the people of the earth.(42)

According to Maimonides, the prophets are the supreme philosophers. [Because of Revelation they (the prophets) are endowed with intuitive knowledge, which is not available to other philosophers, who must learn from them, as, for example, they must learn the principle of the creation of the universe - the creation of something out of nothing.] It is written in the Bible "angels of God were ascending and descending on it." This could not refer to the Ministering Angels, nor to the Aristotelian Intelligences whom he identifies elsewhere in The Guide of the Perplexed as the "Angels of God"(43). The term "angels" (Mal'ahim) in this context could only be a synonym for "messengers." This is not a capricious interpretation, but is in accordance with Biblical usage: "And Israel sent messengers (Mal'ahim) unto Sihon the King of the Amorites."(44) It is not a matter of chance that this socio-political conclusion of Maimonides is in the Platonic spirit. Some scholars, among them S. Pines, commented on the fact that all of Aristotle's work was translated into Arabic except, for some reason, for his Politics, which remained unknown to Arab philosophers. Since Al-Farabi, whom Maimonides regarded as the foremost Arab philosopher, was mightily impressed by Plato's Republic, it is reasonable to assume that he transmitted the principal concepts contained in The Republic to Maimonides. The great Arab philosopher Averroes, who was a contemporary of Maimonides, also interpreted The Republic in the spirit of Al-Farabi, who in turn was influenced by Plato, and comes in this manner to stress the philosopher's (the prophet's) involvement and commitment. It is incumbent upon him to "lead the people of the land." Whether Pines' conclusion, that both The Guide of the Perplexed and Mishne-Torah ("Repetition of the Law") - Maimonides's great Halakhic work, classifying by subjects all the talmudic (and post-talmudic) literature have an explicit socio-political purpose, is right or not, is a question that is beyond the scope of this work.

It may be assumed that the allegorical interpretation of Maimonides and the words of Judah Halevy, both cited above, express the special value that Judaism has always assigned to the practical dimension. (Further comment below.)

Parenthetically, it is of interest to note that the Maharal of Prague (Rabbi Judah Loew), who also emphasized the importance for the sage of being involved in the life of his society (v. ff.), used the image of the ladder to clarify the relationship between "wisdom" (the sciences) and the Law (the

Torah.) In his book, The Wall of the Exile, he writes that the everyday "way of the world" is the ground on which a house stands, but man should aspire to dwell in its uppermost floor, namely the dwelling place of the Law (the Torah.) "Wisdom" is the ladder by which one reaches the top, the Torah. The quality of the ladder may change according to circumstances and time, but the ladder itself remains necessary for the achievement of the goal, which is the Torah. [Incidentally, the figure of the ladder as a means to achieve a theoretical goal is also found in the works of modern philosophers. An example may be cited from Ludwig Wittgenstein's well-known saying, albeit in an entirely different context, that when a man reaches his goal, "He must, so to speak, throw away the ladder after he has climbed up it."(47)] In truth, however, it may be said, that such Platonic influences are few and sporadic in the history of general philosophy. In fact the Aristotelian concept, that, in order to arrive at an overall view of the universe and of man, philosophy must depend on observation, and contemplation, has been dominant for about two thousand years. Among the three distinct activities that Aristotle describes (v. supra), primacy is given to Theory, since it alone has no relation to external aims.

> Evidently they (the earliest philosophers - Z.L.) were pursuing science, in order to know, and not for any utilitarian end ... Evidently then we do not seek it for the sake of any other advantage; but as the man is free, we say, who exists for his own sake and not for another's, so we pursue this as the only free science, for it alone exists for its own sake.(45)

> All the sciences indeed are more necessary than this, but none is better.(46)

The function of the philosopher, as it has been understood for two thousand years, is centered on observation and understanding. The superiority of this activity lies precisely in that it does not seek to interfere with life's practicalities. This is an aristocratic point of view, according to which philosophy becomes a sort of intellectual luxury, suited, by its very nature, to a society based on slavery. Only citizens who are free from work and worry can afford to indulge in philosophy.

A similar view of the purpose of philosophy can be discerned in the thought of one of the greatest philosophers of our time, Bertrand Russell, a man who was very much involved in social and public conflicts. In his opinion, the sciences are of direct use to meet people, however ignorant they may be, whereas philosophy may be of worth to the ordinary man only indirectly.(48) Philosophy is of value only to those who are engaged in it:

> It is exclusively among the goods of the mind that the value of philosophy is to be found; and only those who are not indifferent to these goods can be persuaded that the study of philosophy is not a waste of time.(49)

At times Russell was ambivalent on the subject. He declared more than once that philosophy should concern itself with, and give advice concerning, public affairs, but it may well be that in such cases the personal temperament of Russell the militant man-of-action prevailed over his basic philosophical tenets.

The above concept of identifying philosophy with observation is clearly reflected in the terms used to characterize this activity, both in Hebrew and in the European languages. Perhaps this may be due to the prevailing general view of philosophy. The close linguistic relationship in Hebrew between the words for "observation" and "insight,""contemplation" and "intellect," "theory" and "eye" is very remarkable. The same holds true for the Greek word for "theory," which is derived from theorein, to see, and the Latin words contemplatio and speculatio, that also mean "sight" and "observation." The idea of philosophy's supremacy because of its relation to observation was already present in the thought of the pre-Socratics. The famous allegory about the Olympic Games, sometimes ascribed to the Pythagoreans, tells of the three types of people who attended the games in great numbers: competitors, vendors, and spectators. Whereas the competitors and the vendors come to the Games for defined purposes - the ones seeking glory, and the others a livelihood and profit - the spectators represent the philosophers, whose entire enjoyment is in observation alone, unmixed by concern with other matters. Their entire attention is given to "theory," to "consideration." The word "theory" in Greek also had a religious connotation. The representative whom every Greek city used to send to the Olympic Games and to other public competitions was called Theoros, namely "an observer." Thus, theory was not merely looking, but observing events that were sacred. Later on this meaning of the word was transferred, in philosophy, to the observation of the cosmos.

The perception of philosophy as an occupation for people who have no need to work was opposed to the widely held basic Jewish view in Talmudic times: "Make them (the words of the Law) not ... a spade wherewith to dig."(50) Many scholars of that period supported themselves by physical labor. Maimonides, as well, did not use his endeavors in philosophy, Halacha, or communal affairs as a source of income. At first he was a merchant of precious stones, and thereafter he became a physician. Traces of this characteristically Jewish approach may still be discerned in the case of Spinoza - probably on the unconscious level - who earned his livelihood as a grinder of optical lenses. [Spinoza was certainly also attracted by the scientific problems of optics.] Similarly, Moses Mendelssohn (Mendelssohn himself was a bookkeeper, and later partner of a silk factory] wrote in his book, Jerusalem, in the spirit of the Talmud, that teachers of religion should be compensated only for the time lost from productive endeavor.(51) However, a distinction should be made between two matters bearing on this point: It is one thing to appreciate the superiority of man's philosophic activity, having no purpose other than investigative observation, i.e., the aristocratic aspect of the philosophic endeavor as such, and another thing entirely is to regard philosophy itself as lacking in practical value. Despite the seductiveness of the connection that is made between the "allegory of the Cave" and the well-known Eleventh Thesis of Marx (v. below), the fundamental importance of philosophy, especially in its educational and didactic aspects, lies in its being a domain belonging to theory. It turns man's attention to matters that pertain to the nobility of mind, to considering the problems of the universe and his relations to God. It should not be judged by its purely practical worth in imparting values - moral, social, political, or religious - at all events, not directly. Philosophy should and, indeed, does concern itself with these values, which stem from its very essence. Nevertheless, its major purpose is to be found on the theoretical level: urging man on to consider the problems that touch upon his life and status in the universe and in society, that relate to science, ethics, art and religion. It should foster in him a critical approach, namely, not to accept matters as given. (v. supra. This subject will be mentioned more than once.)

Hence, the dichotomy that exists between emphasizing theory and stressing practice, one that has driven philosophy since its earliest days to now, should not cause us to lose sight of other changes in the views on the aims of philosophy that have taken place over the years. In the beginning, and for a long time thereafter, philosophers regarded the primary function of philosophy in one of two ways. One approach, the Aristotelian, viewed the aim of philosophy as setting forth theses about the universe, man and God. It regarded wisdom as a search for knowledge, or as a guide toward the Good. The second outlook, the Socratic - Platonic, regarded wisdom as a search for the good life, or even as having a function in religious education, an attitude very much in accord with the Jewish view. However, in the ensuing periods, a large part of these functions was transferred to the natural sciences, the social sciences, and religion. (Extended further discussion will be found below.) Thus, during the past two centuries the major subjects of philosophy have been transferred to other disciplines for analysis and criticism. Perhaps this conclusion may cause disappointment to those who expected to find in philosophy adequate and clear answers to the various problems in life that are of concern to them. It may arouse, and actually has aroused, doubts in relation to the validity of rationalism itself which lies at the base of philosophy: what is the use in rationalism, if it failed to prevent the First World War? This was one of the principal themes in the writings of Franz Rosenzweig and the existentialists. The same may be said about the Second World War and the Holocaust that befell the Jewish People. It may feed strong tendencies toward irrationalism, as occurred in the United States after the Vietnam War. Something of the sort took place before our very eyes in Israel in recent years. Rejection of reason contains many perils, since it is likely to foster intellectual blindness and to strengthen movements of religious, national, or even social, fanaticism. Irrational slogans are very effective in inflaming passions. For this reason, while recognizing philosophy's inability to provide final answers, one must emphasize the importance of the function of criticizing, which philosophers are required to fulfil and to educate others to its worth.

Let us return to the dichotomy between Theory and Praxis, which is the crux of this chapter dealing with the aim of philosophy. During the Renaissance, when interest was re-awakened in Plato's teachings, Aristotle's concept concerning observation began to be questioned. A philosopher of Spinoza's calibre, the type of philosopher who sits within the four walls of his small room, weaving the threads of his pure theoretical philosophy, found it ethically and socially imperative to put aside temporarily his work on his <u>Ethics</u> in order to write a topical essay in political philosophy, designed to further his beliefs in a concrete political situation. The <u>Theologico-Political Treatise</u> sought to show that

> Freedom of philosophical investigation is not only possible without damage to God-fearingness and the welfare of the state, but, moreover, it is impossible to extirpate it without extirpating at the same time God-fearingness and the welfare of the state themselves.(52)

This does not refer to the individual preference of the philosopher. It is the philosopher's explicit duty to serve and strengthen political goals and purposes that concern the relations between religion and state.

However, the real philosophical - ideological polarization on the subject occurred at the beginning of the 19th century. Broadly speaking, Hegel continued in the Aristotelian mode.

> Philosophy in any case always comes on the scene too late to give it sense. As the thought of the world, it appears only when actuality is already there cut and dried after its process of formation has been completed ... The owl of Minerva spreads its wings only with the falling of the dusk.(53)

But - in opposition to Hegel - J.G. Fichte, and later A.V. Ciekowski, Moses Hess and Karl Marx took the stand that it was incumbent on philosophy to include the practical dimension as an inseparable component. The new trend received its sharpest expression in Marx's Eleventh Thesis on Feuerbach: "The philosophers have <u>interpreted</u> the world in various ways; the point however is to <u>change</u> it."(54) The main idea of this Thesis, and of those that preceded it, was that henceforth theory turns itself into praxis. Knowing reality and changing it are bound together as one. Thinking, too, is a type of activity, in fact, the activity, which, more than any other, makes man unique. In it man's superiority is revealed. The accepted interpretation of the Thesis, principally by dogmatic Marxist commentators, did a disservice to philosophers. It unwarrantedly placed them in a tendencious light. The great philosopher, by his original thought, contributes in one way or another to the changing of the existing world - often in a very marked manner - and does not leave it as he found it. To the contrary, to accept the abovementioned Thesis, in its simplistic form, might condemn philosophy to a narrow-minded pragmatism. There are things in the universe that cannot be changed and at most can only be interpreted. However, the new interpretation also brings about a change in the perceptions that existed until that time. In order to change, one must know that which requires change. From this aspect alone one cannot claim that the function of the philosopher is at an end. But this is not the place to elaborate on the subject. The basic importance of the Eleventh Thesis is that it serves as a symbol for the crucial change that took place in philosophy about more than one hundred years ago. It was a striking expression of a radical change, not only as to how the function of philosophy was perceived, but as to how the function of the philosopher came to be understood. Among modern philosophers, Franz Rosenzweig successfully described these phenomena. As opposed to "the old type of thought," wherein the abstract concept was at the center of philosophy, the "new type of thought" places at the center the living philosophizing man. (cf. supra comments on "the new type of philosophy" and the "new type of philosopher".)

Thus did the problem of the "involvement" of the philosopher in the life of his society take its place on the agenda of the new era. The Hebrew word for "involvement," in its modern use, first appeared in the philosophical writings of the Maharal of Prague (Rabbi Judah Loew). He based his essay on the Talmudic saying: "Always should the disposition of man be pleasant with people,"(55)using it to explain the reciprocal relationships in ethical consciousness and the solidarity and mutual responsibility that prevails among humans.(56) A man is "involved," when he determines - on the basis of inquiry and thought - to entertain certain values, which he prefers to other values and is prepared to act to advance and execute them. The essence of the problematic character of philosophy that emerges in this connection is the question whether the involvement of the philosopher (or the scientist) can affect the objectivity of his theoretical and scientific endeavors. In other words, what should be the philosopher's system of relations as one who contemplates the objects under his observation? In this respect, modern philosophy returns, on a higher level of sophistication, to the same problem that created the gulf between Aristotle and Plato: If and how to intervene in a process which is being observed.

This topic has another aspect, which Plato and Aristotle ignored completely, and which was not given due attention in the Eleventh Thesis of Marx (even though it was hinted at in several of the prior Theses on Feuerbach). The question is, what is the degree of influence of the various philosophical doctrines on the social, spiritual and political reality, if one does not take into consideration the immediate attitude of the philosophers themselves to this reality. A further question is, whether it is legitimate to hold philosophers responsible post factum for what occurred to their doctrines, especially when such doctrines were exploited to justify vile deeds. The problem becomes even more severe when one considers philosophical doctrines that were used to justify totalitarian ideologies, as, for example, the Nazis did in calling upon the teachings of Hegel and Nietzsche for support. [Eichmann, too, sought to justify his actions by citing Kant's ethical concept of "duty."] Again, here one can only hint at the problem and its implications, that also concern Jewish philosophy in the past and, more particularly, in the present. (The subject will be discussed further in one of the following chapters.)

CHAPTER SEVEN

THE VALUE and USEFULNESS of PHILOSOPHY

Philosophy, without a doubt, is the most inclusive discipline of all the sciences and fields of intellectual endeavor; it encompasses almost everything. True, since ancient times certain changes have taken place in it. Initially, all the sciences were an integral part of philosophy - Aristotle's oeuvre is an admirable example. But in the course of time ramification and specialization have occurred. Hegel's work, perhaps, represents the last daring attempt to embrace all the sciences within a philosophical system. Nor was it mere chance that Hegel concluded his most systematic work - the Encyclopedia of Philosophical Sciences (the name speaks for itself) - by a citation from Aristotle.(57) Indeed, up to Hegel's time, there were not many who cast doubt on the unity of philosophy and the sciences, even if only a few dared to deal with all of these subjects. As early as the Middle Ages the beginnings of a differentiation became apparent. A distinction was drawn between the descriptice sciences - historiography, geography, and the like - which were regarded as being outside the bounds of philosophy, and the theoretical sciences - mathematics, physics and the like - which were regarded as part of philosophy. A radical transformation occurred when in the course of the development of the natural sciences a growing tendency to make use of mathematics became the norm. Nevertheless, throughout the 18th century the sciences were still considered a part of philosophy and termed "natural philosophy" (philosophia naturalis). [Newton called his main work The Mathematical Principles of Natural Philosophy (1687). His stated intent was to supplement by his activities the work begun by Descartes in his Principles of Philosophy (1644). As late as 1808 the celebrated chemist John Dalton called his book A New System of Chemical Philosophy. Many more examples of this sort can be cited.]

But when the sciences began to seek verification for their assumptions, not only in philosophy but in experimental investigation, the process of differentation could no longer be halted. The injunction that had characterized philosophy: "Sit and think!" no longer satisfied scientists, who changed it to: "Go and check!" Slowly the various sciences separated themselves from philosophy. The process began with astronomy and physics, soon to be followed by chemistry. Biology and psychology came of age in the 19th century. More recently political philosophy has established its identity as political science, as have logic and scientific methodology. Bertrand Russell tried to explain this process schematically. He held that as philosophy acquires more knowledge in a specific area and becomes capable of giving answers (albeit not final ones) to questions in that area, it gets separated from philosophy and becomes independent. "As soon as definite knowledge concerning any subject becomes possible, this subject ceases to be called philosophy, and becomes a separate science."(58) This is what happened to astronomy, physics, biology, psychology, et al. According to this view, philosophy engages in speculation about problems for which the exact sciences have not yet found a solution. Therefore, science is what we know and philosophy is what we do not know: "those questions only to which, at present, no definite answer can be given, remain to form the residue which is called philosophy."(59) In the past, philosophy took precedence over the sciences, but today the reverse is true. All that is left for philosophy, as it were, is to deal with those areas that science does not deal with.

Such a determination has its problems, and it is doubtful whether Russell himself remained faithful to the above conclusion in his philosophical work. He not only maintained that the sciences, in which knowledge was acquired, be separated from philosophy, but he also held that whole philosophical branches - such as Ethics and Aesthetics - be excluded from philosophy, because in his view these disciplines could not be put on a suitable cognitive foundation. Therefore, I prefer the Confucian precept: "To know what one knows and to know what one does not know, only that is true knowledge." Russell himself admitted that there will always be problems that are in principle insoluble. From this premise he concluded: "In philosophy, what is important is not so much the answers that are given, but rather the questions that are asked."(60)

On the other hand, there is, of course, no ignoring the influence that the sciences have had on philosophy. In the 17th century it was affected by mathematics, in the 18th, by psychology, in the 19th, by biology; and in the 20th century the sciences, with mathematics in the forefront, continue to influence philosophy. True philosophical knowledge cannot be completely identical with scientific knowledge in its modern sense. However, the goal should be to lessen the gap between the two, especially in matters that are bound up with scientific methodology. The latter maintains a position of crucial importance for both science and philosophy. In consequence a new discipline has come to the fore, the philosophy of science. There seems to be a dialectic process in force that may be outlined schematically as follows: At first philosophy included all the sciences; then the sciences freed themselves from philosophy; and now, it would seem, most of the sciences - the natural sciences, the humanities and the social sciences - are, in turn, developing specific philosophies for their areas of interest, e.g., philosophies of mathematics, physics, biology, linguistics and social philosophy, and so on. Thus the scientist cannot remain unconcerned about the philosophical aspects that are implicit in his endeavors. On the other hand, in equal measure the philosopher should be acquainted with science. It would seem that it is incumbent upon a modern philosopher to be familiar with the problems that face at least one science.

Nevertheless, it should not be forgotten that philosophy has a special function that is not a matter of concern to the rest of the sciences. It is embodied in the very act of philosophizing. It was in this spirit that Kant spoke to his pupils when he said that the major importance of philosophy is that it teaches man to think for himself. Russell expressed a similar thought: the importance of philosophy is not merely in asking questions, but in asking the right questions. (v. supra). This concept is nowadays acquiring acceptance among a number of scientists. The anthropologist Claude Levi-Strauss wrote: "The scientist does not supply true answers; rather he asks true questions."(61) This is a problem of great methodological significance today for both philosophy and science. However, philosophy seeks to emphasize an additional special point:

> There is no method peculiar to philosophy ... And yet, I am quite ready to admit that there is a method which might be described as 'the one method of philosophy'. But it is not characteristic of philosophy alone; it is, rather, the one method of all rational discussion, and therefore of the natural sciences as well as of philosophy. The method I have in mind is that of stating one's problems clearly and of examining its various proposed solutions critically.(62)

Even though these words of Karl Popper may seem trivial at first glance, they deal with one of the basic problems of philosophy. Descartes was conscious of its fundamental nature, when he wrote in his Discourse on Method the famous four rules that must always serve as a condition precedent for all philosophical and scientific inquiry:

> The first was never to accept anything as true that I did not know evidently to be so; that is, carefully to avoid precipitous judgement and prejudice; and to include nothing more in my judgments than what presented itself to my mind with such clarity and distinctness that I would have no occasion to put it in doubt.
>
> The second, to divide each of the difficulties I was examining into as many parts as possible and as is required to solve them best.
>
> The third, to conduct my thoughts in an orderly fashion, commencing with the simplest and easiest to know objects, to rise gradually, as by degrees, to the knowledge of the most composite things, and even supposing an order among those things that do not naturally precede one another.
>
> And last, everwhere to make enumerations so complete and reviews so general that I would be sure of having omitted nothing.(63)

We may sum up what has been said on this subject heretofore in the following way: Since there are no answers to all the philosophical problems, it is, on the one hand, important to formulate the questions that should be asked, while, on the other hand, to examine critically the answers offered. If the answers are unacceptable and the solution to the problem still lies in the future, one cannot draw the conclusion that the very attempt at rational search should be abandoned. The answer should be sought on the intuitive or revelatory level. (Further comment in chapters below.) Theoretical criticism is of no less value than some "positive" formulation.

On the contrary, a critical analysis is one of the safeguards against slipping into dogmatism. Polemics and debate, when conducted on a theoretical level and with suitable intellectual equipment, are always to be preferred to the negation, rejection or ignoring of a hostile viewpoint.

Moreover, judgment and criticism are within the reach of a man who may be unable to formulate an original concept like the one he is criticizing. [The American-Jewish philosopher Walter Kaufmann once commented that even though one cannot lay an egg, one is capable of judging whether it smells bad.(64)]

There is no denying that the study of philosophy requires that the student, or whoever shows some interest in it, must have a considerable capacity for abstraction and conceptualization. The complex subjects of philosophical inquiry affect the form of expression and types of formulation of ideas. This is especially so when dealing with philosophical texts from early periods, which are written in the style of their time. This is important when dealing with philosophers who often had to be careful to express their ideas in Aesopian language. (This subject will be elaborated upon in one of the chapters below.) This phenomenon is quite common in medieval Jewish philosophy, and is especially true of the Cabbala, portions of which are written in Aramaic, so as to increase the difficulties evolved in studying it. These unavoidable difficulties in the study of philosophy, especially those connected with the deciphering of philosophical texts, may well put off some people, interested in philosophy and its problems. The words of Franz Rosenzweig, addressed to potential readers of philosophical books, are worth citing:

> The first pages of philosophical books are held by the reader in special respect ... He thinks the (philosophical books) ought to be 'especially logical,' and by this he means that each sentence depends on the one that precedes it, so that if the famous one stone is pulled, 'the whole tumbles'. Actually this is nowhere less the case than in philosophical books. Here a sentence does not follow from its predecessor, but much more probably from its successor. If one has not understood a sentence or a paragraph, he is helped but little by reading it again and again, or even by starting all over, in the conscientious belief that he is not allowed to leave anything behind that he has not understood. Philosophical books refuse such methodical <u>ancien regime</u> strategy; they must be conquered a la Napoleon, in a bold thrust against the main body of the enemy; and after the victory at this point, the smaller frontier fortresses will fall of themselves. Therefore if one does not understand a certain point, he may most securely expect an elucidation if he courageously goes on reading.(65)

The study of philosophy requires a minimal quantity of knowledge or training. Studying it also has influence on the practical world, as stated above. And yet, there exists in philosophy, as in every other area, the subjective aspect.

A subject that is of interest to one person does not necessarily interest another. However, in its process of development philosophy has begun to shed increasingly its tendency to intellectual isolation. Even though the great philosophical creations are the fruit of the thinking of persons of unusual intellectual ability, the importance in philosophical activity of interpersonal relations, whether direct or indirect, has grown considerably. Both the historical and the social reality, and the intellectual and scientific milieu have left their imprint on the philosophy of every period. They have created a general-objective background for personal-subjective concerns.

Yet, as J.P. Sartre has correctly indicated the essential thing:

> If a society philosophizes, it means that its mechanism allows for a certain amount of free play, that there is room for the individual dream, for each man's fancy, for questioning and incomprehension. It means, in the last analysis, that there is no perfectly rigorous social order.(66)

There is no doubt that philosophy is vitally necessary for man. To the extent that he encounters problems that arouse his intellectual interest, that cause him to wonder at, and doubt, truths and conventions, and that arouse in him intellectual confusion, philosophical activity will never disappear. (The concepts of wonder and doubt are discussed at greater length below.) In this sphere philosophy is, as has been noted, of importance to education. It develops man's critical faculty, and in consequence is expected to make him a more tolerant and broad-minded human being. The contact with philosophy may be expected to affect favorably the mode of one who "burned his fingers trying to get a taste of it." [Reference is to a phrase (literally) "he peeked in and was hurt," found in the post-Talmudic parable of the four wise men who entered the Sphere of Divine Knowledge. Of the four, three were hurt by their contact with philosophy, in one way or another, and only one - Rabbi Akiba - came out whole in body and spirit. However, subsequently he attacked philosophy and eschewed its study. The reasons for the reserved and pessimistic attitude toward philosophy on the part of the Sages of the Talmud, as expressed in this parable, will be discussed below.] Philosophy or, more accurately, the capacity to philosophize, implies an ability to think independently, to present closely reasoned arguments, and, most important, to develop a critical approach in dealing with the subject under study. It is of value to end this introductory discussion on the quiddity and the aim of philosophy by returning to Russell's words. Even though his Logical Positivism is opposed to Sartre's Existentialism, these two not only concurred in their public and political struggle, but quite remarkably found themselves to be in a good deal of agreement in their perspective on the value of philosophy. Thus, the following quotation from Russell complements the preceding ones from Sartre:

> Philosophy, though unable to tell us with certainty what is the true answer to the doubts it raises, is able to suggest many possibilities which enlarge our thoughts and free them from the tyranny of custom. Thus, while diminishing our

feeling of certainty as to what things are, it greatly
increases our knowledge as to what they may be; it removes
the somewhat arrogant dogmatism of those who have never
travelled into the region of liberating doubt, and it keeps
alive our sense of wonder by showing familiar things in an
unfamiliar aspect.(67)

Russell adds, and his words are specially deserving of attention by one who intends to study Jewish philosophy:

Philosophy has a value - perhaps its chief value - through
the greatness of the objects which it contemplates, and the
freedom from narrow and personal aims.(68)

Philosophy is to be studied ... above all because, through
the greatness of the universe which philosophy contemplates,
the mind is also rendered great, and becomes capable of that
union with the universe which constitutes its highest
good.(69)

Philosophy, then, is the attempt to grapple with problems and important subjects, which we would otherwise tend to pass by apathetically. The foregoing quotations from Russell seem to us a fitting conclusion to a discussion of the quiddity of philosophy. Let us now turn to the special problems which this book has undertaken to examine and clarify.

PART TWO: PHILOSOPHY AND RELIGION

CHAPTER EIGHT

IDENTICAL IN CONTENT, DIFFERENT IN FORM?

For many generations religion and philosophy were so closely associated, that there was difficulty in differentiating between the theoretical subjects they discussed. To a degree it may even be said that they had common roots which, with the passage of time, produced different branches and emphases. In the Middle Ages, the prevailing doctrine taught that philosophy was subordinate to theology, indeed, its handmaiden. It was only in modern times that the philosophers began to consider the relationship between these two disciplines. One of the classical formulations on this subject was offered by Hegel. In his overall system of thought the "Absolute Spirit," which is the pinnacle of the spirit of philosophy (its antecedents were the "Subjective Spirit" and the "Objective Spirit)" has three states - art, religion and philosophy. These are the three most spiritual - and consequently supreme sections of the Idea in its process of progress and perfection. The _form_ of perceiving the Idea is common to art and religion. They both perceive it by means of a mental picture ("the drawing," in the language of Medieval Jewish philosophy); however they differ greatly in the ideational _content_ of their concerns. The content of the subjects that art deals with is human, whereas the religious content relates to the Divinity. As against this, Hegel's argument runs, philosophy and religion are the same as to the content - which is the Divinity, the Absolute - but differ as to the form in which they perceive the content. Religion, as has been said, perceives content as does art, by means of a mental image, whereas philosophy perceives it by means of a concept. Religion's mental image refers, indeed to the same content as does the concept, but it still retains vestiges of observation through the senses. The following chart presents the situation schematically:

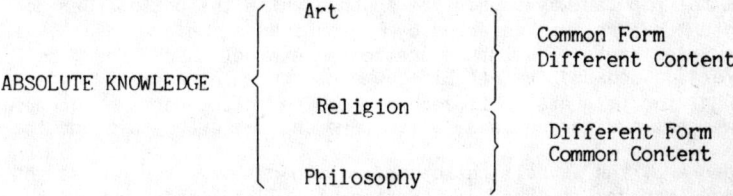

Accordingly, philosophy is superior to religion (theology), since it alone is able to comprehend the Divinity (which embodies the absolute truth) without resorting to the senses, as mental images must do. Religion, as it were, prepares the ground for philosophy in attaining the Absolute.

This speculative outlook of Hegel's is a continuation of philosophical thought on this subject, whose beginnings are rooted in the Middle Ages. For example, Maimonides' idea, that the Prophet is a philosopher possessed of extraordinary resources and able to grasp intuitively metaphysical truth, i.e. the Word of the Lord, anticipated Hegel's philosophy of religion - the understanding of philosophical content by a mental picture. However, for Maimonides this was the final stage, whereas Hegel understood it as the stage before the final one because a conceptual perception is of greater cognitive force for Hegel than one drawn from a mental image. While in Maimonides's thought the mental image is a basic element in achieving divine truth, Hegel holds that it is only a transitional phase: When one enters the final phase, the philosophical one, the mental image becomes superfluous, and even burdensome.

Hegel based his analysis of the difference between religion and philosophy on an explicit principle, whereas the philosophers of the Enlightenment who preceded him sought to make the distinction solely by a historical criterion. Lessing held that the various religions - Paganism, Judaism, Christianity - constituted phases in the "Education of the Human Race" (Erziehung des Menschengeschlechts), as he called his book. He regarded the philosophical religion as the final, longed-for stage. According to Lessing, religion is the stage that precedes philosophy historically speaking, while Hegel regards it as the stage preceding philosophy dialectically speaking.

Furthermore, the similarity between Maimonides' and Hegel's thought on this subject is greater than one might think at first glance. Maimonides saw philosophical religiosity as the highest phase of religion. While simple people accept what is written in the Torah literally, and imagine God in accordance with the anthropomorphic images of the Bible and the Talmud, the philosopher, by revealing the allegorical basis of these images, achieves the religio-philosophical truth that is hidden in the Torah. Hugo Bergman once said about Hegel that to him "religion is philosophy without philosophers, or if one wishes to put it that way, philosophy for the common people."(1) This dictum holds for the distinction that Maimonides made between popular and philosophical religiosity. A similar distinction was expressed by the Arab philosophers, especially Al-Farabi, who exercised considerable influence on Maimonides's general thought. This idea, that religion is the popular way to achieve truths, while the philosopher does so by intellectual effort, was accepted by many thinkers before Hegel, e.g., Spinoza or even Kant. The latter created an ethical theory for "the plain people", based on God and Eternal Life, whereas the Categorical Imperative was intended to persuade philosophers. The philosopher has no need of religion, whereas ordinary humans, as it were, cannot get by without it.

Some years ago, the Israeli philosopher Nathan Rotenstreich sought to sharpen and improve on the distinction that Hegel made, by using terms borrowed from the Phenomenologists, primarily, Husserl. Religion is close to philosophy in the noema (the content of thought), whereas the difference between the two depends on the character of the noesis (the act of relating to the content).(2) The relating is behavioral and not necessarily cognitive. In this manner he sought to break down the hierarchy implied by Hegel, namely, that there are two kinds of knowledge of the one Divine content - one superior (philosophy) and one inferior (religion). In the phenomenologist's view, there are no two levels, but only two types of relationship: the religious form of relationship is different from the philosophical, but not inferior. However, the contents are identical: the reality of God, the creation of the universe ex nihilo, an Omniscient God, free will, reward and punishment, the survival of the soul, and the next world. All these are subjects common to philosophy and religion, even though the former may cast doubt upon them. To what extent they constitute a subject for knowledge, will be discussed below.

It would seem that these distinctions would be of singular importance in clarifying the status of religion in Jewish philosophy. In the Hegelian scheme of things, the philosopher who achieves Divine Truth conceptually would not be interested in achieving it by mental image. He sees himself as having reached beyond the "popular" level. One who has achieved a conceptual perception does not wish to regress to an image type perception. No such opposition exists in the relations between knowledge and behavior. A philosopher may reach, or at least approach, knowledge of Divine Truth as he understands it, by way of thought, but this does not prevent him from worshipping God in one form or another. Hegel dealt only with the knowledge of God, on the religious and philosophical levels. On the other hand Rotenstreich's definition broadened the range, even if he does not say so explicitly, to the possibility of distinguishing between the knowledge and the worship of God. The one does not preclude the other, as does "concept" as opposed to "mental image". This is perhaps the intellectual base that is characteristic of the religious philosopher in our day. It is especially true of the Jewish religious philosopher for whom the behavioral relationship - the Commandments - are inseparable from his religiosity.

On the contrary, for the religious philosopher even "concept" and "mental image" are not necessarily opposites. It is reasonable to assume that for him, too, "concept" is a way of knowing that is suitable to the realm of knowledge, but if he places at its side a realm that knowledge, by definition, is unable to achieve and is unable to create a concept in it - namely, the realm of faith - then the concept a priori has no place in it. What "concept" does for knowledge, "mental image" does for faith. For a believing philosopher the "mental image" can be a source of knowledge of equal validity to the "concept" of the secular philosopher.

CHAPTER NINE

KNOWLEDGE versus ENCOUNTER

There exists, nevertheless, a more basic and essential difference between philosophy and religion, or, more precisely, between philosophy and theology: the dimension of form alone does not exhaust the problem. Firstly, one must not disregard the fact that it is "philosophy that interprets and formulates the essence of religion, whereas religion does not interpret or formulate the essence of philosophy."(3) True, it has happened that men of religion have sought to prescribe the forms and functions of philosophy. As has been pointed out, in the Middle Ages it was customary to regard philosophy as the handmaiden of theology. Also, the dividing line between the two disciplines became blurred from time to time. Both philosophy (at least most of its schools of thought until the present day) and theology are concerned with the concept of God. The first seeks to clarify the concept by its internal logic, without any conscious presuppositions, while the latter purports to justify the concept in open opposition to non-religious stands taken both by science and philosophy. For this reason, "philosophy-of-religion" is philosophy and not theology. Theological dealing in religion is a philosophical investigation by a man who ab initio holds with religion and interprets it for the express purpose of justifying it. On the other hand, a philosophical concern with religion is not necessarily the act of a believing person, even though such a possibility is not to be excluded.

This problem may be illustrated by Maimonides's polemic with Aristotelian philosophy on the subject of the Creation. The conflict between the Aristotelian view concerning God as an "Unmoved Mover" and the Jewish concept of Creation ex nihilo is the equivalent of choosing between an impersonal God, who, of necessity, was compelled to put the universe in motion, and a personal God, who created the world of his own free will. According to Maimonides, neither thesis is subject to rational proof, therefore the decision has to be left to the Prophets, whom he regards as the supreme authority, the highest level of philosophers. It is they who experience true revelation of sudden brilliant intuitions,(4) [In Hebrew the words "lightning" and "a sudden stroke of intuition" are derived from the same word.] which the ordinary philosopher is not privy to. It is the philosophers' task to interpret, in allegorical fashion, the revelatory visions of the Prophets. All in all, the philosopher examines religion and the concept of God in the same way that he deals with his other philosophical activities.(5)

The philosopher selects a number of problems for theoretical inquiry: a) the nature of God; b) proofs for His existence; c) the attributes of God; d) God's relation to the universe and to man. On this point, Hugo Bergmann's position presents a problem. He negates philosophy's ability and right to investigate and validate the truth of religion, since it belongs to a sphere which is beyond man's intellectual ability to comprehend. (More on this matter below.) However, surprisingly, he does not hesitate to interpret philosophical texts "from the depth of our religious feeling."(6) In other words, he grants the religious thinker a right with respect to philosophy which he denies the philosopher with respect to religion. Such a position, especially taken by a philosopher for whom tolerance of the opinions of others was a cardinal test, is quite startling (This subject of imbalance between philosophy and religion will also be discussed from the opposite viewpoint.) Incidentally, if there is a particular subject that philosophy, as it were, cannot consider, this would ipso facto cast doubt on philosophy's competence in dealing with any subject whatsoever. Assuredly, such was not Bergmann's intention. In this matter, he not only took his inspiration from Jewish religious tradition - wherein the Deity is generally perceived as being a personal, living God - but also from the philosophy of Blaise Pascal, who differentiated between the God of the philosophers and the God of Abraham, Isaac and Jacob.(7) (As is well known, Pascal carried a note, sewn in the lining of his coat, which read: "God of Abraham, of Isaac and of Jacob, not of the philosophers and not of the learned.") Bergmann, on the basis of his affinity to Martin Buber's doctrines, characterizes and interprets this difference as being the difference between knowledge and encounter: if I am able to encounter someone, then I am ab initio freed from the necessity of considering his reality. Religion (theology) relates to the Divinity as an existing God. He exists as a problem only for the philosopher, whereas the believer has no difficulty in this sphere.

A different argument could, of course, be presented on this subject. If it is impossible to know the quiddity of God, how can there be an encounter with Him? What could be the possible nature of such a connection between God and man? This is the starting point for the thought of Maimonides. The answer found in the Bible, as a sort of remedy for the "blow" that was to come in the future, was that a Covenant had been made between man and God, or, more precisely, between Israel and God. This is a perception that is distinctly at odds with the theoretical viewpoint of philosophy. God, according to the Biblical perception and to that of the philosophers who are in agreement with it - Judah Halevy, Pascal, Rosenzweig and Bergmann - makes himself known to man through His actions, His revelations. The connection, then, is in that God, for His part, reveals His love for man, while man has trust in God, namely, adopts a posture of faith toward Him. One can only pray to a living God, not to a reasoned concept. Belief in God includes belief in His existence, whereas philosophy is not barred from doubting the existence of any subject that it studies.

> God in religion is the object of religion's relationship. God, in a philosophic system, is a concept in the system and for it. This holds true even if the philosopher has religious motives, in the circumscribed meaning of this concept. Philosophy changes everything with which it deals to a concept, to wit, to a concept within its own methodical system.(8)

It is like the story of King Midas of Greek mythology: everything he touched turned to gold. For the philosopher, God is an abstract concept that makes no demands on him beyond his theoretical concern, whereas for the religious man He is a living God, who generally also imposes on him a specific way of life. This poses a very difficult problem, of special significance for Judaism. When an individual believes in God's existence and that He created the universe, it does not necessarily follow that he is obliged to "worship" him. Man's decision, therefore, to worship the Deity - in Judaism this involved the observance of His Commandments - is not a consequence of his faith, but rather of additional motives. Yeshayahu Leibowitz is very insistent on this point: the Commandments, he maintains, are meant to "force man's nature into worshipping the Creator."(9) He strongly supports the thesis of the Sages: "He who fulfills a Commandment out of a sense of commitment is greater than one who does so without such a sense."(10) Here, then, is another matter, distinguishing the philosopher from the religious person, which cannot be overlooked. While it is perhaps difficult to explain the reasons for it, religiosity influences rules of behavior more than philosophy does.

It would seem that even Rotenstreich's clear and equivocal statements (supra) fail to exhaust all aspects of the questions. How would one characterize, for example, Rene Descartes, one of the greatest philosophers of the early modern era? At the beginning of his philosophical inquiries he systematically cast doubt on everything, including God, in order to achieve a certainty that would provide him with a sort of Archimedean principle, on which he could establish his philosophical system; and so he acted fully as a philosopher, by carrying out his inquiry free of precedent assumptions. However, he was conscious ab initio of the fact that his doubting was only valid on the methodological level. In practice he never abandoned his Christian faith in God. This later enabled him to reinstate God in his system, having previously cast Him out on methodological grounds. He had no intellectual difficulty in finding proofs for the existence of God and in attributing to Him every perfection, including the capacity to create heaven and earth. After having provided a basis for his cogito - "I think, therefore I am" - he went on to claim that man is able to know truth, because it would be inconceivable for God, the embodiment of the highest good, to deceive him. In other words, Descartes relied on an argument that could be regarded either as rational, or as a matter of faith.(11) Yet, no one doubts that he was a philosopher and not a theologian, since his philosophical thinking was not motivated by his religion. His aim was to lay the ground for a system of philosophical principles.

CHAPTER TEN

RELIGION and SCIENCE

At this juncture it might be worthwhile to consider the relationship of science and philosophy to religion. Science, or more precisely, a specific science, investigates questions that pertain to a certain defined area of reality. Its purpose is to suggest an adequate explanation of the phenomena in the particular area under consideration. It does so in order to arrive, with the highest degree of certainty possible, at understanding the processes that are occurring. Thus science, or, better still, the scientist, can permit himself a degree of indulgence, flexibility, or even indifference, to the claims of religion. It is as if one domain were unaffected by the other. Great scientists, such as Newton and Darwin, held firmly to their religious faith. The religious dimension has had relevance not only in times when religion was central to men's lives, but also in our time, when the process of secularization seems to be accelerating. It may well have been that in previous generations the battle between religion and science was harsher, because both religion, relying on Scripture, and science sought to explain the phenonema of nature. Consequently, the conflict between the two types of knowledge was inevitable, as it was expressed in the case of Galilei, or in the objections to Darwinian theory. On the face of things, all this would seem to be a matter of the past. The scientist, in carrying on his research, does not depend on God, even though he may as yet have no scientific explanation for the phenomenon under investigation. God belongs to another sphere, to which science has no need to relate. In Randall's words,

> Few today, outside the definitely old-fashioned, any longer believe that there is an essential 'conflict between science and religion', or between 'science and theology' - though most of us would be hard put to offer any reasoned explanation of just why.(12)

All over the world there are outstanding scientists who are religious. This phenomenon is even more common among Israelis, and Jews in general, than among other peoples. The reason for it is that, generally speaking, Judaism, unlike Christian dogmatics, never based itself on rigid and binding principles of faith. (More on the subject below.) It emphasizes primarily the worship of the Lord and observance of His Commandments. But even a Jewish scientist of Einstein's stature - who had no particular ties to the Jewish religion - when explaining his Weltanschauung resorted to religious-metaphysical language in discussing God. [This position also influenced his scientific considerations, as, for example, in the matter of determinism, when he declared, "I cannot believe that God plays dice with the universe."]

The question of the relation between religion and science was first dealt with lucidly, in the new Jewish philosophy, in the philosophical teachings of the Maharal of Prague (Rabbi Loew). In his view, the Wisdom of the Gentiles and the Torah of Israel both lead to truth. (Cf. supra his comments on the "ladder".) All the sciences are a part of wisdom. The sciences that the Talmud explicitly lauds - philosophy, the science of nature, astronomy - constitute, in his words, Absolute Wisdom, and it is incumbent upon a Jew to study them as valid intellectual sources of knowledge. Yet, Torah and Wisdom are separate spheres that require different kinds of relationships. The Torah belongs to the metaphysical dimension, and Wisdom to the physical one. Everything written in the Torah is of metaphysical significance, namely supernatural and secret, and its contents can only be comprehended after deep exegesis and not from its literal meaning. In this matter, the Maharal adopted the position taken by Maimonides (more on the subject below). He did so in order to avoid, right from the start, the rise of possible contradictions between Scriptures and science. He was quite alert to the scientific progress of his age, the waning days of the Renaissance. A completely opposite view was taken a hundred years later by Spinoza, who argued that Scripture was to be interpreted literally. According to him, the authors of the Scripture had not been acquainted in their day with what the sciences were to teach man many years later. Thus there exists a conflict, on the metaphysical level, between religion on the one hand, and science and philosophy on the other. Consequently Spinoza assigned to religion an entirely different function: it was to serve as the educator toward respect for the Almighty and towards obedience. In the Maharal's view, which some modern religious philosophers are inclined to accept, no conflict of a metaphysical nature is possible, because Wisdom can only explain physical causes. For example, science explains the astronomical causes of a solar eclipse, whereas in the Talmud we find the metaphysical explanation: it is caused by man's sins, which must be punished. ["Our Rabbies taught, On account of four things is the sun in eclipse. On account of the Ab Beth Din (the vice-president of the Sanhedrin) who dies and was not mourned fittingly; on account of a betrothed maiden who cried out aloud in the city and there was none to save her; on account of sodomy; and on account of two brothers whose blood was shed at the same time."(13)] Scientific knowledge is a human creation, and can without difficulty exist compatibly with the revelational-metaphysical knowledge found in Scripture.(14) It is certainly no coincidence that one of the Maharal's pupils, David Gans - author of The Plant of David, which, in its time, was one of the most popular Jewish history books - was an astronomer, one of the closest assistants of Tycho Brahe and Johannes Kepler.(15)

In dealing with the subject of the relationship between religion and science it is well to note another, somewhat paradoxical, matter. In traditional debates in the past the major argument of the representatives of science was that religion, because of its dependence on Scripture, was incapable of offering a suitable explanation for objective reality, whereas science did so. Now, however, some modern scientists seem to be taking an almost completely opposite view. They argue that science no longer claims that it can reveal the secrets and nature of reality. To explain some of the reality, it merely offers hypotheses which are dependent on theoretical elements, e.g., electrons, genes and the like, all products of the human mind. Einstein, for example, wrote:

> Science ... is a creation of the human mind, with its freely invented ideas and concepts. Physical theories try to form a picture of reality and to establish its connection with the wide world of sense impressions.(16)

It would follow, then, paradoxically, that everything has been stood on its head: religious studies deal, as it were, with the description of objective reality, while scientific researchers no longer make such claims. Pierre Duhem, one of the greatest scientists and philosophers of science, a devout Catholic (and a confirmed anti-Semite), expressed this view sharply and unambiguously:

> This will not be the case with those whose reason has accepted the interpretation of physical theory we proposed, for they will never speak of a conflict between the principles of physical theory and metaphysical or religious doctrines; they understand, in fact, that metaphysical or religious doctrines are judgments touching an objective reality, whereas the principles of physical theory are propositions relative to certain mathematical signs stripped of all objective existence. Since they do not have any common term, these two sorts of judgments can neither contradict nor agree with each other.(17)

This, undoubtedly, is an extreme position that contains a hasty conclusion. From the assumption that the theoretical hypotheses of modern science do not reveal objective reality as it is, but for the most part are only attempts at clarifying its structure, it by no means follows that the religious judgments are the relevant ones to the given reality. The only conclusion that one may draw from the relations now prevailing between science and religion is, as has been said, that one sphere does not touch upon the other. When matters go well for man, it is a revelation of God's mercy and love for humanity; and when they take a turn for the worse, it is a sign that our path has not found favor in the eyes of the Lord. In both instances the existence of Divine Providence is "verified." Therefore, the very "hypothesis" concerning God is outside the scope of science, and therefore raises no theoretical difficulties for the religious scientist. However, religious thinkers, especially the Jews among them, have begun to wrestle with, and even to have reservations about, this simplistic view, in the wake of the tragic events that have befallen mankind, and the Jewish people in particular, in the 20th century.

Such a seemingly idyllic condition, as some tried to describe it between science and religion does not obtain between philosophy and religion, or, more precisely, between most of the movements in philosophy and religion. Generally, philosophy requires that reason be the sole arbiter, even though it recognizes, in principle, that reason has its limitations. And so, philosophy is likely to come into conflict more readily with religion than science does. There were philosophers who refused to accept a hierarchic schema, wherein religion was either subordinate or superior to philosophy.

The Christian Scholastics held that philosophy was theology's handmaiden, and Hegel declared that religion was epistemologically and conceptually inferior to philosophy. Those who rejected either view saw a possible solution to this dilemma in placing philosophy and religion in the same relation to each other as science and religion, namely, claiming that "philosophy and religion are two entire separate spheres."(18) The first to make such a suggestion, perhaps, was Levi Ben Gershon (Gersonides). The editor of the first edition of The Wars of the Lord, 1560, noted in the preface to the book, that the writings of Gersonides seem to be inconsonant with the teachings of the Torah and the Sages. However, in his own introduction and in the last chapter of the first section Gersonides explained that the Torah and philosophy are two discrete entities, and each deals with its own subject matter. (The special Jewish problem arising from this view, namely the problem of being a Jew and a philosopher, will be considered in later chapters.)

Spinoza was perhaps the most illustrious philosopher, in both Jewish and general philosophy, to adopt this stand. However, he did so out of completely different motives and for purposes other than those that guided Gersonides in the Middle Ages and Hugo Bergmann in modern times. In Spinoza's view, philosophy and religion were two entirely different domains: the first was engaged in seeking truth, whereas the second had the function of educating toward a life of morality, Godfearingness and obedience (obedience by understanding, and not by compulsion). Thus, since their goals and activities are different, there neither need, nor can, be conflict between them. If the representatives of religion (who, for Spinoza, were mostly Dutch Calvinist preachers) sought to harness philosophy to serve the needs of religion, [The problem of the relations between religion and the state, which, for Spinoza, was a matter of overriding interest, is beyond the purview of this study.] Spinoza held that they were guilty of a serious theoretical error. To dispose of this error, Spinoza wrote:

> Theology is not bound to serve reason, nor reason theology, but ... each has her own domain. The sphere of reason is, as we have said, truth and wisdom; the sphere of theology is piety and obedience.(19)

Spinoza's concern was basically political. It is in the public interest that men of religion should not be permitted to meddle with the freedom of philosophical investigation. It is, of course, of equal importance that philosophy should not be permitted to interfere with the useful educational mission of religion. However, in the final analysis Spinoza regards religion as inferior to philosophy, not only metaphysically, for being "the sanctuary of ignorance" (ignorantiae asylum), (20) but for serving as a means to evoke obedience, a quality that the philosopher can acquire by way of reason, without having to resort to the ministrations of religion. In any event Spinoza clearly explains the utility of religion, Scripture and revelation:

> I consider the utility and the need for Holy Scriptures or Revelation to be very great. For as we cannot perceive by the natural light of reason that simple obedience is the path of salvation, and are taught by revelation only that it is so by the special grace of God which our reason cannot attain, it follows that the Bible has brought a very great consolation to mankind. All are able to obey, whereas there are but very few, compared with the aggregate of humanity, who can acquire the habit of virtue under the unaided guidance of reason. Thus if we had not the testimony of Scripture, we should doubt of the salvation of nearly all men.(21)

On the other hand, when Bergmann declared philosophy and religion to be two discrete entities, he relied on the ideas of Pascal, Buber and Rosenzweig (and also on the latter's friend Eugen Rosenstock, a Christian of Jewish origin.) According to Bergmann, the philosopher speaks about God, whereas the man of religion speaks to God. At the same time he was not ready to accept the idea that "philosophy does not seek to desire, and religion does not seek to know."(23) On this point he opposed Spinoza's view.(24) He believed that God for the man of religion is a reality, and he aspires to know Him, as well. "Knowledge of God" has always been one of the cornerstones of the Jewish religious perception. (cf. above: "knowledge of God" and "love of God.") Consequently, the major difference between philosophy and religion, as Bergmann saw it, was that philosophy is a science like all sciences, it is a system of objective truths, or, to avoid the troublesome term "truths," a system of objective propositions. But, if so, what happens to the characterization of philosophy as a search for truth, a notion which Bergmann usually emphasized, and cited in its support the ideas of Nicholas of Cusa (among others)? Thus, in his opinion, religion was, on the other hand, not a science, but rather an encounter with the Deity, or, perhaps, the road to such an encounter. Religion, as seen by philosophers such as Pascal, Kierkegaard, Buber, Rosenzweig and Bergmann, to name some of the more prominent ones, is on the subject-experimental plane, and does not provide cognitive-objective knowledge. Philosophers can be religious believers - the fact is that there are such - but the two domains should not be commingled. The philosopher must not prove the truth of his scientific claims by resorting to evidence from the domains of faith and religion. To do so would call in question the scientific value of his philosophical work, and, in consequence, the loss would outweigh the gain. By the same token the religious thinker should not try to justify his religious perception and way of life with logical and scientific reasons, as was done in the past. Jewish and non-Jewish philosophers of the Middle Ages undertook as their primary goal to prove the existence of the Deity on rational grounds, to defend the validity of the two truths, to concern themselves with Divine Providence, to uncover the reasons for the Commandments, and the like. But in the age of Enlightenment all this went by the wayside. Ever since Kant, the world of knowledge and the world of faith have become two separate entities. Nor have theologians, beginning with Schleiermacher in the early 19th century and ending with Rudolph Otto, Paul Tillich and Karl Barth in our time, challenged this bifurcation. Jewish theologians, from Ludwig Steinheim to Franz Rosenzweig and Martin

Buber, have adopted similar positions. The attempts of Hegel and, in Jewish philosophy, Rabbi Nachman Krochmal (Ranak), for example, to encompass the concepts of the Deity and of religion within a systematic philosophy were the last two "heroic" efforts to follow the traditionally rationalistic attitude toward religion. Despite their impressive ideational breadth of vision, such speculative positions were not acceptable to the philosophers of their day or of the following generations, neither in general nor in Jewish philosophy. In brief, ever since Kant the schematic distinction has been generally accepted, that as philosophy deals with knowledge, so does religion deal with faith. Religious philosophers who tended to accept this view did not, by any means, regard the elimination of the cognitive dimension from the religious sphere as implying any diminution of religious faith. On the contrary, the dimension of faith remains the main motif, and ipso facto constitutes the crux of the religious relationship.

This sense that attaches significance to the concept of faith in modern theological thought has, as has been mentioned, penetrated Jewish religious philosophy as well. It took the place of the view that supernatural revelation was the sole necessary source for religion. In contemporary Jewish philosophy, the new religious sense of the concept of faith has gained recognition mainly in the wake of Rosenzweig's philosophy and under its influence.

CHAPTER ELEVEN

LOGICAL, AESTHETIC, MORAL and RELIGIOUS UTTERANCES

The aspect of faith as the cardinal dimension of modern religious philosophy stems primarily from the fact that religious utterances differ in essence from other utterances, and are different because of their unique nature. The logical problem that is involved in the uniqueness of religious utterances can be illustrated by comparing the four utterances in the table below:

```
1. The slate is black.
2. The picture by Chagall is beautiful.
3. Charity is a good thing.
4. God is the Creator of the universe.
```

In the first place, these four utterances make two very important points:

a) The problematic character of the assertions that are expressed in the sentences above cannot be considered, nor even perceived, apart from the language in which they are expressed. The linguistic dimension is a condition precedent for the very comprehension of this problematic character. This, among other things, is the reason for the extreme importance that religious philosophy ascribes to what is called "religious language," a subject dealt with by Franz Rosenzweig.

b) The above utterances emphasize the premise that human beings have a certain capacity for abstraction and conceptualization. Could one possibly imagine that creatures without linguistic ability and incapable of conceptual thought would be able to understand these utterances that state that something is true or false, right or wrong, good or bad, beautiful or ugly, exists or does not exist?

The linguistic capacity and the conceptual capacity are both preconditions for the very possibility of making a definitive judgment on these utterances. All four are declarative sentences: they are similar with regard to grammatical structure, but they differ in their logical and cognitive nature.

Only the first utterance presents a proposition in the strict logical sense, i.e., it is either true or false. This group of utterances may, of course, include some that we are unable to verify. Nevertheless, they have cognitive validity, because we know that the proposition that they express is necessarily either true or false, even though we do not know, and in many cases will never know, whether they are true or false. An utterance like "Organic materials are found on the planet Pluto" asserts a proposition of this type, because when man acquires the necessary scientific and technological means for investigation, perhaps in the not-to-distant future, it will turn out to be either true or false. (This holds also for utterances that make assertions for which it is doubtful whether science will even find answers, as, for example, assertions about very far-off galaxies, and the like.)

An utterance like "the sky is blue" is a proposition that reflects conceptual activity and provides us with knowledge about a certain characteristic of the sky, i.e., about a phenomenal aspect of its color and not its physical one. However, an utterance like "the sky is beautiful" expresses the subjective, emotional impression of the speaker. It differs from the preceding utterance, even though the grammatical structure is the same. The fundamental problem that becomes manifest in the above four utterances (or sentences - for the purpose of this study the terms are synonymous) belongs to the field of epistemology. The question immediately arises: what is the status of the propositions in the other three sentences, and do these sentences really express propositions? The first sentence provides us with a concept; the second and third sentences deal with values, and as for the fourth sentence - its uniqueness lies, as we shall see later, in that its subject is faith. The concept in the first kind of sentence concerns the object discussed; the values - good, beautiful - that appear in the second and third sentences, are dependent on an evaluation by the subject; whereas the content of the fourth sentence - there is a question as to whether to define it as a concept or as a value - has to do with faith. The question of truth seems to be only relevant to propositions of the first kind.(26) This was, inter alia, the position of Analytical Philosophy (Logical Positivism), which denied the cognitive significance of sentences that express "propositions" [The quotation marks that enclose the word "propositions" are intended to suggest that the capacity of such sentences to express propositions is doubtful.] of an ethical, aesthetic, or religious nature. This did not imply that other types of meaning cannot exist - non-cognitive ones, such as commendatory, emotive, religious or the like.

The schema of these four sentences shows that the value "truth" pertains to propositions, the value "beauty" relates to an evaluation of objects; the value "good" is revealed mostly in human conduct; while the fourth sentence raises the question as to what faith is about. As far as the aesthetic propositions are concerned, no one denies that the aesthetic evaluation and response are basically subjective. True, one's evaluation is also affected by external factors - historical, social, cultural and so on. If a certain artistic creation, be it in the realm of painting, music or literature, is pleasing to me, I would like it to please others. However, if someone should differ with me on the subject, I would not regard it as anything unusual, nor would it make me specially unhappy. Reference is not made here to an aesthetic evaluation that is influenced, or even dictated, by extra-aesthetic considerations, such as moral or educational factors. Religious perceptions have always had a very powerful influence in the field of art, both positive and negative. Evidence for this thesis is to be found in the Commandment: "Thou shalt not make unto thee any graven image or any likeness of any thing."(27) This is found in the Torah; its main purpose was to prevent idolatry, as is evidenced by the sentence that follows: "Thou shalt not bow down to them, nor serve them." There are similar prohibitions, even more extreme, in Islam, which limited painting to the creation of arabesques about the sentences of the Koran. Catholicism, on the other hand, has encouraged the plastic arts - painting, sculpture, architecture - while both Catholicism and Protestantism have always nurtured music. Nor was Judaism indifferent to the aesthetic aspects of the objects of religious worship. Among the extra-aesthetic influences, religious morality played a greater role. For generations it dictated to art and literature what was permitted or forbidden, especially with regard to the subjects of sex, nudity, etc. However, all these problems do not directly affect the purely aesthetic judgment on Chagall's painting, that was contained in one of the sentences above. For it, and for those like it, the subjective aesthetic evaluation is determinative, though it may well be bound with a considerable degree to intersubjective convention. In this case, no one would want to apply the criteria of truth and falsity, as in the case of the black slate, and argue that an opinion different from ours is false.

The situation is different in the case of the third sentence. Sentences that express moral "propositions" immediately arouse controversy because of the problematic nature of the subject matter. Certain moral behavior, which seems to me to be good, is not automatically so regarded by others. For instance, the sentence that was cited as an example - "Charity is a good thing" - would not be accepted by Spinoza. He would interpret it as an emotional reaction, i.e., as passively following one's feelings. In his view, there is no place for private charity. The governing bodies are responsible for providing care for the needy, as part of their overall responsibilities. Thus he defined pity as something bad: "In the man who lives by the guidance of reason, pity is in itself bad and disadvantageous."(28) Spinoza's view evoked the wrath of Samuel David Luzzatto, who regarded pity as being one of the three cornerstones of the Torah.(29) For this reason, among others, he totally rejected Spinoza's philosophy. However, even though moral value judgments may be open to disagreement, one would still be unwilling to leave them to the subjective evaluation and decision of the individual, as in the case of aesthetic judgments. When I make value judgments - that helping others is good, that equality is good, that murder, adultery, bearing false witness, exploitation of others and so on are bad - I would not like to regard them only as matters of personal taste. To the contrary, I would hope that others would feel as I do. In this instance, there is a definite goal of universalization, i.e., value judgments and moral norms are to be seen as almost a matter of consensus gentium for all times and for all cultures. The question whether a universalism of this sort actually exists or is achievable is the axis around which philosophical discussion revolves. It is not our intent to go into this matter here.(30) In any event, we would like to assign to the sentence, "Charity is a good thing," the same cognitive status, more or less, that applies to the sentence, "The slate is black." In other words, we would like to regard it as a sentence, whose proposition as presented can be confirmed (at least in part), and that the criteria of truth and falsity can be applied to it. We would not like to regard it as a purely emotional, subjective expression.

The philosophical problem that has arisen from these sentences - and it applies as well to the fourth sentence to which we now turn - is brought about because in living linguistic reality the logical and epistemological differences among the four sentences are disguised by the capacity to express all four of them in declarative sentences. A declarative sentence is an utterance that contains a certain assertion - as opposed to interrogative sentences, or imperative ones. (These are very important in religious language - more about them below.) The contrary possibility of expressing a declarative sentence in an interrogative form - "Am I my brother's keeper?" -is not philosophically germane in the present context. Only one sentence really expresses a proposition, i.e., something capable of absolute verification or refutation. In pronouncing these sentences, which are in part value judgments, one cannot avoid using the copula "to be." In addition, these sentences must be constructed by creating subjects and predicates, even though their grammatical constructs do not automatically express a descriptive or factual proposition. (More below on the function of the copula.)

This matter is of extraordinary importance when dealing with the propositions of "religious language." We now turn to the fourth sentence in the above list: "God is the Creator of the universe." It differs from the three preceding ones in that its subject is God. The proposition that it sets forth can neither be confirmed nor disproved by conventional epistemological criteria, logical or empirical. Neither is it similar to the second sentence. One who utters this sentence does not intend that it should be regarded as merely a matter of personal taste. He quite clearly seeks to express an objective "proposition," i.e., that God exists and that He created the universe. The second sentence in the above table ordinarily does not undertake to set forth an objective proposition, whereas the fourth sentence definitely does. Nor does the latter bear any resemblance to the third sentence in the table. A moral value judgment seeks, as has been pointed out, to achieve universalization. It tries to validate its universal content (more precisely, almost universal) by epistemological (or partially epistemological) criteria, derived from logic and experience. Thus, a sentence of the third type seeks to approach as closely as possible, cognitively speaking, the status of a sentence of the first type.(31) The fourth sentence also wishes to approach the first, cognitively speaking, and to be considered verifiable. But, as will be seen below, it cannot make use of experimental or logical criteria, contrary to what was thought by most of the religious philosophers and theologians up to the middle of the 18th century.

In conclusion, the first sentence expresses an objective proposition, capable of being verified (or confirmed) or refuted. The second sentence does not express a proposition at all, but rather a subjective judgment of taste. The third sentence expresses a moral value judgment that has the nature of a proposition which seeks to, and may, gain partial epistemological status. The fourth sentence also seeks to state a proposition, just like the first one, but is not served by the epistemological instruments on which the third sentence rests. Its object, by definition, is beyond human understanding. However, since it is not satisfied to accept the status of the sentence dealing with aesthetics, it adopts another kind of epistemological capability, faith. This criterion was not resorted to in the preceding three sentences. The correct phrasing of the fourth sentence is: "I believe that God created the universe." All the difficulties that this sentence faces actually arise from the deletion of the first two words ("I believe"), turning the sentence into a simple declarative one ("God created the universe"). This kind of sentence can certainly have meaning and importance, and should not be dismissed as meaningless, as has been done by Analytic Philosophy. However, one must be conscious of the fact that a religious proposition is valid only for the realm of faith. It does not belong a priori to the category of declarative sentences, whose criterion is cognition. In other words, when one expresses an utterance that presents a scientific proposition, one ipso facto confirms or refutes the objective situation, to which the proposition refers; whereas, when a religious utterance is made, it contains, as a matter of fact, no proposition: it is only an expression of a subjective faith. The scientific proposition deals with knowledge beyond the words of the sentence itself, whereas the religious utterance is limited to faith, as expressed by the words of that utterance, and contains nothing more. Thus these are two completely distinct utterances. Another matter should be clarified here. It would be incorrect to state that the religious utterance is dependent on Holy Writ, which confirms its truth, in the same way that facts confirm (or negate) an ordinary utterance. It is unthinkable for a religious utterance that relies on Holy Writ ever to be refuted by it, as occurs with some facts with respect to other utterances. On the other hand - and this is the essential point - the religious utterance cannot be confirmed by Holy Writ, but it derives its seeming validity from the belief that certain books - the Torah and the Oral Law in Judaism - are indeed Holy Writ.

Concerning the various problems that arise from the phrase "I believe," more will be said in Chapter Thirteen of this Part. However, before turning to them, it is necessary to consider the status of the copula to which, in the religious sentence, special significance and functions, which are absent from the other sentences, have been assigned. This may shed some light on the special status of the religious utterance as presented in the latter part of the present chapter.

CHAPTER TWELVE

THE COPULA in RELIGIOUS LANGUAGE

In the four utterances that served as a point of departure for examining the epistemological problem of the previous chapter, the copula was a link between the subject and the predicate. Its function was grammatical, and it turned the utterances, as regards their formal structures, into declarative sentences. However, the status of the copula in religious language is, in fact, different. True, in the Hebrew language the matter is not quite clear. The characteristic copula in European languages - is in English and ist in German, and so on - does not have an exact parallel in Hebrew. The pronouns he and she are used, and occasionally they are omitted. But this does not alter the basic aspect that will be considered below. This problem, which is of considerable importance for the religious perception, will be illustrated by a consideration of the views of Hegel, Feuerbach and Rosenzweig.

In the speculative system of Hegel, the subject of philosophy was truth, and therefore, Hegel treated it as a grammatical subject, and was able to formulate sentences such as "the truth is a totality," "the truth is Absolute Spirit," "the truth is God," and so on. In all these sentences the predicate is a sort of idea that is thought about and thus the function of the copula is purely grammatical. The predicate gives expression to the subject. Without it, the subject would lack both content and meaning. As opposed to Hegel's sentence "Truth is God," Rosenzweig offers the sentence "God is truth."(32) He explicitly states: "Truth is not God, God is truth." The change of the order of the subject and the predicate is of great significance. Rosenzweig elaborates on the Biblical concept: "God is the truth." ("But the Lord is the true God.")(33), which both Christian and Jewish medieval philosophers, such as Augustine and Maimonides, cited very frequently. Thus Maimonides wrote: "This is what the prophet means when he says, 'But the Lord is the true God' (Jer. 10:10), that is, He alone is real and nothing else has reality like His reality."(34)

In the sentence "God is truth" the subject alone, without the predicate, still has meaning: "God is" - means "God exists." (This is grammatically correct in German, sounds awkward in English, and hard to translate literally into Hebrew.) What Rosenzweig meant was that God is not a philosophical concept, but a living, personal Deity, who maintains a relationship with man. His existence is experienced through faith. According to this view, God exists before and beyond thinking. The concept of truth merely connects with Him. It is of interest to note that Rosenzweig's perception is amazingly similar to that of Spinoza who wrote: "God being the Truth or that the Truth is God Himself."(35) Spinoza's God - substance - is self-causing, and from this aspect is antecedent to human thought. The latter merely partakes of His infinite wisdom. Rosenzweig was conscious of his close intellectual relation to Spinoza, and discussed it in his essay, New Thought, which was a sort of belated introduction to his presentation of his philosophical system.(36) The three elements of his philosophy are something like the Spinozistic "substance" - each is "self-causing."(37)

It is even more interesting to compare Rosenzweig's position with that of Feuerbach (who, in a number of instances, exercised considerable influence on Rosenzweig's doctrines). Feuerbach, as well, in clarifying the concept of God, devoted a great deal of attention to the question of the relationship between subject and predicate. He attacked the assertion that he who denies God's being as a subject becomes an atheist, whereas he who only denies Him his attributes (predicates) may be regarded as belonging to the minions of religion. In this fashion Feuerbach distanced himself from the line of thought of the "Negative Theology," of which Maimonides was one of the most fervent supporters in Jewish philosophy. Feuerbach felt that the negation of the predicates - "Bestimmungen" was his term - was the equivalent of negating the subject. A subject without predicate is "a being without qualities...is virtually non-existent, (ein nichtiges Wesen)"(38) Feuerbach discussed, in the main, the anthropomorphic attributes of the Deity, but the fundamental conflict between his outlook and that of Rosenzweig is quite clear. In Feuerbach's words, "What the subject is lies only in the predicate; the predicate is the truth of the subject - the subject is only the personified, existing predicate, the predicate conceived as existing. Subject and predicate are distinguished only as existence and essence. The negation of the predicates is therefore the negation of the subject."(39) Rosenzweig, on the other hand, emphasizes that God as a subject is greater than the truth about Him.(40) To him, the Divine subject is self-sufficient, independent and significant without the predicate. Gott ist means that "there is a God," whereas Feuerbach argues that: "The predicates ... have an intrinsic independent reality."(41) As to Divinity - the true and primary subject is the predicate. "What the activity of the reflective power has converted into a predicate, distinguishable or separable from the subject, was originally the true subject."(42) In other words, man is the one who created the concept of God, by ascribing to Him attributes usually of an anthropomorphic nature, which in his opinion were suitable for the Deity.

The negation by Feuerbach of God as an independent existent in human thought and the belief in God on the part of Rosenzweig therefore expressed themselves by divergent attitudes to the Hegelian assumption described at the beginning of this chapter. Each interpreted the assumption according to his fundamental philosophical views. As regards the meaning of the concept of God, Feuerbach gave preference to the predicates, and based it on logic and thought, whereas Rosenzweig preferred the subject, and assigned to the concept of God an existential base, which embraced more than mere conceptual truth.

> Consequently, God, of necessity is 'more' than truth, just as every subject is 'more' than its predicate, everything is more than its concept. Even if the truth is the last and only thing that one can experience of God's essence, nevertheless there will still remain in God something more than his essence.(43)

In other words, God's existence, which has independent value, encompasses within itself something more than His essence. Truth is only God's predicate, but it lacks the power to exhaust Him. Thus Rosenzweig conceives of God on the faith-existence level. He can never be completely known on the basis of his predicates. However, one may know Him, because, since one believes in Him, one can turn to Him and maintain contact with Him.

The conclusion one can draw is that every sentence that has God for its subject is different in essence from all other sentences, even though they may be similar in their grammatical and formal structure. In this instance, the difference cannot be reduced to the validity and meaning of the propositional content of the sentences that were discussed in the previous chapter. (It should be emphasized that the difference is in itself of very great value in understanding the cognitive distinction between assertions of fact, aesthetic judgments of taste, and ethical value judgments.) Above all, the difference lies in the function of the copula. In the first three sentences, regardless of logical differences between them, the copula fulfilled a grammatical function, and so without the predicates they were completely meaningless; whereas in a sentence like "God is truth" (Rosenzweig) or "God is the Creator of the universe" (author's example) the copula, in addition to its grammatical role, has primarily an ontological function that derives its confirmation only from faith.

Faith, therefore, is the deciding factor in modern religious philosophy, from Kant to the present day. It determines the nature of contemporary religious language. We must therefore turn to a more thorough examination of faith in philosophical and theological thinking.

CHAPTER THIRTEEN

FAITH and BELIEF

It would be well to clarify the unique philosophical and religious problem that inheres in the concept of "faith" from the terminological and substantive points of view. As a result of the too-frequent use of this concept and of the ambiguity prevailing in some languages, notably German [One should remember that most of modern Jewish philosophy that flourished up to World War II, was centered in regions where German philosophy and culture reigned. For this reason, German linguistic problems had implications for modern Jewish philosophy.], a certain equivocalness has developed in its use. This ambiguity exists in the Hebrew language too.

In English, there are two separate terms, "faith" and "belief." [The difference in French between foi and croyance is somewhat less clear. Likewise, the English word belief has two meanings, but this is of no relevance to our problem. In everyday English the distinction between the two terms is not always adhered to; nevertheless, the various errors, described below, are avoided.] In German, the word Glauben serves for both. In Hebrew, an attempt was made to preserve the distinction by using the term ha-amana for "belief" (as first suggested by Professor Yehoshua Bar Hillel), and emuna for "faith." The distinction was first made by the greatest medieval Jewish philosopher, Maimonides, who used these two words in the same sense. The discriminative definitions that he gives relate precisely to a question that will be discussed below: "Belief is the affirmation that what has been represented is outside the mind just as it has been represented in the mind."(44) In the very first sentence of the chapter Maimonides notes: "Belief is not the notion that is uttered, but the notion that has been represented in the soul when it has been averred of it that it is in fact just as it has been represented."(45) Nevertheless the attempt to maintain the distinction between these two words was unsuccessful. On the one hand, the term ha-amana is already used in Hebrew as a term for the "accreditation" of an ambassador. On the other hand, both terms use the same verb form - in the present tense it is ani ma'amin - and the distinction between them is again blurred. In the first case, there is a close relationship between ani ma'amin - "I believe" - and ani savur - "I am of the opinion." In both these instances we are dealing with an utterance, which is subjective and reflects knowledge that is not beyond doubt, but can, in principle, be verified and become certain knowledge. This kind of utterance refers to existential reality, and therefore "belief" may be called an "existential utterance." Incidentally, there is perhaps more than a bit of the paradoxical in that, in Hebrew, "I believe" sometimes tends to contain a higher degree of certainty (empirically speaking) than "I am of the opinion," since an opinion is clearly much more an expression of the subjective, personal view of its holder. [The same phenomenon occurs in German: The verb meinen and the noun Meinung are derived from the word mein (mine), i.e., it is my personal opinion, and not a general one.] On the other hand, belief alludes to the fact that there are data of a more objective nature, on which I am entitled to rely in expressing my belief (see below). Yet, there is something in the use of the term that nudges us gradually toward faith. The very use of the concept belief in place of knowledge suggests the hidden assumption, that incontestable knowledge is lacking. It is a proposition concerning knowledge, which ab initio contains a certain reservation. It would certainly be strange were one to say: "I have faith that 2 and 3 are 5," or "I believe that 2 and 3 are 5." Even as great a skeptic as David Hume, who, on philosophical grounds, hesitated to state, "I know that the sun will rise in the east tomorrow," would not regard the rules of mathematics as a matter of "belief."

This problem, too, can be illustrated schematically by a number of sentences, five in all. Each one offers a proposition of different cognitive value. (Further distinctions could be made by adducing additional utterances, but for dealing with the subject at hand this is not necessary.)

> 1. I know that 2 and 3 are 5.
> 2. I know that a tree is growing in back of the house.
> 3. I believe that it will rain tomorrow.
> 4. I believe that Simon will keep his promise.
> 5. I believe that there is a God.

The first sentence expresses a logical proposition that deals with mathematical "truth." The second presents an empirical assertion, which can be directly tested by observation. True, the proposition presented in the first utterance, viewed from a given aspect, can also be regarded as a result of experience, by virtue of the fact that the individual acquired the knowledge as a school boy, by doing exercises in arithmetic. However, its verification - and this is the point - is not dependent on experience; whereas in the second sentence empirical verification is required. In the second sentence observational experience is a condition precedent for verification. Moses Mendelssohn, in dealing with the stratum of "the eternal truths" in his treatise Jerusalem, took note of this fundamental difference:

> Those principles which are independent of time and remain forever unchanged, are called eternal truths. They are either necessary, and, as such unchangeable, or contingent: that is, either their permanence is grounded in their essence (they are what they are because logically they cannot be anything else and are not conceivable in any other way), or it is based on their reality (they are universally true because they occurred and became real in this and in no other way, and they could not have achieved reality in any other or better way than they did). In other words, necessary as well as contingent truths have a common source - truth.(46)

The distinction - borrowed from Leibnizian philosophy - that Mendelssohn made between "necessary" and "contingent" truths, corresponds to the distinction above between the first sentence, which is based on internal logic, and the second, which requires empirical observation.

The situation is different in the third and fourth sentences. If "I believe" that it will rain tomorrow, I rely on my observational experience and on meteorological data. Nevertheless, as is known, even today a weather forecast, made with the aid of sophisticated technological equipment, such as computers, is not absolutely certain. But the important point in the above sentence lies in the fact that what today is still a "belief" will tomorrow become certain "knowledge," i.e., tomorrow we will know whether the proposition in the above sentence was true or false. Thus, in essence, it is a subject for verification or refutation. The same holds true for the sentence which states that "I believe" that Simon will keep his promise. In this case, as well, the belief is founded on known data - personal acquaintaince with the man, knowledge of his character, the circumstances surrounding the promise, and so on. In this instance, as well, the keeping or non-keeping of the promise will, in fact, become known and will clarify whether the proposition contained in this belief - utterance was true or false. That is to say, it is in principle possible, by experience, to confirm or deny the proposition expressed in the above sentences. [Another logical problem arises here: Every sentence that begins with the words "I am of the opinion," "I believe" and so on, expresses, at first glance, a true proposition, because, unless I am a liar or a hypocrite, then, when I say "I am of the opinion" or "I believe," I must be telling the truth. However, this logical problem is not relevant to the present discussion.]

The problematic nature of the fifth sentence is another matter entirely. "I believe that there is a God." In this case, <u>ab initio</u>, there is an intention to be completely detached from even attempting to confirm the proposition expressed in the utterance by giving any kind of explanation or reason other than one of <u>faith</u>. (Note: faith, no longer belief.) Again, in this discussion we are interested in the modern problem, not in the problem that dominated the thinking of the medieval Scholastics. Their main concern was proof of the existence of God, or, as the Jewish philosophers put it, "the knowledge of God." In truth, the correct formulation of this sentence should be "I believe in God." Faith is unique in that one does not "believe that," but one "believes in." The problem here is psychological rather than logical. The determination that religious faith has imbedded in it a faith in a man or in some thing, and not a faith that a certain proposition is true, does not, of course, render faith superfluous or meaningless. However, it must be put in its proper place from a theoretical point of view. There is, in fact, only one exception, which confirms the rule. The English philosopher Antony Flew, among others, commented on it: The religious proposition "I believe in God," assumes God's existence as self-evident; whereas from propositions such as "I believe in socialism," "I believe in international brotherhood," or in any other such idea, it does not follow that they actually exist. To the contrary, these propositions denote their non-existence and a desire to realize them. But he who says, "I believe in God," most certainly does not intend to say that God does not exist, and that he wishes to bring Him into being...(47) For this reason Buber and others formulated a sort of revision of the distinction between "belief in" and "belief that." They found support in Maimonides's utterance: "I completely believe that ..." (Thirteen Principles of Faith). They sought to present every sentence, which permitted the reduction of the first version to the second, as belonging to religious language. From "I believe in God" or "I believe in angels" one can derive "I believe that there is a God," or "I believe that there are angels," whereas from "I believe in justice" and the like, one cannot derive "I believe that there is justice." However, the very assumption that the existent constitutes the predicate (see preceding chapter) was refuted by Kant in his time, and today, as well, this entire distinction is extremely problematical.

Therefore, the sentence "I believe that there is a God," must be treated quite differently from the four preceding sentences. Faith, in this sense, does not require the acceptance of things not known to us as true. It has nothing whatsoever to do with acceptability, probability or the like. The atheist can use exactly the same argument for the sentence: "I do not believe that there is a God"; a sentence such as "I know that there is no God" has a peculiar ring to it in almost everyone's ear. Every discussion of the question of the existence of God, by its very nature, goes beyond the bounds of knowledge. The use of the word "knowledge" in every case - in the negative sense, as well - is improper. A modern philosopher will not respond to the claim that "God exists" by saying "That is a false proposition." Instead, he will ask: "What do you mean by your assertion?" A shift has taken place from dealing with the problem on the traditional, ontological level - now considered obsolete - to the dimension of meaning, on the one hand, and to that of faith on the other. Logically speaking, one cannot derive from the connotation of a certain entity (noting its meaning and characteristics) its denotation as well, (that there actually is an entity possessed of such qualities, an entity paralleling the connotation). Understanding the meaning of the concept God does not ipso facto guarantee His existence, as the Cartesian ontological proof would have it. Here we are in the realm of faith. Were we able to prove God's existence, faith in Him would be superfluous.

Every religious utterance, such as "there is a God", or "God exists," is bound up with an element of faith that is antecedent to any acquired knowledge. That very element of faith is what creates the utterance. (Rosenzweig dealt with these problems in extenso, mainly in the first part of his book The Star of Redemption.). It is true that such an utterance includes, as Rotenstreich has pointed out, an explicit determination with regard to existence - to God's existence. Ab initio, however, it does not require verification, as is necessary in the realm of knowledge, but is grounded in faith. "The realm of faith includes behavior that partakes of the Holy, and a relationship with faith."(48)

In this respect, it may be that in the Hebrew word emuna there is a certain significant aspect that is not present in the terms "belief," "faith" and "Glauben." It points to the unique mentality that characterized the bond of the Children of Israel to God. The above non-Hebrew terms emphasize the aspect that faith represents a kind of knowledge, short of absolute certainty, while the Hebrew term emuna also includes the meaning of eimun, "trust" (in German: Vertrauen). It implies that what the Torah says will come true. "A faithful witness will not lie."(49) In this spirit,

Maimonides noted in his Thirteen Principles of Faith: "I believe in full faith in the coming of the Messiah." The Hebrew term, as it were, has an element of confidence in it, which is lacking in other languages. Furthermore, the Hebrew word emuna ("faith") is derived from the same root as the word ne'eman, ("faithful"). The Jew, in giving his eimun, "trust," in the Torah and in God, is ne'eman, "faithful," to them - without unduly brooding about how to be faithful.

The meaning of the words Glauben and "faith" constitutes, in fact, a blend of two traditions - Biblical fear of the Lord, relying on faith, and Greek philosophy, which places its trust in reason. "Faith" is a combination of fides (credence) and intellectus (understanding.)

The element of faith includes the subjective, existential dimension of religiosity, as opposed to the "institutionalized" socio-cultural dimension of religion. Various modern religious philosophers, from Kierkegaard to James, have considered the relationships between the two dimensions and have awarded primacy to the element of faith. However, in general, they have ignored the reciprocal relations between faith and knowledge, which existed despite all the differences between the two. This tie was clearly defined by Rotenstreich, when he wrote:

> When a man says, 'I believe that God exists,' he seeks to say two things simultaneously: it is a matter of faith, i.e., the utterance derived from it lacks a complete basis; but he is also implying that the utterance has a unique basis, and that its certainty is not impaired, even though it is not completely verified by the instruments of knowledge.(50)

He related the second meaning of the utterance, which is characteristic of the modern approaches to faith, to the words of the Jewish philosopher Joseph Albo, who lived in the latter part of the Middle Ages, and was one of the apologists for the Jews at the Colloquium of Tortosa (1413-1414). Albo wrote:

> Belief in a thing means a firm conception of the thing in the mind, so that the latter cannot in any way imagine its opposite...(51)

There is no connection whatsoever between Albo's perception and the well-known Credo quia absurdum ("I believe it because it is contrary to reason"), an adage erroneously attributed to the Church Fathers Tertullian and Augustine. The foregoing credo refers to a faith that is ab initio opposed to all knowledge acquirable either by the senses or by reason. In modern times it has attracted certain Christian philosophers, who have sought to break religion off from any affinity to reason (ratio), such as the theologian J.K. Lavater and the philosopher F.H. Jacobi, Mendelssohn's adversaries in the 18th century, or the Dane, S. Kierkegaard, in the first half of the 19th century. Their perception can be traced directly to Martin Luther's arbitrary and extreme declaration that "... in opposition to all reason and to the evidence of the senses, one must learn to hold fast to faith." Or, as he put it in his pungent language, "Reason is a whore." Kierkegaard used the phrase: "Religion crucified the mind." It is to be wondered whether Kierkegaard did not sense that his blunt pronouncement might not contain a hint that the crucifixion of reason was analogous to the Crucifixion of Jesus, and was likewise the source of Salvation... . Protestantism has from its very beginning been far more hostile to philosophy than Catholicism. For the latter, philosophy was an integral part of theology. Judaism, on the whole, tended to a rationalistic position (cf. Albo's view supra). But the reservations of Protestantism concerning reason had an unanticipated result: since it expelled philosophy from its sphere, philosophy, in consequence, adopted a generally secular position in the Protestant countries.

All this has had far-reaching implications for man's behavior. The believer places his faith in Divine Providence, giving emphasis to the moment of "trust," as discussed above, whereas philosophical knowledge imposes on man freedom and responsibility that develop from his use of his reason. Faith, too, may resort to man's capacity to weigh options, as, for example, in the case of Pascal's well-known "wager": If I wager that God exists and I win, I gain Eternal Life and unlimited happiness; if I lose, all I have lost is a life fraught with illusion. But if I wager on the non-existence of God and I win, all I have gained is a short life and nothing else; if I lose, the everlasting tortures of Hell await me.(52) What sensible man would wish to wager on the second option? Without going into the moral problem of employing utilitarian arguments in justifying faith in God, the wager, per se, is not reasonable, since Pascal puts up the non-existence of a God against the existence of the Catholic God, who sends the unbeliever to Hell. Incidentally, inadequate attention has been paid to the underlying agnostic premise that guided Pascal, perhaps unwittingly, in his considerations for justifying faith.

As opposed to the above positions, Albo in his day, and Rosenzweig and Buber in the present age, wrote about faith in an entirely different manner. They continue the line of thought that was first formulated in the Middle Ages by one of the most important theologians and philosophers of the scholastic period, Anselm of Canterbury. He said: Credo ut intelligam, ("I believe so that I may know.") It is in this spirit that Rosenzweig argues in The Star of Redemption that faith indeed antecedes knowledge, but it need not forego the dimensions of knowledge. And so, Rosenzweig's philosophical aim is to achieve knowledge grounded in faith, or, as Hugo Bergmann defined it, in "believing thought."

Let us now return to our principal subject. General and Jewish religious thought in our day (the term "thought" is to be understood as religious philosophy, and not in its institutionalized forms) proceeds from the assumption that the word "faith" "... possesses a degree of certainty that is greater than that inhering in factual knowledge, and a fortiori than that inhering in a guess or hypothesis."(53) It is true that religious philosophy has a certain element of the same kind of knowledge that we find in the third and fourth sentences set out in the table above. Such knowledge is no more than a general hypothesis, as expressed in the fifth sentence. But the religious man, the man of faith, from the very beginning does not need all the criteria that are necessary for ordinary knowledge. Faith does not require verification on the cognitive plane, since in any event it holds that it cannot be refuted on that plane. It regards its subject, as has been said, not as open to hypothesis or speculation, but rather as one of certainty. Rabbi Israel Meir Hacohen of Radin, the author of the work Hafetz Hayim, (d. 1933), is said to have once remarked: "For the man of faith there are no questions and for him who lacks it, there are no answers." Nevertheless, the philosophical man of faith is aware of the basic and essential distinction between faith and philosophy. He chooses the first by a conscious decision, fully aware of its implication. It follows, then, that that which turns faith in the eyes of the non-believer into an untrustworthy and uncertain type of cognition, i.e., a lesser plane than knowledge, turns it in the eyes of the man of faith into certain cognition, freed from the need to report to cognitive criteria. It stands on a higher level than knowledge.

Finally, one can derive from the foregoing a social and moral lesson of prime importance. To the extent that the reasons for the different relation to faith are clear to both parties, those who do and those who do not have faith, there is room for mutual tolerance and for overcoming the tendencies for "ideological" confrontation in so sensitive an area as that of religious faith. The man of faith should recognize, and accept, the fact that faith is unable to refute the philosophical position that denies the existence of the Deity - it may merely reject it. He can, and is entitled to, reject the non-believer's position, but since he cannot refute it, he should respect the holder of the opposite opinion and his right to it. On the other hand, philosophy is indeed able to refute the position that argues for the existence of the Deity (in fact, it has been refuted by Kant and others), but it is incapable of rejecting faith in God. It would then seem that faith cannot refute the philosophical position, but can reject it, and philosophy can refute the position of faith, but is unable to reject it. Thus, the understanding of the theoretical problem here discussed and, in consequence, the mutual understanding that can be achieved by a balanced consideration of the data, can contribute to the prevention of a "cultural war" which, as is well known, is one of the dangers that is constantly facing the State of Israel's spiritual life in all its social implications.

CHAPTER FOURTEEN

KNOWLEDGE versus FAITH; AUTONOMY versus HETERONOMY

Thus far our investigation has been focused on the ties between philosophy and religion, on the epistemological problem of knowledge versus faith. However, this subject has another aspect - that of the relation of knowledge obtained by means of reason to knowledge acquired through revelation. The first view eventually became bound up with a trend termed "negative theology," i.e., opposition to all anthropomorphic attributes and images for the Deity. The contrary view is connected with "positive theology," namely a view accepting the existence of a personal God who reveals Himself to man. Jewish philosophy had certain theoretical problems in this area, because it negated God's corporeality, on the one hand, and, on the other, it saw Him as a "Living God" who reveals himself to man. This distinction was also of considerable importance for the moral question, that of autonomy versus heteronomy. Does the validity of moral norms depend on the independent, intellectual activity of man? In other words, is it dependent on an internal, human criterion, or is it derived from a Divine commandment, i.e., from an extra-human criterion?

In treating this subject we encounter some very difficult problems, and it was only after Kant's time, that their full significance was realized. For Kant, a moral law is one that is autonomous and is not imposed on man by an external force. Consequently, a law imposed by God on man would apparently not be moral. This conclusion might be moderated by arguing that Divine Law acquires moral force only when it is freely adopted by man. Nevertheless, the source of the law is Divine, and is, as it were, not subject to question; therefore it has no moral significance. Kant himself tried to avoid the dilemma by imposing on it a kind of "Copernican Revolution," ["The Copernican Revolution" which Kant discussed in his preface to The Critique of Pure Reason referred to the thesis that it is the subject that dictates the code of rules to the objects.] as he did in his general philosophy: It is incumbent on man to attribute the laws of morality, which are moral in themselves, to the Deity. Man first accepts the validity of the moral laws, and thereafter he determines that they were given by God, on the assumption that only a superhuman intelligence could have established them. But the question still remains: Why should man attribute the moral laws to a Divine Legislator, if he is capable of comprehending their morality by his own intelligence? For Kant, this remained an open question. Of course, the problem had existed before Kant defined it in its starkest form, and it was constantly present in Jewish philosophy.

In Jewish philosophy of the medieval and modern periods, no thinker challenged the status of God as the Supreme Legislator. Nevertheless, certain trends were discernible that seemed to oscillate between autonomy and heteronomy.

The Aristotelian and Neo-Platonist schools of the Middle Ages, for example, held to autonomy. When Maimonides considered the question of Divine Providence, he followed the line taken by the Mu'tazala, whose philosophers emphasized "the wisdom of God."(54) He criticizes the Kalam, who combined their a priori religious concepts with the Aristotelian system, whereas he held that

> Belief is not the notion that is uttered, but the notion that is represented in the soul when it has been averred of it that it is just as it has been represented ... as if what we aimed at and investigated were what we should say and not what we should believe ... belief is the affirmation that what has been represented is outside the mind just as it has been represented in the mind.(55)

Priority is obviously given to reason. Thereafter, this point of view found its clearest expression in the natural religion of the Enlightenment. Moses Mendelssohn, who was one of its outstanding spokesmen, argued in his Phaidon that immortality, namely, the survival of the soul, is not a dogma of any religion, but can be comprehended by an intelligent man. This treatise by Mendelssohn had a hidden aim as well: If immortality could be understood by any man of reason, this would ipso facto refute a charge leveled by Christian theologians of his day against Judaism. They, and Kant as well, claimed that Christianity was religiously more spiritual than Judaism, because the New Testament attained the concept of the survival of the soul, whereas the Old Testament did not. But this aspect of the problem is of marginal significance for the present discussion. In a similar fashion, Mendelssohn emphasized in his Jerusalem, as well, that the "eternal truths" (v. supra), which he identifies with "religious doctrines" and which are

> about God, His rule and Providence, without which man cannot be enlightened or happy ... were ... addressed to man's reason, for his rational understanding and acknowledgement according to the nature and evidence of eternal truth. These truths could not have been inspired through direct revelation; indeed, they could not have been made known through speech or writing, which can be understood only here and now. The supreme being has revealed them to all rational creatures through concepts and events inscribed in their souls with a script that is legible and intelligible at all times and in all places.(56)

Incidentally, Mendelssohn went on formulating his ideas on these matters, unaware that Kant, in his Critique of Pure Reason, which appeared two years earlier, had already demolished his arguments. In his critical philosophy Kant - contrary to Mendelssohn - negated the very possibility of human reason achieving knowledge of "transcendental ideas," namely, ideas of God, Freedom (in its philosophical sense, as opposed to determinism) and Immortality (the survival of the soul.) However, in his philosophy of ethics, Kant gave the conception of autonomy its fullest expression.

Man establishes moral law based on the concept of obligation, duty. However, just as many philosophers before him - Maimonides, Spinoza and others - had differentiated between the intellectual capacity of philosophers and that of the common people, so also Kant believed that his ethical doctrine, derived from the Categorical Imperative, could not be grasped by the common man, and, therefore, it was not adequate for his education in moral behavior: he needed another, simpler type of motivation. In any case, his conclusion in favor of autonomy can be derived - both from his book on ethics, The Critique of Practical Reason, and from his view of religion as an aid to morality (v.ff.) - from his subordination of the epistemological problem to moral requirements. Indeed, it is possible to think about God, the world and the soul, but they cannot be known, since they are transcendental concepts. Thus the existence of God, the survival of the soul and the freedom of the will, according to Kant, are postulates (theoretical demands) that are necessarily derived from moral doctrine. In his famous saying, in the introduction to the second edition of The Critique of Pure Reason, he writes: I have therefore found it necessary to deny knowledge, in order to make room for faith"(57). Kant did not intend to refer, as some of his interpreters have erroneously thought, to the faith of the Christian Church. He meant to adopt a voluntaristic position, no longer based on theoretical foundations, but on moral postulates. According to Kant, religion is in fact nothing but the moral law dwelling in man's heart. In consequence, religion cannot, and is not intended to, establish the truth of the idea of the supreme Divine law-giver and judge, but only to make it real, and to emphasize it. "There is only one (true) religion, but there can be faiths of several kinds."(58) And so there is no room for "revealed religions," only for "revealed faiths." However, Kant is not always consistent in his use of this terminology. The main point is that man tends to regard his moral duties as Divine Commandments.

Kant's position on religion as a motivating force for morality can be outlined schematically. If God, Freedom and Immortality are "transcendental ideas," which human reason cannot grasp but in which man must believe, then man has conceived on the practical level something that he could not attain on the theoretical one: If we believe (since we cannot know) that man is free, and is always at any moment capable of initiating a new causal chain - in other words, is free to choose between good and evil, without prior conditioning; and if we believe (again without capacity to know) that a God exists who will reward man for his good deeds and punish him for his bad; and, finally, if we believe (once again, without the capacity to know) in immortality, namely in the survival of the soul in the next world, where man will receive his due reward or punishment, it follows (at least Kant believed so) that there exist potentially all the elements of a moral motivation for ordinary men to behave in accordance with the principle of duty. Since Kant is discussing popular motivation, he does not hesitate to use the conventional, anthropomorphic images that expect God to reward the righteous and to punish the evil. People believe that God behaves according to certain values. But even in his main philosophy of ethics Kant perceived God as the embodiment of morality and its realization. Of course, this leads to a contradiction between his basic philosophical view, which places God on the transcendental level, that man is incapable of knowing, and the view that the concepts of God, Freedom and Immortality make for moral distinctions, from which it follows that man has some positive knowledge about God. Kant neither succeeded in overcoming this contradiction, nor did he, perhaps, want to. In short, since the bases of religion are found in the above three ideas, in which one can only believe, it follows that religion fulfills a very important function in guiding man toward the moral life. Even though the moral law is engraved on man's heart, still one must do something to activate it. Needless to say, turning religion into an adjunct of ethics was regarded with little favor by the men of the cloth, who comprehended quite well the agnostic structure that underlay this view. One should add that after completing his three Critiques Kant approached the problem of religion as a subject for independent study. In his treatise, Religion Within the Limits of Reason Alone, he allowed religion a more independent status, and did not regard it merely as an instrument for achieving morality.

We have discussed at length the autonomic aspect, and will at this stage deal with the heteronomous position only briefly. It was supported, inter alia, by the "Ash'ariya" school in Arab philosophy, which forbade one to entertain any doubts concerning God's will. Maimonides, in his discussion of Providence,(59) argued against this school of thought as well. The Arab philosopher el-Gazali held to the heteronomous view, as did, in his footsteps, Judah Halevy. The Scholastics Duns Scotus and William of Occam and later Calvin, Pascal and others also supported the concept of heteronomy. In modern times, this view has been favored by religious Existentialists, including Rosenzweig and Buber in Jewish philosophy. In the nature of things, this line of thought became the major trend in Jewish philosophy. It will be dealt with extensively below.

CHAPTER FIFTEEN

PHILOSOPHY of RELIGION and THEOLOGY in JEWISH and GENERAL PHILOSOPHY

As a result of the encounter between philosophy, as an expression of one spiritual world, and the monotheistic religions, based on the Scripture, as the expression of another, two basic disciplines emerge:

I. Philosophy of religion, which became a branch of philosophy. (Part of its subject matter and some of its problems have been discussed above.)

II. Theology, which became the theoretical basis of religion.

At the outset there was no clear difference between philosophy of religion and theology, as there was none between theology and philosophy, and even later on the differences often became blurred. Let us take Hegel as an example. Even though between 1821-1831 he had devoted much attention to the philosophy of religion, (60) he was not comfortable with the term "philosophy of religion" itself, because it might create the impression that philosophy deals with religion as, say, engineering deals with research in space. After all he believed religion and philosophy to be the two supreme stages of the Absolute Spirit (v. supra), dealing with the same content, and differing only in the manner in which they dealt with that content, and so it would be impossible for the one, namely religion, to constitute the content, or the subject of investigation of the other, namely, philosophy.

Yet, today philosophy of religion deals with exactly the subject matter which Hegel sought to deny it. There is even something of a paradox in the matters that are of concern to the philosophy of religion, as it seeks to establish itself as a scientific discipline, employing logical propositions and rationalistic arguments in the investigation of matters that, seemingly, mind and reason do not apply to. This logical vulnerability, of employing rational thought in an area where reason does not apply, did not bother Hegel, who consciously pinned his hopes on philosophical speculation. Thus, in his view, philosophy of religion is essentially only theology.

Rabbi Kaufmann Kohler, one of the founders and leaders of the Reform Movement in the United States in the 19th and early 20th centuries, expressed a similar idea, but from a distinctly Jewish standpoint. Since "philosophy of religion" is philosophy dealing with religion, there is nothing particularly Jewish about it. There is no more room for a Jewish philosophy of religion than there is for a Jewish mathematics. (The general principles involved in the problems here raised will be dealt with in the coming chapters.) But there definitely is room for a Jewish theology, that will consider the unique Jewish perception of God.(61)

Despite his reservations concerning the term "philosophy of religion," Hegel refrained from using the term "theology" in its stead, since it was already reserved for "church dogmatics." However, after Hegel the term "Theology" was rehabilitated to a certain extent. Beginning with the "Young Hegelians" of the thirties and forties of the last century up until the Christian and Jewish thinkers of the present century, theology freed itself to a considerable degree from the chains of the Church, its institutions and its dogmas. It became once more a field of pursuit for the independent religious philosophers, at least for the more important among them. Hence it was not paradoxical that there were even theologians who did not believe in God, such as D.F. Strauss and Ludwig Feuerbach, in the middle of the 19th century. God as a subject of philosophical inquiry - the "Doctrine of God" - does not require, a priori, acceptance of His existence. For Feuerbach, theology, a creation of man's spirit, was nothing other than anthropology; the concept of God is a self-projection of man's mind, and therefore the true Godhead is nothing other than man's quiddity, perceived as free from the corporeal limitations of the real man. "Love of God" should be turned into "love of man" as the only true religion. (He developed these ideas, for the most part, in his books, The Essence of Christianity, 1841, and The Essence of Religion, 1851.) For this reason, Rosenzweig later accused Buber, because of certain motifs of Feuerbach that appeared in his early teachings, of "Atheistic Theology." (62) These are extreme examples, but it is worthy of note that in this fashion theology, ever since the 19th century, has also become an area of theoretical inquiry for philosophers who have no ties with religious institutions. Secular philosophers, as well, have succeeded in pointing out the humanistic and moral foundations that may be revealed in traditional theological thought:

> Man creates God, all-powerful and all-good ... In this lies Man's true freedom: in determination to worship only the God created by our love of the good, to respect only the heaven which inspires the insight of our best moments ... not by renunciation alone can we build a temple for the worship of our own ideas ... In this way mind asserts its subtle mastery over the thoughtless forces of nature.(63)

In modern Jewish philosophy, theology was dealt with along similar lines by such 19th century thinkers as Samuel Hirsch, Solomon Formstecher, Ludwig Steinheim, Abraham Geiger, Moritz Lazarus and Heymann Steinthal. In the 20th century one should mention Hermann Cohen, Rosenzweig (even though he had reservations about the term), Buber, Felix Weltsch, Max Brod, Margareta Susman, Max Wiener and Leo Baeck. All of these writers were brought up upon classical German philosophy, though some of the latter ones rebelled against it in different ways and tended toward existentialist interpretations. Later on, the preoccupation of the major Jewish thinkers with theology shifted to the United States, as evidenced by the writings of Solomon Schechter, Kaufmann Kohler, Abraham Yehoshua Heschel, Mordecai M. Kaplan, Emil Fackenheim, Will Herberg, Milton Konvitz, Milton Steinberg, E. Berkovitz, Steven S. Schwarzschild, Jacob Neusner, Arthur A. Cohen, Jacob Agus, R. Rubinstein, Eugene Borowitz, [Borowitz published in 1977 a detailed platform for Liberal Jewish theology.] and others. While it is true that the latter group does not, perhaps, equal the preceding generation of German-Jewish scholars in originality of thought, nevertheless the long list of names cited above speaks for itself, and points to the great interest that Jews have in the theological problems of our day. It is premature to comment on certain initial attempts that have been made in Israel in the field of Jewish theology. They are few, for two reasons: The real religious philosophers, like Rabbi Kook, with all the daring originality of his thought, are inseparably bound up with orthodoxy; whereas others like Hugo Bergmann, Yehoshua Gutmann, Julius Guttmann, Moshe Schwarcz, Baruch Kurzweil and the like are primarily philosophers and scholars, and theological investigation is not one of their priorities. It can be readily understood why "theologians" of Feuerbach's kind are rare in Jewish philosophy, in spite of Rosenzweig's accusations against Buber, and similar strictures by Jewish religious thinkers against the naturalistic "Reconstructionism" of Mordecai Kaplan. The only Jewish philosopher who might fit the designation of "Atheistic Theologian" was Hiwi al-Balkhi, who lived in the 9th century and against whose views Sa'adia Gaon and Abraham Ibn Ezra leveled sharp criticism.(65)

CHAPTER SIXTEEN

WHAT is JEWISH THEOLOGY?

"Theology" means the "theory about the Divinity," the science concerning God. As such, it has been a subject for investigation throughout the generations; however, it was the influence of the Christian Church that turned it into a systematic discipline. As its name suggests, from the very beginning it was meant to function in a specific and defined area of philosophy - the subject of the Godhead, and in this domain it posed four basic questions: 1) the quiddity of God; 2) the proofs for the existence and for the knowledge of God; 3) God's attributes; 4) God's relation to man and the universe - creation, revelation, redemption, providence, predestination, miracles, prophecy. With the passage of time, theology no longer limited itself strictly to subjects that dealt with God alone, but broadened its areas of investigation to include some of the more general areas in religion, like prayer, worship, free will, sin, repentance, the problem of evil, survival of the soul, the status of the angels and the like. It also devoted a very large part of its efforts to the hermeneutics of the Holy Script, and to ethics. For example, the question of the reasons for the Commandments occupied an important place in Jewish philosophy from the Middle Ages onward.

The term "theology" was first mentioned in Plato's Republic: "What are these forms of theology which you mean?"(66) However, philosophic investigations as to the quiddity of the Gods, as opposed to mythological fables, could be found as early as the days of Xenophanes (c.570-c.480 B.C.), the pre-Socratic who fulminated against the anthropomorphic images attributed to the Godhead. By identifying the Deity with nature he anticipated, to a certain extent, Spinoza's pantheism. Later on Plato - especially in the later dialogues, such as Timaeus (whose influence on Judah Abarbanel's Dialoghi d'Amore was very marked(67)) - and Aristotle in his Metaphysics paid a good deal of attention to theological subjects. Up to this period, theology, as its name implies, has been the science of the Godhead.

In the 13th century, Thomas Aquinas, following Aristotle, enunciated the principles of natural theology (Theologia naturalis) as opposed to revealed theology (Theologia revelata). By connecting the teachings of the Christian Church with Aristotelian philosophy, he laid the foundation for the system of theoretical dogmatics of the Christian Church. [In 1879 Thomas was declared the official philosopher of the Roman Catholic Church, and in 1924 the Fourteen Theses of his philosophy were declared to be the authoritative expression of his teachings.]

The relations between natural and revealed theology also engaged the attention of Jewish philosophy in the Middle Ages. The problem was first known, through Sa'adia Gaon's philosophizing, as "The Rule of the Two Truths," namely, rational truth and revealed truth (v. chapters infra). However, what was unique in Christian theology was to be found in the formulations of the Principles of Faith - dogmas - that were binding upon the believer - and without which Salvation and Redemption were not possible.

Natural theology was not regarded as opposed to revealed theology, but rather as complementary to it: it provided the rational basis for the religious content. In this respect some philosophers considered theology as a part of philosophy, even as philosophy's crowning activity. But Aristotle himself already identified theology with metaphysics, or, as he called it, "Primary Philosophy." The Godhead is the supreme principle of reality, the ultimate cause of all causes, the "mover unmoved," the "form of forms," and so on. It embodies the unity of "the intellect, as well as the intellectually cognizing subject and the intellectually cognized subject"(68) - an idea that had a far-reaching influence on the teachings of the medieval Jewish philosophers Abraham Ibn Daud, Maimonides and Levi Ben Gershon (Gersonides). From them it found its way, through a number of channels, to the writings of Judah Abarbanel, Spinoza (from the pantheistic aspect) and Salomon Maimon (from the idealistic viewpoint).

In the 18th century, the philosophers of the Enlightenment, following Christian Wolff and his adherents (among whom was Mendelssohn), changed the term "natural theology" to "rational theology" (theologia rationalis). They did so in order to emphasize its independence from revelation - anyhow, revealed theology was abandoned by the philosophers of the Enlightenment. So came into being - first in England, and then in France and Germany - the school of "deism," which held that God is the First Cause of all causes, but that after Creation there is no further Divine intervention in the events of the universe and no Divine Providence. The basis of this school of thought was natural religion, and its doctrine - rational theology. Influenced by these teachings, Mendelssohn sought to found the uniqueness of Judaism not on religious truths, but on the Commandments (the "Law"). Of all the traditional proofs of the existence of God, deism retained only Anselm's most sophisticated ontological proof. This proof rapidly became one of the important principles of natural and rational theology - in Descartes's philosophy in the 17th century, to a degree for Spinoza, for Leibniz and later also for Hegel. The "ontological proof" provides that the objective existence of God is derived from a subjective idea concerning a supreme and perfect existent. In other words, it rests on the argument that were God not real, but merely an idea, the concept of God as a completely perfect existent would be deficient. This argument was very attractive to the philosophers of the Enlightenment, because of its logical structure and reliance on exclusively rational reasons. In that same period, Kant was engaged in refuting the various proofs for God's existence. He demonstrated that they all depended on the ontological proof, which was itself in grave error, because it made no distinction between "concept" and "existence": "existence" cannot be an attribute (a predicate) and can never serve as an attribute of God.

But by this argument Kant, willy-nilly, indirectly strengthened the position of supernatural, revelatory theology. It is not a matter of chance that Rosenzweig, a modern Jewish philosopher, found inspiration for his belief in revelation not only among philosophers like Judah Halevy, Pascal, Kierkegaard, and the later Schelling, but also in the necessary conclusions that follow from the philosophy of Kant. In short, after Kant, natural and rational theology lost their attraction. As pointed out in previous chapters, today religious thinkers again tend to accept supranatural concepts of a "positive" theology. Faith and reason are regarded as two necessary faculties, belonging to different and separate domains, with no connection between them whatsoever. The well-known anecdote that Rosenzweig told about Hermann Cohen is illustrative: "Cohen once explained 'the concept of God' to a simple Jew from Marburg. The Jew listened closely and finally asked: 'Professor, and where does the Creator of the Universe come in?' And then - so it is told - tears rolled down Cohen's cheeks."(69)

A certain interesting dialectic development is revealed here. Religious dogmatism, the legacy of the Scholastics, has, since the 18th century, gradually given place to the aspirations of the Enlightenment to objective certainty. As a reaction, these, in turn, gave birth to an irrational mysticism, especially since the Kantian critique seemed to have uncovered the vulnerable points in the position of the Enlightenment. A new kind of dogmatism developed on the fringes of the Romantic movement, especially among its chauvinistic, racist and religious elements, but this is not the place to enlarge on the subject.

Thus, the problem of God, in fact, exists only for philosophy, but not for theology, and certainly not for a man of faith, as the above anecdote about Hermann Cohen illustrates. And so, supranatural theology preserves the barrier between religion and philosophy; whereas the "negative," traditional, theology, just as in the case of the speculative philosophy of Hegel hundreds of years later, sought to identify the God of religion with the God of philosophy, by identifying God with the Absolute Truth. Thus, almost paradoxically, it was philosophical skepticism that led its adherents to "Fideism," a simple faith in the truths of revelation, that foregoes attaining them by way of reason, of which it is occasionally sharply critical. In the history of philosophy and theology one encounters a great many variations, both of Anselm's view that intellectual attainment is the reward of faith, and of the would-be Tertullian approach that faith exists despite, and because of its absurdity. It is in this way that theology tries to widen the gap and sharpen the antagonism between philosophical investigation on the one hand, and the fear of Heaven and obedience to religious dogmas on the other. For completely different reasons, and on the basis of a completely different line of argument, Spinoza, in his time, claimed that the goal of philosophy was to seek the truth, whereas it is the duty of religion and theology to educate to fear of Heaven and to obedience to constituted authority. The crucial difference, one with very far-reaching implications, between Spinoza's views and the theological views expressed above is that the obedience to which religion educated man, according to Spinoza, does not pertain to matters of thought and faith.

All these problems existed and were discussed in Jewish philosophy, as well, especially in medieval times. However, they never developed into a special systematic discipline. It surely is not accidental that the Greek word "theology" never became a part of the Hebrew language; while the term "philosophy" became a part of the Hebrew language without difficulty, because it answered an intellectual need. The reason may be very simple. All the Talmudic authorities and Halachists, except for a very few well-known converts, were born Jews. They did not come to Judaism from the outside, and therefore never felt the need to be persuaded of its validity in order to accept it; whereas most of the Christian scholars in the early centuries of the Common Era were not born Christians. They adopted Christianity by an act of conscious free will (there may have been other factors involved as well, but they do not affect the matter in principle), and theology was, as it were, forced upon them, as they sought to examine and evaluate their former pagan beliefs against the basic religious tenets of Christianity. None of this was present in Judaism, and therefore theological writings, in the strict sense of the word, were, for a very long time, foreign to Judaism. Philosophy, and philosophy of religion, as well, i.e., the philosophical interpretation of the Jewish religion was acceptable, but systematic theology as it existed in Christianity was not.

As noted previously, theoretical theology deals with enunciating the principles of faith, which constitute a necessary condition for Salvation. Judaism, too, incorporated faith in revelation, but this faith contained no promise of salvation as it did in Christianity (and in Islam). Nevertheless there was a controversy on the question of whether Judaism is dependent upon dogmas, and, in consequence, whether there is such a thing as Jewish theology. The principles of faith make a claim to explicit cognitive status, in which case they must perforce be the consequence of a theoretical, systematic theology. In the philosophy of the Sages there appears the phrase "one who denies the principle of Jewish religion" (agnostic).(70) This phrase can be interpreted to mean that even in earliest times there was a kind of theology that held to at least one principle, namely, the faith in one God. There is no doubt that medieval Jewish philosophers, who discussed the subject of The Principles of Faith, dealt with something that may be called "theology" - Ibn Da'ud, Maimonides, Hasdai Crescas, Joseph Albo and others.

Each of these various authorities set forth a different number of "Principles of Faith" - Ibn Da'ud, six; Maimonides, thirteen; Albo, three - and they were never accepted in Judaism as binding. The very fact that what seemed binding in the eyes of one authority - be he even as illustrious a philosophical and religious authority as Maimonides - was not necessarily so in the eyes of another, was sufficient to cast doubt on the very existence of a Jewish theology. As a matter of fact, every single one of the Thirteen Maimonidean Principles of Faith, was rejected by one Jewish authority or another in the generations to come. In retrospect one might say that this testifies to the intellectual tolerance that prevailed, which is one of the distinguishing characteristics of true philosophy. Moreover, except for the last two of the Thirteen Principles of Faith enunciated by Maimonides, all the others are unlike the dogmas of Christianity, because they are derivable from reason as well as from faith. This idea is lent force by the order of appearance of the problems discussed in The Guide of the Perplexed (even though this book often seems to be intentionally muddled because of Maimonides's esoteric style. On this subject, more infra.) In any event, Mendelssohn, the first of the Jewish philosophers of the modern era, was right when, in dealing with this problem in a systematic fashion, he held that Judaism has no binding principles of faith, only binding rules of behavior, and so there is no place for a Jewish theology.

At this point, one may sum up as follows: Jewish philosophers did deal with questions, which, strictly speaking, belong to theology; however up to the 19th century there was no "Jewish theology" comparable to the Christian (and Islamic) theology that has existed from the Scholastics to the present day. And so the Encyclopedia Judaica is in error in holding that the Jewish philosophy of the Middle Ages was not philosophy, but theology.(71)

Beginning with the latter half of the past century, modern Jewish thought has looked upon theology as a kind of intermediary between philosophy and religion, whose aim is to subordinate the former to the latter, but without blurring the principled differences between them, and without causing philosophy to retreat to the status of a "handmaiden." Unconsciously, these aims have expressed a preference for the religious truth over the rational one. Prior to this period, Sa'adia Gaon, Maimonides, and most of the Jewish philosophers of the Middle Ages held that the two truths were identical in content: Religious truth was derived from the belief in Revelation, and philosophical truth was the fruit of reason. Consequently, there was no need either for theology or for some conciliation between philosophy and religion, since they were not considered as being inconsistent with each other. In the modern era however many theological subjects relevant to the fundamentals of faith of the Jewish religion have been discussed. But the Jewish philosophers dealing with theology have not neglected their investigations in the fields of philosophy, history and the other fields of Judaic studies. One of the tasks undertaken by Jewish theology has been to defend, in one way or another, the traditional theistic view, and expecially the concept of God as being both transcendent (the Creator) and immanent (the Divine Presence).

Jewish theology, then, is a relatively young phenomenon in the field of Jewish philosophy, one of the expressions of the innovations that occurred in the passage from the Middle Ages to the modern era. The first systematic discussion of "Jewish theology" may be found in the thinking of Abraham Geiger. Beginning with 1835 he published the Wissenschaftliche Zeitschrift fuer juedische Theologie ("The Scientific Journal for Jewish Theology"). Its contributors included some of the most important Jewish scholars in Germany and France, such as Joseph Naphtali Derenbourg, Marcus Jost, Leopold Zunz, Adolf Munk, Shlomo Yehuda Rappaport and others. From 1862 to his death in 1874 he published the journal Juedische Zeitschrift fuer Wissenschaft und Leben ("The Jewish Journal for Science and Life"), which served as the exclusive organ for expressing the views of the editor. The names of the foregoing two periodicals exemplify the new spirit of the age - the investigation of scientific ideas, and revelation of life's realities at one and the same time. Geiger believed that theology should be scientific, but that it should not be divorced from everyday life. His dealing with the practical aspects of the theological studies also underlined the influence that the Jewish spiritual heritage had on his thinking.

Because of the important implications of Geiger's conception of the quiddity and function of Jewish theology - with regard to both principle and methodology - it is well to elaborate somewhat on this theme. He felt that theology should not limit itself only to cognitive matters, but should also reflect a serious moral concern. This principle held for science, and, even more so, for theology.(72). In the first two paragraphs of his essay <u>Introduction to the Study of Jewish Theology</u> Geiger states:

> 1) Theology involves getting to know the religious truths and the lives that have to be led in accordance with them. It is every person's duty to attain this. However, when theology becomes a science (as it must), a defined discipline, <u>ipso facto</u> it assumes the additional task of helping others, who are unable to traverse this difficult path by themselves, to reach this knowledge by easier means, to make sure that they hold firm to it. To achieve this end there are special means, and theology adds to its purely theoretical contribution a practical one as well, which includes the instruments by which one may influence others to achieve this specific aim.
>
> 2) Theology that is Jewish determines the two parts of this investigation more clearly. On the theoretical level it now reflects an awareness of the religious truths and the life led in accordance with them on the basis of the Jewish Torah. The achievement of such a consciousness, were it not presented to us in a certain manner, would only constitute an intellectual aim, a goal for philosophical observation. However, since it is also <u>given</u>, it becomes a goal for history.(73)

It is easy to discern in these programmatic assumptions, <u>inter alia</u>, the intellectual influences of Maimonides - religious truths, principles of faith - and those of Kant - the supplementing of the theoretical dimension by the practical one. However, the unique aspect of Geiger's thinking was his attempt, in his theology, to link philosophy to history. In his opinion, the two are inextricably intertwined. Whoever confines himself to one of the two, cannot be a Jewish theologian, because he will either lack a historical perspective or an epistemological perception.(74) A certain similarity to the thinking of Nachman Krochmal is sensed here, be it conscious or unconscious. There is a reasonable probability that Geiger was acquainted with Krochmal's book <u>A Guide for the Perplexed of the Times,</u> which had just been published by Zunz.

Citing Maimonides in support, Geiger declares that a genius does not arrive at truth by gradual, logical steps - he does so by a sudden intellectual <u>inspiration</u>, which is a <u>revelation</u>. [Parenthetically, the question of the nature of inspiration, which was raised in the introduction of <u>The Guide of the Perplexed</u>,(75) has, in recent years, been of great interest to philosophers and psychologists who have sought to clarify the creative moment in scientific research and artistic endeavor(76)]. Geiger thought that the phenomenon of "revelation" was characteristic of ancient times, when spiritual chaos reigned. It was at this juncture that Judaism gave of its religious light to mankind. The Prophets were geniuses of this type. Their message was the equivalent of the Act of Creation. [The parable of the creation of light was very congenial to the writers of the Enlightenment ("<u>Haskala</u>") period. The English words "enlightenment" and "illumination" give evidence of this. The English philosopher-poet Alexander Pope used this parable in connection with Newton, and, following him, one of the Jewish scholars of the end of the 19th century did the same for Moses Mendelssohn ("And God said: Let there be Moses; and there was light.")]

In accordance with Geiger's description, the following diagram may be drawn to represent Jewish theology:

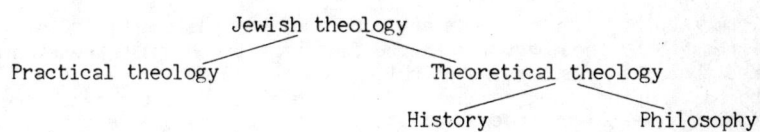

Here again are reflected the problems of the relations between theory and praxis, which have already been considered in the First Part, in discussing the differences between the views of Aristotle and Plato on the function of philosophy. Geiger transfers the discussion to the theological plane. Influenced by his Jewish heritage, he gives special weight to the practical aspect. Of particular interest is the function that he allots to history, and, in its wake, to Judaic studies in general (v. infra). History, to him, serves as a mediator and a bridge between theoretical and practical theology. Whereas philosophy presents the questions and suggests a method for the attainment of the idea, history examines the manifestations of the idea. (He refers especially to the idea of monotheism in Jewish history.) Its purpose is to make available to practical theology the conclusions of the investigation of the history of the idea, whose quiddity is revealed, in its many incarnations throughout the generations, by philosophy.

> The main aim of science is thoroughly to explore, critically and without bias, the sources of Judaism and its historical development. In this fashion, it can, on the one hand, learn the essential truth about the sources, and, on the other hand, it can point out the changes brought about in the historical development. The practical religious interest in the matter is to use the results obtained by such research for present requirements, so as to consciously forge a link between that which occurred in ancient times (in accordance with historical discoveries that have come down to us in the form of tradition) and the present historical process. Furthermore, to turn the past into a living reality, relevant to the present and its attendant circumstances.(77)

This opinion was strongly seconded in our day by Eugene Borowitz, a scholarly Reform rabbi, who declared: "History is the laboratory of Jewish theology."(78) One of the results of this sort of historical investigation, Geiger believed, would be that, in view of the metamorphoses that have taken place in the spiritual realm from early times to modern days, it would be legitimate to relate to a given idea in a light different from that of the past. It then follows that corrections (reforms) in the Jewish worship of God would be justified. From this point of view, the theologian differs from the philosopher of religion in that he must <u>live and act</u> in accordance with changed circumstances, to advance his faith. He cannot be satisfied with a mere theoretical comprehension. He is an active partner in the practice of his faith, whose basic premises he has undertaken to elucidate. However, there is no possibility for a Jewish theology to exist, that is not grounded in philosophy.

From the above schema one might conclude that philosophy is only a part of theoretical theology. On the surface, the erroneous impression might be gained that Geiger subordinated philosophy to theology, as had been the standard in the Middle Ages. But this is not the case here at all. Philosophy, as Geiger understood it, is the point of departure and the condition precedent for theological studies. As such, its function is self-sufficient and independent. Moreover, there is another essential difference between the two, which has been touched upon previously: philosophy holds to no presuppositions as to the matters it considers. (Whether this is possible, is another question.) It professes to have no aim other than to accept as true everything that it discovers objectively, through the philosophical endeavor. On the other hand, theology, its goals and assumptions are <u>ab initio</u> consciously guided by a faith in the existence of God, and by an aspiration to strengthen such a faith.(79) The lesson to be learned from this is of paramount importance in perceiving the quiddity of religion, even though it entails a theoretical difficulty. According to Geiger, theology, which accepts, <u>ab initio</u>, the truths of religion, undertakes to rely on philosophy, which, for its part, is free of presuppositions. Only in this manner can philosophy be of theoretical value for theology. Were philosophy also to be based on previous assumptions, it would be of no real theoretical value to theology. Yet the argument has something of the <u>petitio principii</u> in it. What can the theologian do if the objective "unbiased" investigations lead him to conclusions that are contrary to his goals and aspirations as a theologian? It would seem that a theologian who seeks to ground his religious position in the objective findings of philosophy and Geiger argues that such must be the case - evidently hopes that such findings will be in consonance with his religious view, or perhaps he is even completely certain <u>ab initio</u> of what the results of such philosophical investigations will <u>be</u>. It is his subjective aspiration that dictates to him what his "objective" philosophical conclusions will be - those that he is supposed to discover and confirm. Borowitz in our day has sought to overcome this difficulty. It is his opinion that Jewish theology, unlike Christian theology, which is fundamentally dogmatic, does not put limits to one's freedom of thought. It is systematic, but not authoritarian. It seeks to achieve its ends by persuasion. It may well arouse debate and controversy, but these will only be helpful in achieving the aims set forth. (On this point he is doubtless right.)(80) Theology's conclusions can be binding only for him who accepts its theses. Yet, the basic difficulty of the "persuaded" theologian remains.

One might argue that Geiger's problem, in the final analysis, is a dilemma which every cultured man, every individual who philosophizes, not only the theologian, encounters at least once in his life time. J.G. Fichte, in the introduction to his Wissenschaftslehre ("Science of Knowledge"), has already stated: "The kind of philosophy you choose depends on the kind of person you are."(81) Nevertheless, there does exist a difference between the philosopher and the theologian that cannot be blurred or ignored. A philosopher, even if he tends to a particular view - idealism or materialism, determinism or indeterminism, or the like - will not undergo intolerable pangs of conscience if he comes to the conclusion that his philosophical position is indefensible and that he has to adopt a new standpoint that seems to him more reasonable and better than the one he held heretofore. True, it is often very difficult to shed accepted, conventional ideas. Yet, to approach a theoretical subject without any prejudices is the only valid road for scientific investigation in any sphere, including philosophy. Many examples can be adduced of philosophers who because of their intellectual integrity, abandoned previously held positions. We do not mean to refer to those well-known cases, where an individual underwent some personal experience that brought about a change in his viewpoint, but rather to instances, where philosophical inquiry per se brought about a change in a scholar's thinking. There is practically no major philosopher who did not revise his philosophical views: the early Kant versus the Kant of The Critique of Pure Reason; the Schelling of "Transcendental Idealism" versus the Schelling who held to a view rooted in mythology and revelation; and, in our time, the examples of Husserl, Whitehead and Russell come to mind. A most remarkable example is Ludwig Wittgenstein. In the late twenties he radically reversed his position, which he formulated in the Tractatus Logico-Philosophicus only ten years earlier, and which he had regarded as the last word in philosophy. A similar case in point is Martin Buber, in the field of Jewish philosophy. In the early twenties he revised his earlier position and adopted a dialogic view of a personal God. This change was expressed, as is well known, in an impressive discourse in his book, I and Thou. This occurred in 1923. His friend Rosenzweig tended to define this revision as a Return to the Faith. Buber reacted positively to the designation even though the Hebrew term "Return to the Faith" (Hazarah bitshuvah) meant originally repentance for one's sins; it is certainly doubtful whether Buber's earlier philosophical position can be regarded as a "sin".

However, the problem is fundamentally different for the theologian. It is, of course, possible to cite examples of theologians, priests and ministers who abandoned their faith as a result of philosophical speculation. In addition to Giordano Bruno and Spinoza, one might recall what happened to Franz Brentano, Buber's and Bergmann's teacher, who left the priesthood and was excommunicated by the Roman Catholic Church. Sometimes it also happens the other way round, namely that a secular thinker returns to the world of faith. The conservative Rabbi and theologian Will Herberg was in his youth a Marxist and an active member of the Communist Party.(83) However, it is certain that Geiger did not have in mind the possibility that Jewish theologians, who are obligated to study philosophy in depth, would be lured by their investigations into giving up their faith. Nor did he envisage that such studies would determine the validity of religion. He believed that their philosophical efforts would strengthen their religious faith and would be of assistance to them in their religio-moral mission in practical life, and not the opposite. The inescapable dilemma - perhaps Geiger, personally, was not aware of its gravity in principle - remains a problem. Further, Geiger warned Jewish theologians that in dealing with philosophy they might unwittingly succumb to the covert Christian assumptions that are to be found in western philosophy.(84) Yet, in this very warning there is an adoption of an a priori standpoint, correct or not, concerning conclusions to which philosophical inquiry might lead, or, in the given case, might prevent.

However, the theoretical difficulties that may be found in Geiger's theology in no way derogate from its value in clarifying the problem. Geiger explored the principled aspects of the relationship of theology to philosophy from a standpoint that was explicitly rooted in Jewish theology, as Spinoza had done previously (cf. Theologico-Political Treatise, especially Chapter 15), and as Mendelssohn had done (especially in the first chapter of Jerusalem). However, Spinoza had held that philosophy and theology dealt with matters that were discrete and that the two had no point of contact. Mendelssohn had rejected the need for theology as far as Judaism was concerned; whereas Geiger was the first Jewish scholar who believed that Jewish theology was vitally necessary as a spiritual-intellectual ground for Jewish religious life in the modern world. Yet the practical application of his assumptions did not always allow him to remain faithful to the theoretical beliefs that underlaid his theology and that were meant to illustrate the importance of the Science of Judaism in general, and not only from the historical aspect, as set forth in the above schema.

For Geiger, practical theology, that is to say, the concrete component in Jewish theology, was meant to spread the ethical message of Judaism and at the same time to ensure the full implementation of religious ethics in Jewish life. The bearers of these moral tidings were to be the rabbis and preachers. However, since their authority was not sanctioned by the State, it had to be based on knowledge.(85) The theoretical grounds of the Jewish religious morality had to be clear to the congregants so that they could apply them in everyday life. These rested on three main factors:

1. The eternal content of Judaism.

2. The religious outlook, rooted in the soul (Gemuet), and bound to ancient tradition.

3. The modern spirit.(86)

The third factor was of the highest importance to Geiger, the Reformer. "The function of the theologian is to be aware of the spirit of the times and of the present. A rabbi should proclaim the religious verities attuned to the era." He who knows only the way of the Shulhan Arukh (the Jewish Code of Laws) of the past is unworthy of the title "theologian" or "rabbi." But here lies the difficulty: a religious system, by its very nature, has strong conservative and patriarchal tendencies. It seeks to inculcate in its communicants a feeling of intellectual and spiritual inferiority vis-a-vis the founders, the elders, the fathers, side by side with the need for accepting their authority. The Bible already refers to "the elders of the congregation."(87) In Talmudic times the old people were regarded as the truly wise. "The elders of the Court delivered him to the elders of the priesthood."(88) "The elders of Bet Shammai and the elders of Bet Hillel" are mentioned in a similar spirit,(89) and it was even stated explicitly that "there is no old man but that he is wise."(90) This aim of assigning authority and prestige to the founders, whose judgments we are commanded to accept, is well expressed in the following quotations:

> Moses received the Law from Sinai and committed it to Joshua, and Joshua to the Elders, and the Elders to the Prophets, and the Prophets committed it to the men of the Great Synagogue.(91)
> If the earlier (scholars) were sons of angels, we are sons of men; and if the earlier (scholars) were sons of men, we are like asses.(92)

This attitude is to be found not only in Judaism. It exists, perhaps to even a greater extent, in Catholicism and Islam. It follows, then, that the spiritual leaders are the wise men of the past, who of course have no connection with present experience and problems. This trend in Judaism has led to the complex of anachronistic religious law and religious intolerance that is vexing the public in Israel today. It was against this that Geiger rebelled. He believed that it was on this essential point that the men of the Science of Judaism must make their contributions, through the disciplines which they nurtured and developed since the twenties of the 19th century. These were the studies that would provide the historical and ideological substructure for the new theoretical and practical theology.

> The aim of the Science of Judaism ... is to get to know the total religious and ideological content of Judaism, which characterizes it as an unique life-force. This kind of knowledge can be acquired only by observing the manner in which the idea has gained entry into the phenomenal world; the manner in which it is reflected in the word and in the language; the way it embodies reality and history. Only after one uncovers, by induction, the spiritual motive power of Judaism, can one truly achieve a full knowledge of its philosophical religio-ethical views which is liberated from its temporary embodiment and from the seedlings concealed in it which, as yet, have not attained their full development. The Science of Judaism consists of three main parts:
>
> 1. Linguistics;
>
> 2. History, especially that of literature and of culture.
>
> 3. Religio-philosophical studies.(93)

In summing up the subject of the relations obtaining among philosophy, theology and religion today, one gets a different picture from the one that Geiger drew when he began his theological studies. In reality, theology functions as an intermediary between philosophy and religion. In the past - during the Middle Ages - it understood its task as that of subordinating philosophy to religion: philosophy was considered the handmaiden of religion. Nowadays there is no longer any aspiration of subordinating philosophy to religion - today theology seeks the aid of philosophy in reaching its religious goals. Yet the main identifying mark of traditional theology holds for modern theology, namely, the preference given to religious, believing truth over its rational counterpart. When the two are congruent, when the religious truth and the philosophical truth are perceived as one sole truth (without returning to the problem of the capability of achieving truth, discussed in the first chapter), theology would seem to be entirely superfluous. Examples may be cited from the teachings so diverse in time and in content as those of Maimonides and Hegel, or even Rosenzweig. In such an event, there is no need for an intermediary (v. supra). Thus, whereas philosophy is an independent discipline, theology is only a functional one.

Of course, the goals of Jewish theology may turn out to be very different, in accordance with the philosophical preferences of its practitioners. Philosophers like Rosenzweig and Emil Fackenheim seek to emphasize what one might term a Theology of Commandment; whereas Moshe Schwarcz or Borowitz speak about a "Theology of the Covenant," whose aim it is to emphasize the existential dimension in Judaism. These are only two of the trends current in our day. Other outlooks are connected with the names of Leo Baeck, Mordecai Kaplan, Buber, Heschel, Soloveitchik and many others.

PART THREE: WHAT IS JEWISH PHILOSOPHY?

CHAPTER SEVENTEEN

JEWISH PHILOSOPHY and the PHILOSOPHY OF JUDAISM

Most of the attempts to define the quiddity of "Jewish philosophy" have been made in the 20th century. It has become clear that what seemed at first glance to be self-evident and simple, was really fraught with a diversity of problems. The concept itself gave rise to differences of opinion, and the problem of terminology is an expression or a cover for substantive theoretical difficulties. Was the subject "Jewish philosophy," or "a Philosophy of Judaism," or, perhaps, "a Philosophy of Jews"? Latterly, the term "Jewish Thought" also has come into use. This has raised a new problem: how to treat the relations between "Jewish philosophy" and the "Philosophy of Judaism." Are they identical in content? Is one included in the other? Additional questions of this sort have appeared.

These are not merely pedantic questions - they extend beyond the bounds of terminology and definition. The various aspects are so significant as to justify extensive consideration. Up to the present time, no didactically satisfactory solution has been suggested for integrating Jewish philosophy within the teaching of general philosophy. This fact, as well, lends added energy to the necessity of addressing this subject in a more fundamental manner. Of course, the question might be posed: "What business is it of yours?"

Why should those concerned with Jewish thought be required to answer a question as to the quiddity and the uniqueness of Jewish philosophy? These questions were not of concern to Maimonides and other medieval Jewish philosophers; nor did they trouble Krochmal in the 19th century, or Buber and Rosenzweig in the 20th. What moves modern Jewish philosophers to reflect more deeply on the raison d'etre for their activities? This book opened with the premise that philosophy is the sole discipline that investigates its own quiddity, and, therefore, it would seem only natural that Jewish philosophy do the same. Nevertheless, the question does arise as to whether such concern is the expression of an ideological crisis that did not exist previously. It seems to me that one of the reasons for the rise of these questions is the traditional reserve that has existed in Judaism vis-a-vis philosophy and has resulted in a constant tension between the Philosophy of Judaism and philosophy as a whole. This matter will be considered below, among other questions.

Philosophy, by its very nature, deals with problems that are not peculiar to any specific national culture. Fundamentally, it is universal in scope. It is as general as mathematics, physics, astronomy and the like. Thus, ab initio, one must approach with a certain degree of scepticism any attempt to describe or define philosophical doctrines on the basis of national criteria. This is different from one's attitude to literature, especially to poetry. In these the determining criterion is the dependence on the language. The national language, including all its components with their particular forms, plays a significant role in the determination of the content of a literary work, and a fortiori, of poetry. Indeed, one cannot ignore the linguistic aspects in the field of philosophy either. As has been mentioned several times, these have overriding importance with regard to meaning, the presentation of propositions and so on. [The subject of linguistic problems, such as the concepts of emuna and ha'amana, the Hegelian term Aufhebung, the differences between declarative sentences that may be identical in external form, and the like have been considered above.] Language has its influence on the ways of philosophizing. Philosophers such as Hegel and Heidegger could only have emerged from a German-speaking society. Yet, all this has only an indirect effect on content, which does not belong to any specific cultural or national milieu. (An example to the contrary may be cited in the case of Logical Empiricism, which grew out of both the German-speaking "Vienna Circle" and British Analytic Philosophy.) In this respect, the distinction between philosophy and literature is clear: The fact that universities the world over (including Israel) maintain separate departments for literature in the Hebrew, Arabic, English, French, Russian or German languages is accepted without any questions. Yet it would cause astonishment were separate departments instituted in universities for English, French, German, or even Greek philosophy.

Incidentally, when one turns from literature to other departments in the arts, e.g., music, painting, sculpture, once again, from the methodological and disciplinary aspects, the uniqueness of the national contribution becomes blurred and tends to vanish. When one speaks about classical Greek sculpture, which is doubtless one of the salient expressions of ancient Greek culture, one does not search for the unique elements which distinguish this sculpture from that of other places and periods, though, of course, artistic styles keep changing. The same may be said of Flemish painting, which, in essence, differs from Italian or French painting of the same period. Differences do exist in choice of motifs, techniques, types of design and expression, and so on: Flemish artists painted figures taken from the Old and New Testament and from Greek mythology, dressed according to their current local fashion; their landscapes were replete with windmills, canals, seascapes and the like; whereas Italian artists painted figures dressed according to their local fashion, and put into their landscape mountains, vineyards, olive trees and the like. But no one will contend that these identify national cultures to the extent that would justify dividing up painting into categories of Flemish art and Italian art, and regarding them as two discrete artistic disciplines. The same holds true for music. Here, as well, one can doubtless discern influences of a unique cultural and national environment, but no one will undertake to present German music as being different in essence from French, Italian or Russian music. Many more examples could be cited.

Nevertheless, the fact remains that there is no Jewish mathematics, no Jewish physics, no Jewish biology or psychology, yet there is a Jewish philosophy. Terms, such as "Jewish mathematics," "Jewish physics," "Jewish psychology" may well evoke unpleasant associations, since in their time, they were the stock-in-trade of various anti-Semites and racists. [One of the reasons that Freud was interested in cooperating with the Swiss psychoanalysts in Carl Jung's circle was his fear that psychoanalysis would be regarded as an exclusively Jewish affair. The fact that most of the founders of psychoanalysis were Jewish has already produced some interesting studies.(1)]

Such is not the case with Jewish philosophy. Jews who were outstanding in the fields of mathematics and psychology (Einstein, Freud) made their mark as scientists and not as Jews; whereas a very large number of Jews who took an interest in philosophy did so because they were Jews, and because they were moved to do so by explicitly Jewish-religious motives. In other words, mathematics, physics and so on, even when dealt with by Jews, do not take on a Jewish coloration; whereas when Jews work at philosophy, it is possible - though not necessary - that their work will take on a Jewish coloration and significance, i.e., that it may turn into Jewish philosophy. Furthermore, one is not inclined to seek in a physicist's teachings the "Jewish moment," whereas, in the case of a Jewish philosopher, even if he devotes himself entirely to general subjects, one tends to search for a connection with Judaism. (More about that later.)

Thus, even if we posit as a working hypothesis that there is such a thing as Jewish philosophy, i.e. a philosophy that has a unique Jewish coloration, ipso facto, a number of vexing theoretical and methodological questions arise: Can we speak of a Jewish Marxism or a Jewish Existentialism? Rosenzweig and Buber are known as Jewish existentialists. Yet the difference in principle remains: There are Jews who are Marxists, and some of them even use Marxist theory to explain unique phenomena pertaining to Jewish existence; moreover, Borochov, in analysing the Jewish Question and in dealing with its theoretical aspects, refined the general Marxist theory. (For example, he emphasized the importance of "conditions of production" side by side "with the "forces of production" and "relations of production" - the two central concepts in Marxist theory up to that time.) But did Borochov's emendation create a Jewish Marxism? The answer is in the negative. The same is true of a term like "Jewish Existentialism." There were and are Jewish thinkers with existentialist tendencies, but there is no validity in ascribing a particularly Jewish dimension to their existentialism. The existentialist elements in the teachings of Rosenzweig, Buber, Heschel and others are a part of their general Weltanschauung. True, Buber sought to reveal existentialist moments in Hasidism, and his own personal existentialist leanings were rooted in and influenced by his Jewish heritage and sources. However, it would not be accurate to speak of a "Jewish Existentialism," which, as existentialism has, as it were, a Jewish coloration and reflects a specific Jewish problem. The contrary is true. There are not only "existentialists" among Jews, but there is also "existentialism" in modern Jewish thought, i.e., a particular philosophical trend that serves as a common denominator for a number of Jewish thinkers. But there is no Jewish Existentialism.

The foregoing only fortifies the contention that philosophy in its very nature has universal significance. It deals with problems that man has raised and will raise, in every period, in every place, in one way or another. Therefore, let it be stated quite clearly: The fact that Jewish philosophy exists as a discrete discipline for study and research does not free us from the need to explore, from a theoretical point of view, and to examine, impartially and unemotionally, whether there is actual scientific justification for such existence, and not only pragmatic convenience. It is still an open question, and the subject warrants further inquiry. It is not the expression "Jewish philosophy" that creates problems and difficulties.

After all, we unhesitatingly speak about Greek philosophy, Arab philosophy, Eastern philosophy (Chinese and Indian), British Empiricism, classical German Idealism, American Pragmatism, Continental philosophy and the like. In other words, various subjects, periods and streams of philosophy are characterized by a national label, as it were. Sometimes it is done in a narrow sense, and sometimes in a broader one. Yet, do we regard any of these as an independent discipline standing on its own? One can study Greek philosophy as a branch in classical studies, as one can study Chinese philosophy as a part of Far-Eastern studies. It is exactly in this manner that Jewish philosophy is studied as a part of Judaic studies in the universities in the Diaspora. [It is included even in the departments of Judaic and Near Eastern Studies, but this is an administrative matter and not one of principle.] There is also no problem for an individual to concentrate in Greek or Chinese philosophy, just as it would be natural, and even be made obligatory by circumstances, for A to specialize in the teachings of a certain philosopher or a certain school, whereas B would devote himself to a specific subject, such as logic, ethics, aesthetics and the like. However, we would be justified in casting doubt on a scholar's philosophical competence and ability, were his knowledge of philosophy confined only to Greek or Chinese philosophy. Nevertheless, such a phenomenon exists, nor is it regarded as abnormal, with respect to those who concern themselves with Jewish philosophy. Especially is this so in those branches of the Philosophy of Judaism where the philosophical patterns are not rigidly systematic or defined, such as the thought of the Sages or the ethics taught by Hasidism. Whether such a condition is desirable or not is beyond the purview of our study at this point. The inferences that relate mainly to the didactic side will be considered in later chapters, but what has become clear so far is that there will be important didactic implications for the questions of principle in the coming discussion as well. The problem which has to be clarified is centered, schematically speaking, on the question: Why is there no such thing as "English philosophy" (or German, or French), side by side with general philosophy, while there is "Jewish philosophy" that exists as a separate academic discipline, especially in the universities of Israel? What has caused it? Is it justified? Is it needed? It has already been stated, and it is necessary to repeat it once again as we are about to study the quiddity of Jewish philosophy, that no satisfactory answers to the questions raised above have so far been found. The problem of the special status of Jewish philosophy within the structure of general philosophy remains unsolved and requires looking into. The remarks that follow are not intended to furnish a complete and final answer to those knotty problems. Their main intention is to make something of a contribution to the clarification of these patterns and to place them on the philosophical agenda for further consideration.

There is another issue. Even though, as has been said, there is no separate discipline for English philosophy, French philosophy and so on, the works of English and French philosophers and others - not to mention the Greek philosophers - constitute an inseparable part of the study of philosophy and are part and parcel of the spiritual baggage of anyone who concerns himself with philosophy. Such is not the case with Jewish philosophers. To put it bluntly, one cannot complete his philosophical training without having studied Plato and Aristotle, Descartes, Spinoza, Hobbes, Locke, Berkeley, Hume, Kant, Fichte, Schelling, Hegel, Husserl, Bergson, Russell, Dewey, Wittgenstein and many others. Even if one's knowledge of their works is superficial and partial, some acquaintance with them is obligatory. However, a student of general philosophy can complete his studies, even in a university in Israel, without knowing anything about the teachings of Sa'adia Gaon, Maimonides, Judah Halevy, Ibn Gabirol, Krochmal, S.D. Luzzatto, Hermann Cohen (his Jewish doctrines) and Rosenzweig. The fact that one rarely finds their writings in textbooks or anthologies of general philosophy speaks for itself. What is the meaning of the regrettable phenomenon that Jewish scholarship is terra incognita for general philosophy? This is rather paradoxical. Jewish philosophy has practically no place in general philosophy, yet in Israel it is an independent discipline. Does the Biblical saying, "Lo, it is a people that shall dwell alone," (Numbers, 23,9) hold for the spiritual realm as well? Needless to say, such a condition is not only intellectually indefensible, particularly in Israel, but is not consonant with the essential universality of spiritual life. This is, however, only one of the aspects highlighting the complexity of the problem.

But the basic question that will be discussed below may be formulated as follows: How can a certain concept be truly philosophical, and simultaneously Jewish in its essence? How can one make compatible the objectivity and universality that are of the very nature of philosophy with content that is national and particularistic? When one posits certain "values" which are found in Jewish sources, then one of two conclusions must be valid: If the "value" has philosophical meaning, its Jewish origin is merely of historical interest; if it contains meaning, that is uniquely Jewish, it ceases to be philosophical as the term is generally defined. To become involved in dealing with such "values" may be interesting and instructive in both cases, but they are not interdependent. Yet everyone who is familiar with the subject matter being discussed here at close range feels clearly, almost intuitively, that the foregoing two alternatives do not exhaust the problem. This will be the basic subject discussed in the coming chapters, in its various aspects.

CHAPTER EIGHTEEN

IS THERE a JEWISH PHILOSOPHY?
A FEW PRELIMINARY ASSUMPTIONS

The question, "Is there a "Jewish philosophy?" seemingly pertains to four problems that may be reduced to the four questions posed by Isaac Israeli, the first of the Jewish Neo-Platonist philosophers. Chronologically, he was perhaps the first of the medieval Jewish philosophers, an older contemporary of Sa'adia Gaon. In the introduction to his book Book of Fences (Sefer Hagvulim) he sets forth the following questions: Is there? What? How? Why? Israeli described, through these four terms, the four types of Aristotelian inquiry, as they reached him by way of the Arab philosopher el-Kindi, and we are applying them here, perhaps somewhat arbitrarily, to the subject we are considering:

1) Is there such a thing as Jewish philosophy?

2) How does Jewish philosophy relate to its subject matter?
In other words, problems of methodology, such as the interpretation of Holy Script - literal meaning, homiletic or allegorical interpretation, difficult questions, casuistry and so on.

3) What is Jewish philosophy? This is the main question.

4) Why Jewish philosophy? The question is, why is there a need for a special theoretical discipline, either from the philosophical or the Jewish point of view.(1a)

The main points of dispute are to be found in the first and fourth questions. The second and third questions are only the consequence of a prior affirmative answer to the others. And so the problem before us is Janus-faced: the philosophical aspect and the Jewish aspect. The latter is not confined exclusively to philosophy: the question of "Who is a Jew?" is also a good deal more complex than "Who is an Englishman?" Without entering too deeply into the matter of Jewish identity, a subject that seems to have gained a permanent place on the contemporary Jewish agenda, the same problem exists for Jewish philosophy. A person may regard himself as a Jew whilst others do not regard him so. Conversely, a person may be considered a Jew by his society when he does not regard himself as such. [J.P. Sartre wrote penetratingly on this subject in his book, Reflections sur la question juive (1946), especially in Chapter III.] Reference is here made to the philosophic aspects of the problem, not to the Halakhic one. The Halakhic determination is usually unambiguous, even though, regrettably, it often raises human and moral problems, problems of conscience, that are very difficult to solve. What of the Jewishness of one who was born a Jew, but is alienated from and apathetic to Judaism? What of the Jewishness of one who was born a Jew, identifies with Judaism, but, for reasons of belief, has converted to another religion? [There have been several cases of Jews who became Christians for reasons of conscience; one of the most notorious cases in Israel is that of Brother Daniel, who was hidden during the second World War in a Polish monastery, adopted Christianity and became a monk, yet he continued to consider himself as belonging to the Jewish People, immigrated to Israel and joined the monastery on Mt. Carmel.]

What is the Jewishness of one whose affiliation is in dispute, e.g., the Karaites, the Samaritans? Closer to our area of inquiry is the problem of Jewish scholars who converted to Christianity, e.g., Abner of Burgos (1270-1340), whose entire field of work, whether for positive or negative reasons, was confined to Jewish thought. He influenced the thinking of Jewish philosophers such as Hasdai Crescas, who quoted extensively from the writings of Abner in order to refute them. Would anyone question the Jewishness of Heinrich Heine, who converted to Christianity in order, as he acidly remarked, to gain an "entry card" to European society, even though he remained, emotionally, closely tied to Judaism all his life? Much has been written about the Judaism of Marx and other socialist thinkers, some of whom converted to Christianity. This difficult problem was illustrated most strikingly in the case of Spinoza. Although he himself felt estranged from his roots, he remained bound to Judaism, not only because he never formally converted to another religion, but because of his philosophy which, though it is inseparably tied up with general philosophy, was fed by Jewish roots: It is impossible to disregard the influence of the Jewish sources on the shaping and crystallization of Spinoza's philosophy.(2) In addition, his Theologico-Political Treatise which has been commented upon above several times, deals with Biblical criticism, the early Jewish kingdom, the reasons for the Jewish Exile (at the end of Chapter 3), and has had a direct influence on some of the most important Jewish philosophers of future years - Moses Mendelssohn, Moses Hess and others.(3) Even an Orthodox rabbi like Rabbi Abraham Isaac Hacohen Kook, the first Chief Rabbi of Palestine, described Spinoza as "A man sprung from the seed of Israel, in whose soul the unity of God was so deeply imbedded, that only he could have created such a horrible dark shadow side by side with Great Light ..." Nevertheless, "even from this pomegranate with its thick skin we are able to extract some quintessential meaning worthy of preservation after it has been cleansed, bleached and refined."(4)

These are just a few random examples that emphasize the Jewish dimension of the problem.(5) A similar problem exists for "Jewish art," "a Jewish joke," and the like.(6)

The crucial point, however, is that the Jewish dimension is only one of the two dimensions of the problem. The other is - and in this respect the problematic nature of the quiddity of Jewish philosophy is different from that of other Jewish problems, such as "Jewish identity" et al. - the philosophical one, from which will emerge a basic assumption that will serve as the axis around which this investigation revolves: It is impossible to discuss Jewish philosophy apart from, and a fortiori not completely severed from, general philosophy. Salomon Munk held that the mission of the Jews, to know God and to bring such knowledge to the peoples of the world, was not especially tied to philosophy, and so "The Jews as a nation, or as a religious society, play only a secondary role in the history of philosophy."(7) But this position is not tenable, and the fact that it was adopted by one of the first great commentators of the Maimonidean Guide of the Perplexed gives pause for thought: Long before Munk, many Jews contributed to philosophy as Jews. Likewise, the blunt assertion by Isaac Husik at the conclusion of his well-known work, History of Jewish Medieval Philosophy - "There are Jews now and there are philosophers, but there are no Jewish philosophers and there is no Jewish philosophy"(8) - is clearly refuted by the very fact that he made it just when he himself completed a work on Jewish philosophy ... Did he mean to imply that Jewish philosophy had vanished into the thin air after the Middle Ages? In any event, Husik's words express in its starkest form the problem that is to be discussed in the following chapters.

At the opposite pole we encounter the position, which has always had its fervent supporters in Judaism, that a philosophy of Judaism is self-sufficient. This position, which in our times is regarded as nationalistic and provincial, is usually based on one of the following two arguments: a) Judaism is founded in the Torah and in the Oral Law. Since the Torah is the word of God, ipso facto it contains all the answers to all of Israel's problems. Judaism is spiritually autarkic, and is in need of no external assistance. This is a kind of intellectual isolationism. Why should the People of the Book need to have recourse to the wisdom of the nations? b) The Torah is the Torah of truth; it contains all the ideas that man needs, and therefore philosophy cannot contain anything that is not already included in the Torah. This identifies the Jewish sources of Judaism with the universe of ideas. This position, based on either argument, is ab initio not consonant with the philosophical approach, and so cannot be accepted by anyone who wishes to concern himself with Jewish philosophy.

As opposed to such skeptical and negative opinions and to the reservations as to the existence of Jewish philosophy as an independent discipline, it would be well to pay heed to one of the greatest Jewish scholars of our age, Harry A. Wolfson, who stated unequivocally not only that such a discipline exists, but that Jewish philosophy has embedded in it the essence and the seed of all religious philosophy from Philo to the present day.(9) More recently, L.D. Stitskin (professor of Jewish philosophy at Yeshiva University, New York), in a very comprehensive book called Jewish Philosophy, declared: "Jewish philosophy is a genuinely creative scheme, organically Hebraic and typically Jewish"; "Jewish philosophy, whose central thesis is drawn from uniquely Hebraic sources, and its character delineated by the projection of the centrality of man as the focus of concern."(10) All these diverse opinions, for which a number of examples have been furnished, give one some idea of the spectrum of positions taken with reference to Jewish philosophy.

CHAPTER NINETEEN

WHAT IS JEWISH PHILOSOPHY?

One of the first modern attempts in Israel to define Jewish philosophy was made by Felix Weltsch in an essay entitled, "What is Jewish Philosophy?"(11) The remarks that follow stem, in part, from some of the questions that Weltsch raised in his effort to elucidate the unique aspect of Jewish philosophy. However, they are restricted to methodology only, and are not related to his intellectual conceptions or propositions. Although the purpose of what is to follow is to clarify the meaning of the concept "Jewish philosophy," immediate use of the term cannot be avoided. But for the moment, this use is no more than a technical and temporary matter. It is not intended to anticipate the conclusion to be drawn from the inquiry to the inquiry itself.

I. Jewish Philosophy is the Philosophical Work Created by Jews or by Philosophers of Jewish Origin

Inter alia, such was the opinion of the well-known Israeli scholar Joseph Klausner. He believed, for example, that Henri Bergson's philosophy should be classified as Jewish philosophy.(12) Alexander Altmann was of the same opinion. He argued that Bergson's work was inspired by Hebrew prophecy.(13) Altmann includes in Jewish philosophy the writings of Samuel Alexander, an Englishman of Jewish origin, who never dealt with Jewish questions. [Alexander never denied his Jewishness. He even served on the Academic Council of the Hebrew University, but his philosophy in no way pertains to Jewish philosophy.] However, Altmann in his article "Judaism and the Philosophers of the World" seems to be more intent on highlighting Judaism's contribution to the intellectual life of Western civilization than to attempt to define the quiddity of Jewish philosophy. Rabbi Simha Urbach, as well, in writing a book on Bergson's philosophy, sought to align the ideas of the French philosopher with those of Judaism.(14) Such apologetic efforts are, obviously, dubious, and render the term "Jewish philosophy" void of any distinguishing content. True, Bergson never denied his Jewish origin, and when the Nazis came to power he was fully conscious of the common fate that bound him to his brothers, and for this reason, though he was intellectually close to Catholicism, he did not convert. But, as a philosopher, he was remote in his thinking and alienated from Judaism and its sources in all his life. Therefore, all comparisons of Bergson's philosophy to that of Judaism are either generalizations that cannot be supported or arbitrary determinations,(15) and are even partially motivated by a desire to bolster national pride. The criteria that are applied to Bergson would be equally valid for the French assimilationist philosopher Leon Brunschvicg, who had a marked influence on all the French philosophers in the early decades of the 20th century, and for scholars like Emile Durkheim and Claude Levi-Strauss, whose sociological and anthropological research had far-reaching implications for philosophy.(16) The same might be said about Edmund Husserl, the founder of "Phenomenology," who also was of Jewish origin. The list could be extended. Jews have been prominent in philosophy, as in many other scientific disciplines, ever since they achieved equality of rights in the post-Emancipation period. There are, of course, historical and sociological reasons for this phenomenon. A statistical roster of Jewish names in philosophy might indeed be impressive, but it would have no connection whatsoever with the term "Jewish philosophy."

The question will become even clearer, if we recall Ibn Gabirol's Fountain of Life.(16a) For hundreds of years the true identity of the author was unknown. In its Latin edition, Fons Vitae, authorship was ascribed to a Moslem or Christian medieval scholar by the name of Avicebron or Avancebrol. Jewish philosophers like Judah Abarbanel (who may have known the author's identity), and, through him, Spinoza were influenced by it. But its main influence - on Giordano Bruno, on Hegel, and in the 19th century on Schopenhauer - lay in the sphere of general philosophy. However, since the Jewish scholar Salomon Munk (who published the first scientific-critical edition of The Guide of the Perplexed with a French translation; he was mentioned earlier) discovered in 1846 that it had been written by Ibn Gabirol, there was no difficulty in regarding the work as an integral part of Jewish philosophy. This was so, although the word "Jew" did not appear in The Fountain of Life; even though it contained no references to Jewish sources, as was customary in medieval Jewish works of philosophy; and even though there was nothing particularly Jewish about it. The book deals with all the problems that engaged the interest of Jewish scholars of that period, and it fits in organically with their mode of thinking. An even superficial comparison of The Fountain of Life with Ibn Gabirol's great liturgical poem, The Kingly Crown,(16b) (wherein the term "Fountain of Life" is used as a name of the Deity) makes the matter easily understandable. The purpose of this comparison is to show that it is not the philosopher's being a Jew that entitles him to belong to "Jewish philosophy." The criteria are related to the content of his thought. Of course, one might speculate whether, had it not been for Munk's discovery of its Jewish authorship, there ever would have been a scholar who would have included The Fountain of Life in the treasure-chest of Jewish philosophy.

II. Jewish Philosophy is Philosophical Literature Written in Hebrew.

Is Jewish philosophy characterized by the fact that its creators wrote in Hebrew? There is no doubt that language is an important factor in philosophy (v. supra), particularly in the philosophy of Judaism, where, as in Jewish life in general, the Hebrew language served as a holy tongue, performing a function that was unique and unparalleled in the history of other civilizations. It is not to be compared with Latin, which, on the one hand, has become a religio-ritualistic "dead" language, and, on the other hand, was a lingua franca for scholars and intellectuals in a certain historical period. However, it was never revived as a "living" language for a specific nation. Hebrew was for countless generations a sacred language, but, simultaneously, it also continued to function uninterruptedly as a vital national language. Even when it ceased to be a spoken language for everyday use, it was in no sense "dead."

Yet, a philosopher who writes in Hebrew is not necessarily one whose concern is "Jewish philosophy," as has been illustrated by the ramified philosophical activity that has been carried on in Israel in recent decades.

Jacob Klatzkin, an important philosopher of the present generation, has sought to define Jewish identity in modern times - the post-Emancipation period - exlusively by the criteria of country and language. He argued uncompromisingly that everything written in Hebrew, including all translations into Hebrew, belongs to Judaism, while everything written in a foreign language does not. To him, then, a mystery story, translated into Hebrew, was more "Jewish" than, say, <u>Die Religion aus den Quellen des Judentums</u> by Hermann Cohen, who, incidentally, was Klatzkin's teacher. (<u>According</u> to this thesis, Cohen's book became Jewish only when its Hebrew translation appeared some twenty years after Klatzkin's death.) It is quite clear that Klatzkin's thesis is untenable, especially when one casts a glance on Klatzkin's own literary work. He formulated his views on Judaism in two books written in German,(17) which, according to his maximal definition, do not belong to Jewish thought. He was the editor-in-chief of the <u>Encyclopedia</u> Judaica in German, a project that he and Nahum Goldmann had initiated in 1924: should this work be claimed as belonging to Jewish or to general philosophy? Perhaps Klatzkin would have argued in his defense that if one is resolute in his determination to put an end to the Diaspora, and one aspires to acquire a country and a language that are Jewish, then one is no longer a part of the Diaspora. The element of intention is of course important, but it invalidates at once all his basic premises. Furthermore, along with his German essays on Judaism, Klatzkin wrote quite many essays on general philosophy, mostly in the form of aphorisms, in Hebrew.(18) He even composed an anthology of the writings of general philosophers.(19) Do these belong to Jewish philosophical literature, as his criterion would have it? I have cited Klatzkin's rather strange position to illustrate how a schematic - not necessarily dogmatic - perception may lead a thinker astray, even one of the caliber of Klatzkin, whose important contribution to Judaic studies and to Jewish philosophy is beyond dispute, but will not be elaborated upon here.(20)

It is impossible to ignore the fact that Jewish philosophers, throughout the ages, <u>did not write in Hebrew</u>. Philo wrote in Greek; the medieval Jewish philosophers wrote in Arabic (except for the later ones); Judah Abarbanel wrote his book in Italian; Spinoza (whose place in Jewish philosophy will be discussed below) wrote in Latin; and Jewish philosophers of the modern period, beginning with Moses Mendelssohn and Salomon Maimon up to Hermann Cohen, Rosenzweig, and Buber, wrote mostly in German and sometimes in French. Buber alone, after migrating to Palestine, wrote some of his later works in Hebrew, which had become the language of the land. Samuel David Luzzatto wrote some of his essays in Italian and German. The same holds true for the present-day Jewish philosophers, who write in English and sometimes in French. The number of Jewish philosophers, both in the medieval and modern eras, who wrote in Hebrew is very small. Nachman Krochmal, Luzzatto and Ahad Ha'am were among the more prominent who did so. Even Judah Halevy and Solomon Ibn Gabirol, the greatest of the Hebrew poets of the Golden Age of Spain, wrote their philosophical works in Arabic. Maimonides, who wrote the <u>Mishne Torah</u> in clear, excellent Hebrew, developed a fine Hebrew style for his philosophic writing as well - it suffices to examine his <u>Sefer Hamada</u> (The Book of Science), the opening part of the <u>Mishne Torah</u>, to be convinced of his virtuosity - even Maimonides wrote his main philosophical work, <u>A Guide of the Perplexed</u>, in Arabic. That the foregoing philosophers wrote Arabic in Hebrew letters, or that Mendelssohn, following them, wrote part of his German translation of the Bible in similar fashion, is of no moment. That they wrote in a foreign language in Hebrew letters is perhaps an unconscious expression of their yearning to maintain a living tie with the ancient language, which had become a holy tongue and no longer functioned as a spoken language in everyday life. There are various hypotheses as to what moved them to write in the language of their country of domicile rather than in Hebrew. The most reasonable conjecture is that they were guided, primarily, by the thought that philosophy is essentially universal, and not limited to a certain nation or to a particular group of people. (This touches on one of the basic aspects of this investigation.) Even without subscribing to the thesis of Gersonides that the Torah and philosophy are two separate spheres, the philosophers - chief among them Maimonides - whose motivation for their work was chiefly "Jewish," such as the desire to resolve the contradictions between what is demanded by reason and what is written in the Bible and in other sources, attached to their writings general philosophic, and not only purely Jewish, significance. The influence of Jewish philosophy did in fact extend beyond the Jewish sphere: Philo's main influence was on Gnosticism and on early Christian thought, rather than on Jewish philosophy. (It did, however, penetrate, in curious fashion, the early Hasidism in Germany of the 11th and 12th centuries and the Kabbala.) Maimonides's doctrines were known to Christian theologians, and even had their influence on the viewpoints of Albertus Magnus and Thomas Aquinas. The main area of influence of The Fountain of Life was for a very long time only in the non-Jewish world. Judah Abarbanel's Dialoghi d'Amore was one of the most widely distributed philosophical works in the days of the Renaissance. It appeared in very many editions, in Italian and in translation. Finally, it was banned by the Church and placed on the infamous Index of forbidden books of the Vatican. [A copy of the Spanish edition of the book was found in Spinoza's library.] The effect of Mendelssohn's works, or Rosenzweig's and Buber's, in their respective periods, is well known. Many of the thinkers in the field of Jewish philosophy today, in the United States, in England, and in France, have a high reputation in general circles.

Thus, without yet going into the problem of the reciprocal relations between Jewish and general philosophy, one thing becomes clear: Writing in Hebrew cannot serve as a distinguishing criterion for Jewish philosophy.

III. Jewish Philosophy is the Study of General Philosophical Problems in the Jewish Arena.

Is Jewish philosophy, irrespective of its ties to a linguistic dimension, nothing more than a shifting of general problems of philosophy to the Hebrew or Jewish scene? According to this premise, one finds nothing in Jewish philosophy of the Middle Ages other than the philosophical problems that are under general investigation - form and substance, functioning of reason, and the like. In other words, it continues to deal with the subjects under discussion in Aristotelian circles, or with subjects such as inspiration or illumination that occupy the Neo-Platonists, and so on. This in no way means that Jewish thinkers were plagiarists, eclectics, or imitators. All it means is that their original contributions were not, as it were, characteristically Jewish, but only part of the preoccupations of general philosophy. <u>Inter alia</u> this position was supported by the Israeli scholar Joseph Sermoneta, who, in discussing the quiddity of Jewish philosophy, maintained that if in the teachings of Maimonides there was "... a special Jewish element or an element of a true and profound philosopher, he made his contribution to his generation and to those that were to follow, and not necessarily to Jews alone."(21) This is not just a sad conclusion, as Sermoneta evidently thought, it only emphasizes one of the focal points of this essay. Every original philosophical contribution that is made by a thought process that has a certain national flavor, if it is of value and original, is absorbed in general human thought. However, this view does not provide a sufficient answer as to the quiddity of Jewish philosophy. It makes of it a kind of attempt at translation, and it leads to the conclusion that original Jewish philosophy, possessed of a national coloring, does not and cannot exist - the uniqueness of Judaism cannot find expression in philosophy, which is by its nature universal. Jews partake in it as thinking humans, but on another level. Already Mendelssohn thought so: He held that only the Law is unique in Judaism, i.e., the <u>fact</u> that the Torah of Moses had been given to the Jewish People by a one-time act of Revelation. Such a position on Jewish philosophy would seemingly mean its denial, as philosophy and Judaism assume adversarial roles. Furthermore, such a conclusion does not truly reflect the viewpoint of the Jewish philosophers themselves, the vast majority of whom regarded religious philosophy as the apex of Jewish religiosity, and, at the same time, as the apex of religiosity in general. The teachings of Maimonides are evidence of such a position.

IV. Jewish Philosophy is Philosophy Dealing with the Jewish Religion

Can one regard "Jewish philosophy" as thought that deals with the Jewish religion? The term "Jewish philosophy of religion" was quite popular among Jewish scholars in Germany in the 19th century. (As to the problematic nature of the concept, v. <u>supra</u>.) However, it is somewhat reductive, as if only the Jewish religion is a proper subject for Jewish philosophical consideration. The religious dimension occupied a prominent and unique role in Jewish life throughout the two thousand years of Exile, a role that was far more central than that played by religion in other nations, as is well known. But the definition suggested above is not appropriate for any of the great Jewish philosophers throughout the ages. It was made clear in Part II of this book that "a philosophy of religion" means a philosophy whose subject is religion, just as art is the subject of the investigations of a "philosophy of art." There were scholars, Jewish and non-Jewish, who dealt with the Jewish religion, but there was not one Jewish <u>philosopher</u>, who confined his philosophical concerns exclusively to the Jewish religion, as the term is defined.

V. Jewish Philosophy Deals with General Philosophical Problems from the Point of View of the Jewish Religion

Can perhaps the claim be made that "Jewish philosophy" means the consideration of general philosophical problems from the point of view of the Jewish religion and its sources? This was Hermann Cohen's expressed purpose in writing, in the latter years of his life, his book Religion of Reason out of the Sources of Judaism (Die Religion der Vernunft aus den Quellen des Judentums). But, once again, this was not the mainstream of Jewish philosophy. Even Cohen himself did not seek to clarify philosophical problems by turning to the Jewish sources. All he tried to do was to seek support in the sources for specific ideas that he had previously adopted on the basis of his philosophical thinking, influenced by general philosophy - he was particularly affected by the teachings of Kant and the classical German Idealists - as a way of buttressing his ethical position. One of Cohen's principal perceptions was that Hebrew prophecy, ab initio was endowed with a mission of disseminating the moral message to all mankind. This view sprang from general philosophic-ethical considerations, rather than from specifically Jewish ones. Thus, the definition suggested is in no way exhaustive.

The subject warrants expansion through an appraisal of some of the typical propositions of medieval Jewish philosophy. As an example, let us compare the following two sentences:

a) Man lives on earth, and is in the center of the universe, which is composed of a number of concentric circles.

b) The earth sustains man's life and supports man in his spiritual efforts.(22)

From the religio-philosophic point of view, the propositions set forth in the two sentences are identical. They both note the central place that man occupies in the plan of Providence and his status as Creation's crowning glory. Yet, the first sentence expresses the proposition by relying on a certain astronomical theory, whose origin is not to be found in the philosophy of Judaism: The geocentric theory was, indeed, accepted by nearly all philosophers and theologians before Copernicus - Jews and non-Jews alike - but the fact remains that it came to the Jewish philosophers from the outside. The problem of the truth or falsity of the foregoing theory and its refutation by new astronomical theories is not relevant to the subject under discussion - the characterization of the Jewish element in Jewish philosophy. The problem played a very significant part in the struggle between religion and science. The labeling of Copernican doctrine as heresy ,the well-known story of Galilei, and the burning at the stake of Giordano Bruno were some of the sad landmarks in this struggle. It may very well be that there is some validity in the idea that "they (the clashes between religion and science) have usually been between new and better scientific ideas and older scientific ideas that happened to become enshrined as religious beliefs."(23) The problem is, in fact, much broader and is not reducible only to relations between religion and science - it has far-reaching implications for scientific methodology itself.(24) What is of concern here is that in the first of the two sentences a religious belief is expressed (acceptable to Judaism as well) by a conceptual perception that came into Jewish thought from the outside; while the proposition contained in the second sentence expresses a religious perception that is already well known, mainly from Jewish sources.

One might continue to pose vexing problems. Philosophical determinations concerning God and His relation to the world do not belong to Jewish philosophy, in accordance with the distinction made above, when they are expressed by concepts that are foreign to the traditional Jewish view. One must therefore differentiate between sentences like "God created the world" or "God revealed Himself to Moses," and sentences like "The world is an emanation of the eternal God" or "Moses was endowed with Divine illumination." The first two sentences more or less represent the traditional Jewish perceptions, whereas the latter two converted the "Jewish" Biblical concepts of "creation" and "revelation" to the Neo-Platonic ones of "emanation" and "illumination." This is not merely a terminological preference. The Biblical and the Neo-Platonic concepts are not identical. The concept of "creation" in Jewish usage refers to a result of a voluntary act of God; whereas Plotinus, the founder of Neo-Platonism, uses the term "emanation" to describe a necessary, inevitable process of effluence of Divine Essence, similar to the bubbling waters of a spring. Maimonides also used the phrase "an (intellectual) overflow overflowing"(24a) in referring to God. And so, when, in The Guide of the Perplexed, he described the prophecy of Moses as: "Among us there is one for whom the lightning flashes time and time again, so that he is always, as it were, in unceasing light. Thus night appears to him as day. That is the degree of the great one among the prophets"(25) (namely Moses) - he adopts a philosophical procedure that is non-Jewish.

An interesting example may be found on this point in The Kuzari of Judah Halevy. The Khazar king uses the word "nature," whereas his Jewish "companion" does not know the word, because he had been raised on the concept: "heaven and earth and all that they contain."(26) The word "nature" does not appear in the Bible. In Talmudic language, the word denotes a characteristic trait such as "the nature of prayer."(27) The word "nature," meaning an all-embracing cosmos, infiltrated into the Hebrew language from general philosophical terminology. In the parlance of the Midrash it refers to the word "element," in the sense of the four elements in Greek philosophy, following Empedocles, of which the universe was composed: "... the four elements from which the Holy One, blessed be He, created the world ... the earth ... the water ... the air ... and the fire."(28) Here we find an attempt, of sorts, to merge the story of the Creation with the Greek teachings on the elements. Thus when the term "nature" came into use in medieval Jewish philosophy, it reflected, according to the definition set forth, a non-Jewish philosophical tradition.

In all the instances of this kind, and in keeping with the attempt to define Jewish philosophy as "... the consideration of general philosophical problems in relation to the Jewish religion," the opposite seems to have occurred: Jewish philosophical perceptions were integrated into philosophical systems, whose sources and systematic ways of thought were outside the Jewish tradition. In the example cited, does a philosopher who deals with a universal problem, e.g., man's centrality in the universe, belong to Jewish philosophy if he grounds his view on traditional Jewish religious perceptions, and he does not belong to Jewish philosophy if he adopts general philosophical or scientific theories? This is not at all a rhetorical question. Jewish religious thinkers of modern times, at least up to the 19th century, still looked with suspicion, and indeed negated, the "external sciences," and opposed their inclusion in Jewish educational curricula. Samson Raphael Hirsch, a philosopher who had acquired philosophical and scientific training and who had been influenced by J.G. Herder, demanded that the science of Judaism became "autarkic," namely, that one should study and understand all the philosophical problems that pertain to the Jewish religion only from Jewish sources, without using any of the general scientific achievements to support the essence of Judaism.(29) Luzzatto, as well, who was very knowledgeable about general philosophy and science and who had adopted the basic ideas of E.B. de Condillac and of other followers of French Sensualism, criticized Maimonides and Abraham Ibn Ezra for the same reasons that Hirsch had given: Their rationalism was a thorn in his side, not merely because he valued emotion and faith above reason and understanding, but because he was of the opinion that they were, in essence, a foreign element in Jewish philosophy. As opposed to them, he extolled the work of Judah Halevy and Rashi. (Luzzatto ignored the fact, consciously or unconsciously, that Halevy's reservations about philosophy had their roots in the thinking of the Arab philosopher el-Gazali, and that he used the Aristotelian method in presenting his theses.)

In summing up this brief discussion it becomes clear that the definition of Jewish philosophy as the consideration of general philosophical problems on the basis of Jewish religion is inadequate and unacceptable. It would exclude most of the medieval and modern Jewish philosophers.

VI. Jewish Philosophy is a Synthesis of the Jewish Religion and a General Philosophical System of Thought.

Is it possible for Jewish philosophy to serve as a synthesis of the Jewish religion and a general philosophical system? To all appearances, this was the prevailing view in Jewish thought in the Middle Ages. Thus Sa'adia Gaon could be described as a Jewish scholar whose philosophy stemmed from the Arab Kalam; Isaac Israeli, Bahya Ben Joseph Ibn Paquda and Salomon Ibn Gabirol would be regarded as Jewish scholars who had accepted Neo-Platonist philosophy; and Abraham Ibn Da'ud, Maimonides and his followers would be classed as Jewish scholars who relied on Aristotelianism (with its Arab coloration). The description is, of course, advisedly schematic. Without dealing with the question of whether the description above is in any way accurate as far as the above-mentioned scholars were concerned, one should be aware that it is dubious even as concerns Maimonides and Ibn Gabirol. The definition does not at all suit the thinking of later Jewish philosophers, like Gersonides and Hasdai Crescas, and a fortiori of Judah Abarbanel and of philosophers of the modern era, or of contemporary philosophers. These were, first and foremost, general philosophers, and in the case of some of them their philosophical work was independent of their Jewish religiosity. Gersonides, for example, thought, as has already been pointed out in this book, that the Torah was one matter, philosophy another, each functioning in its own separate sphere.(30)

The conclusion reached by Leon Roth, who denied any originality to all Jewish philosophers, beginning with Philo of the Hellenistic period and ending with Mordecai Kaplan of our own age, is not persuasive either. He reduced their contribution to merely attaching the label "Jewish" to one philosophy or another. According to Roth, there is no warrant whatsoever for speaking about "Maimonides's philosophy."

> True, as Philo used Plato, so Maimonides used Aristotle, in an original way with original results. But the originality consisted not in his philosophy, which was that of Aristotle (or rather of the Arabized Aristotle), but in what resulted when he applied his Aristotelianism to Judaism.(31)

In like manner, he maintains that Mendelssohn merely reflected the thought of 17th- and 18th- century philosophy; that Hermann Cohen's work leaned heavily on Kant's philosophical principles; and that Mordecai Kaplan merely rephrased the philosophical insights of Dewey. This is a simplistic and inaccurate interpretation of their work, and is unfair to the Jewish philosophers mentioned.

VII. Jewish Philosophy is a Philosophical Interpretation of the Values of the Jewish Religion.

Is "Jewish philosophy" a philosophical interpretation of values which are characteristic of the Jewish religion? At first glance this would seem to be an acceptable definition, though it is somewhat difficult to make a clear distinction between it and the criterion suggested in the previous section. However, in the present case, the idea is not merely to create a synthesis between a non-Jewish philosophical theory and the Jewish religion, but also to evaluate properly the original philosophical contributions of Jewish thinkers as they relate to Judaism and its religion. Without denying external influences on their thought - was there ever a philosopher who created his doctrine ex nihilo? - the main emphasis is placed on the attempt of these philosophers to contend independently with the spiritual heritage, essentially the religious one, of Judaism. This heritage is the motive force for philosophizing, i.e., an effort not to accept the religious values as something impervious to questioning, uncritically, but to get down to the philosophical and ideological significance of the religious ideas, some of which prove valid under critical examination and others do not. While this definition will not be the final word on the subject, it is helpful in understanding what is uniquely Jewish in the philosophical teachings of Jewish philosophers, especially of those beginning with the modern era to the present day: Judah Abarbanel, the Maharal, Spinoza, Mendelssohn, S. Formstecher, Samuel Hirsch, L. Steinheim, N. Krochmal, M. Lazarus, H. Steinthal, Hermann Cohen, F. Rosenzweig, M. Buber, and perhaps even Rabbi Kook, are some of the more illustrious names.

The uniqueness of the characterization will become obvious if we note an additional matter. In the first steps of Greek philosophy, there was clear manifestation of an abandonment of the mythic world for the logical one. The fact that Plato sometimes, for didactic purposes, resorted to the use of myth, does not alter the matter in principle. As to Jewish philosophy, however, not only did it not divorce itself completely from early Jewish tradition, but the contrary is true: Tradition as contained in the Torah and the Oral Law, was the foundation for Jewish philosophers. They sought to confirm rationally the assumptions made by Jewish religious tradition. There were no two opposing worlds, as in Greek philosophy, but rather, as has been stated, an attempt at a philosophical interpretation of the values of the Jewish religion. [The term "values" is not considered here. It, in itself, is a matter of controversy in general philosophy and among modern Jewish philosophers. There are thinkers, like Isaiah Leibowitz, who deny the existence of Jewish "values." In their view Judaism is expressed exclusively by the Halakha, which is based on commandments, and not on values. In his day, Mendelssohn strongly advocated this position. He considered the uniqueness of Judaism to be its "Law."] This interpretation is very prominent, for example in Sa'adia Gaon's work, Beliefs and Opinions (Emunot V'de'ot). He begins his treatment of each subject by quotations from the Bible, submits philosophical assumptions and proofs related to them, and concludes the consideration of the problem by offering some additional Biblical quotations.

VIII. Jewish Philosophy also Includes the Thought of Jewish Philosophers that Stems Unconsciously from the Jewish Heritage.

Should "Jewish philosophy" include the thought of Jewish philosophers, which has its origins in Jewish heritage and thought, even though the philosophers themselves were unconscious of such an influence, and some of them were even estranged from Judaism? The three names that readily come to mind are Spinoza, Marx and Bergson. (Our discussion is limited to philosophy alone.) Common sense would certainly dictate a negative response. What value is there in characterizing a certain philosopher not on the basis of his oeuvre alone, but rather on the basis of his roots, and the sources that have influenced his teachings - be they conscious or not? Nevertheless, the answer is more complex than it seems at first sight. Of the three names mentioned above, Spinoza is essentially different from the other two. Despite his excommunication by the Jewish community of Amsterdam, and despite his own estrangement from Judaism as the years moved on, Spinoza has continued to be an inseparable part of the stream of Jewish thought over the generations (v. supra). According to most scholars, Jewish sources played a greater role in the formation of his philosophical doctrines (which are outstanding in their originality, the work of a genius) than did other influences, including that of Descartes. Not only is it impossible to understand Spinoza's philosophy correctly without taking into account the Jewish sources that influenced him, but - and here is perhaps the crux - Spinoza continued to concern himself with the problems that Jewish philosophy had dealt with before him. The Jewish dimension in his teachings is not limited to a knowledge of the Bible, of medieval Jewish philosophical literature and its influence on his thought.(33) It is imbedded in Spinoza's very approach to philosophical problems. In the opinion of the American philosopher George Santayana, Spinoza's pantheism reflects the Biblical attitude towards God's omnipotence, bolstered by logical arguments.(34) Many scholars have emphasized that, in the equation Deus Sive Natura (God or Nature), the Godhead is not lowered to the rank of Nature, but rather Nature is elevated to the rank of the Godhead. It is true that Spinoza's philosophy is not in accord with the religious tradition of Judaism, and for this reason the break between Spinoza and the Judaism of his day was inevitable. However, one must not separate his philosophy from the chain of Jewish thought.(35) Thus, even before we clarify what Jewish philosophy is, we are entitled to make the determination that the philosophy of Spinoza, in any event, is not a foreign implant. All the studies in Spinozistic philosophy that have been made since the middle of the 19th century serve to reinforce this assumption emphatically.

The situation with reference to Marx is different. It is true that psychological elements in his attitude to Judaism - without resort to a discussion of the controversial notion of "self-hate" - might explain many episodes in his life, e.g., his ambivalent relations with Moses Hess and Ferdinand Lassalle. Yet, his philosophical thought does not stem from the heritage of Jewish learning. All the talk about the "Hebrew prophetic zeal" to be found in his social doctrines, or the comparison of the socialist vision with the eschatological strains of the prophetic idea of the millenium, which Marx came to - so it was alleged - because he was a descendant of a long line of rabbis, are nothing but apologetic rhetoric. Were Marx not known to have been of Jewish origin, it is doubtful whether any such emphasis would have been placed on these aspects. "Justice, only justice shalt thou pursue"(36) was undoubtedly a central motif in Hebrew prophecy. Moreover, no one will deny that the prophetic vision always had a very great influence on progressive social movements. But it does not follow that every philosophical theory that expresses a longing for social justice ipso facto becomes a part of "Jewish" philosophy, because the propounder is of Jewish origin. There is another question, which is not in the purview of the present inquiry: Why were so many Jews attracted in modern times to revolutionary, socialist movements? This question belongs to the realms of history, psychology and sociology. It is a very important one for understanding the course of development of modern Jewish life, however it is not relevant to the field of Jewish philosophy.

As to Bergson, the fact that he was of Jewish origin left no traces on his philosophy. Buber once tried to discover certain aspects of Hasidism in Bergson's thought. He ascribed them to the fact that one of Bergson's ancestors had been a Hasidic rabbi in Eastern Europe,(37) and in mysterious fashion some Hasidic ideas had come to him. But this was, doubtless, a forced interpretation, which Buber would never have considered making had it not been for Bergson's Jewish origin. The same holds true for the book on Bergson's philosophy by Rabbi Simha Urbach, mentioned earlier. He too would not have undertaken to uncover "Jewish elements" in the thinking of a non-Jewish philosopher.

Every attempt made to include in "Jewish philosophy" the philosophical positions taken by Jewish thinkers, or those of Jewish origin, who had no special relation to Judaism is arbitrary. It is a tendentious hermeneutics that, in most cases, reflects the wishful thinking of the writer, or occasionally his apologetical leanings. He graps at a word or a sentence, here and there, seeking to find in it some ideational connection to the principles of Judaism. In any event, "Jewish philosophy" is not to be found there - perhaps the opposite: Such attempts make things more difficult for those who are trying to present a clear picture of the problem.

IX. The Weight of Methodological Aspects in Characterizing Philosophy as Jewish Philosophy

What emphasis should one place on methodological presuppositions when characterizing a certain set of philosophical doctrines as Jewish? Here, as in the previous section, the question is pertinent only, or mainly, for philosophers who are known as Jews or are of Jewish origin. The question is, whether philosophizing by Jewish writers in the casuistic spirit that typifies the Talmud, and even more so its commentators, is evidence that it constitutes "Jewish philosophy." On the basis of such a criterion a large part of Christian Scholasticism and even of modern concern with problems in Logic (especially those trends that are dominant in the English-speaking world) could be classified as "Jewish philosophy." No doubt, the same scholarly aim that motivates the logician, motivated in its time the Talmudist and his commentator, namely, the complete clarification of a given subject, by adducing extreme examples, often bordering on the absurd, in order to test the validity of the proposition under discussion in every imaginable situation and to verify its universality. There is a certain proximity between logical and legal subject matter. The late Belgian Jewish philosopher Ch. Perelman, a man with an international reputation, devoted most of his intellectual endeavors to philosophy and legal logic. His main works are Traite de L'Argumentation (1958), Justice et Raison (1963) and others. (His small book On Justice appeared in Hebrew in 1962, under the aegis of the Faculty of Law of the Hebrew University, and an enlarged version was published by the Magnes Press in 1981. It was published in English by Random House, N.Y. in 1967). Nevertheless, no one could conceivably suggest that Perelman's work in the fields of logic and law constitute "Jewish philosophy." Even the fact that he was a Zionist and a Jew is irrelevant. It might very well be that there is a disproportionately large number of Jews in the community of modern logicians, larger than in other philosophical fields, such as aesthetics and the like (though there are no reliable statistical data on the subject). A possible explanation of the phenomenon is that generations of Jewish students and scholars have sharpened their analytical faculties by dealing with the subtleties of Talmudic subject matter, but this, again, is an appropriate subject for historians, sociologists and psychologists - it does not pertain to philosophy. (Similarly, one might, from a historical and sociological perspective, explain the presence of a considerable number of Jews in the fields of Linguistic Philosophy and Theoretical Linguistics.)

The problem is really other. Jewish philosophers of the Middle Ages and perhaps some of the later ones - particularly those who wrote in Hebrew - lived as Jews in a unique spiritual climate, where the study of the Bible and, to a greater extent, of the Talmud constituted a very large part of their intellectual activity. Maimonides's writings on Halakhic matters were more voluminous than his philosophical works. It is difficult to grasp how a single person could have written the gigantic work Mishne Torah. It comprises the legal decisions of the Gemara (the main body of the Talmud, consisting of a commentary on and an elaboration of the Mishna), arranged systematically according to subject, as well as final judgments in all fields where the Sages had reached no decision. This in itself was a task for more than one man. Yet, this was only a part of Maimonides's scientific and philosophical work, one facet of his genius. However, his work cannot be compartmentalized into Halakhic and philosophical parts. Just as his philosophical writings invaded, as it were, his Halakhic work - he began the Mishne Torah with Sefer Hamada (Book of Science), a philosophical investigation, and his Shmona Perakim (Eight Chapters) are a philosophical-ethical introduction to his commentary on the tractate Avot -- so is his Talmudic background strongly in evidence in his philosophical treatise The Guide of the Perplexed. Maimonides's philosophy doesn't become Jewish for reasons of method and form - as important as these may be - but because of the content of his philosophical work. The same holds true for many other Jewish philosophers who were very well-versed in Talmudic literature. Their strong Talmudic background is reflected in their thinking, but it did not determine its path or its aim.

Nevertheless, a particular problem does arise concerning Philo and Maimonides. While the content of their work was determinative, as has been pointed out, their method of writing was lineally connected with Jewish pre-philosophic thought. In several important aspects they wrote not only philosophical but also Midrashic books, that undertook to interpret the Torah by way of allegory (v. infra). In this respect they were closer to the interpretative tradition in Judaism, though such a literature of commentary was not uniquely Jewish - works of this kind were frequently found in Christian medieval philosophy.

Let us go on. Klatzkin, in translating Spinoza's Ethics into Hebrew, changed the Latin quod erat demonstrandum ("that which had to be proved"), which Spinoza took from Euclidean geometry, to the letters Sh. M., an abbreviation of Sh'ma Mine, which in Talmudic discourse stands for "(yes) draw that conclusion."(38) This translation adds to the linguistic attractiveness of Klatzkin's Hebrew of the twenties (the translation was made in 1924). It is evidence of the translator's personal taste and of the principles he believed in as to the primacy of the Hebrew language in determining what is of Jewish-national character. However, such a methodical stratagem cannot ipso facto turn Spinoza's Ethics into a part of Jewish philosophy. The fact remains that the philosopher drew on a foreign source for his expression, and not on Jewish sources. If one wishes, nevertheless, to argue that Spinoza's philosophy cannot be separated from Jewish thought, the argument must be based on relevant content, and not merely on method and terminology.

Let us turn to another interesting example that illustrates this major problem. The story is told of Salomon Maimon, the contemporary of Kant and Mendelssohn, that when he would finish writing a philosophical work, he would go to a tavern and get drunk. Maimon's bohemianism disgusted Mendelssohn, who was his patron. There were those who saw in Maimon's behavior an unconscious reversion to the ceremonial festive meal that Talmudic scholars held when they finished the study of a Tractate. This comparison, whether valid or not, may well be of interest to the biographer or the psychologist, but it does not make Maimon's philosophical work more "Jewish." His awkward, unsystematic German style might, to an extent, be regarded to have been the result of Talmudic training in his childhood, again, however, this does not turn his philosophical works such as his

Inquiry into Transcendental Philosophy (Berlin, 1790) and others, into Jewish philosophy. Maimon is justifiably regarded as the most important of the group of philosophers who constituted the connecting link between Kant and classical German Idealism. However, his philosophical contribution was made in the field of general philosophy, and not in the Jewish one. Nevertheless, one cannot sever Maimon's intellectual life from Jewish thought. The name that he adopted is evidence of his great veneration for Maimonides. In his well-known autobiography he wrote at length on the beginnings of Hasidism; included ten chapters on Maimonides's philosophy; distinguished between Mendelssohn's perception of Judaism and his own, and so on.(39) He also wrote, in Hebrew, a book entitled The Hill of the Guide,(40) which is a philosophical commentary, reflecting the spirit of his age, on the first part of The Guide of the Perplexed. It is a long book in the style of the Jewish interpreters of the Talmud. These latter two books of Maimon intrinsically belong to Jewish philosophy. (I have in mind the philosophical chapters in his autobiography, The Life of Salomon Maimon, and not the other fascinating chapters that have no philosophical significance.) As for the rest of his writings, they do not belong to Jewish philosophy. The fact that The Hill of the Guide supported his philosophical perception does not change this evaluation. Again, it is not the methodology, but the content that is the controlling factor. The same holds true for Mendelssohn's books. The great majority of them belong to general philosophy, and only Jerusalem and a few minor works can be categorized as belonging to "Jewish philosophy."

X. Jewish Philosophy is One of the Schools of Philosophy.

Can we possibly look at Jewish philosophy as being one of the many schools of philosophy that have cropped up in its long history? In other words, is Jewish philosophy a kind of tradition (not in the religious sense) of a well-defined, specific outlook, just as one might speak of Greek philosophy, or, more specifically, of "Stoic," "Aristotelian," "Neo-Platonic," "Kantian," "Neo-Kantian," "Hegelian," "Marxist," "Existentialist," "Analytic" philosophy? (One can, of course add more names to the list.) At first glance, this kind of definition might give rise to discomfort and reservations. It might seem - and not unjustifiably so - to be an attempt to reduce the status of Jewish philosophy by describing it as one school among many. Nevertheless, the definition should not be rejected out of hand. From the point of view of general philosophy by which we are guided in the present essay, Jewish philosophy really comes quite close to a teaching of a unique "Tradition of Jewish Philosophy."(41)

But there is a fly in the ointment. Even in the separate philosophical schools mentioned there is a plethora of trends, and not one of them ever represented a monolithic system of thought. The development of sub-schools can easily be discerned in them. What characterizes them is a common denominator within a specific ideological-philosophical tradition, by virtue of which they have been able to crystallize into philosophical schools. However, this phenomenon is not as common in Jewish philosophy. From its very beginning it consisted of separate schools and not just of "sub-schools." The bond to Judaism was the common denominator in Jewish philosophy; its schools, more or less, shared a religious tradition;

however, they lacked a tradition of a common philosophical outlook. Jewish Hellenistic philosophy is not like medieval Jewish philosophy; nor is modern Jewish philosophy similar to that of the Middle Ages. In every era, different Jewish philosophical schools made their presence felt: It will suffice to mention Jewish Neo-Platonism and Jewish Aristotelianism, the two major schools in the Middle Ages. Is it possible to find a common denominator between the philosophies of Solomon Ibn Gabirol, Maimonides, and Judah Halevy, that would be more than a meaningless generalization?

There was, possibly, a period of about three hundred years in the history of Jewish philosophy when some form of a monolithic philosophic tradition did exist. This was in the post-Maimonidean period, in the 12th to the 15th centuries. At that time there was a good deal of homogeneity among Jewish thinkers, as, despite their differences, they all dealt with questions that emerged from Maimonidean philosophy. They really had something like a philosophical tradition. However, that would seem to be the only period in the history of Jewish thought that can be described as having a Jewish philosophical tradition,(42) which was delimited by a specific historical framework. The general philosophical trend in this period was to accept Aristotelian philosophy and to interpret it in the light of a given faith, whether Christian, Moslem or Jewish. From this perspective, the existence of a philosophical tradition for several hundred years is not what made Jewish philosophy specifically Jewish.(43)

The problem comes down to this: Jewish philosophy, throughout the ages, acquired its inspiration essentially from the outside, namely, from the trends that were current in general philosophical thought at the time. This fact, again, raises doubt as to the possibility of characterizing Jewish philosophy as a tradition with a specifically Jewish outlook. It is no accident that we are wont to speak of "Jewish Neo-Platonism" and so on, even though these terms, in themselves, are quite problematical. There were Jews who were influenced by Neo-Platonism, just as in our days there are Jews who are influenced by Existentialism.

XI. Jewish Philosophy is Characterized by the Fact that it has an Apologetic Dimension.

Can a trend to defensiveness, accompanied by an apologetic strain, be considered a characteristic of Jewish philosophy? No one can deny that a considerable portion of Jewish philosophy is tainted with such tendencies. This is probably one of the reasons that medieval Jewish philosophy developed under Moslem culture. It was in this milieu that Judaism was attacked with philosophical arguments and was compelled to conterattack with the same kind of weapons. In Europe, where Judaism encountered physical assault, oppression, massacres (at the time of the Crusades) and the like, its response took the form of strict religious observance and acts of martyrdom. (In the 11th and 12th centuries, the literature that was produced by Hasidej Ashkenaz contained some philosophical strands, especially in the occult studies, but these instances do not change the general picture.) The sub-title of Judah Halevi's Kuzari is a good example of its apologetic purpose: "A book of proof and evidence in defense of a religion that has been debased." [Incidentally, exactly at the same time, in 1141, the approximate date of Judah Halevy's death, the French Scholastic P. Abelard composed his <u>Dialogue between a Jew, a Philosopher, and a Christian</u>. It is difficult to ascertain whether the book was written under the influence of the <u>Kuzari</u> or was a reaction to it.] Mendelssohn's <u>Jerusalem</u> was also written as a direct response to a challenge from the outside, in an attempt to justify Judaism. Even Leo Baeck's book, <u>The Essence of Judaism</u>,(44) written in the present century, was a reaction to the book by the Christian theologian Adolf von Harnack, <u>The Essence of Christianity</u> (1900). These are but a few of the outstanding instances in this area.

Even though the term "apologetics" evokes immediate negative associations, as if one is engaged in apologizing and justifying one's actions, it need not necessarily be so. Rosenzweig once commented that the art of defense (in law) can be one of the noblest of occupations. There is also good apologetics. True, "the attack dictated the subject." (The reference is to the books of Max Brod and Leo Baeck) but "the subject is: our very essence."(45) Is not The Guide of the Perplexed, wherein, inter alia, Maimonides sought to prove that all the anthropomorphic descriptions of the Godhead in the Torah were an allegorical mask for philosophical concepts, also an apologetic book? Does this fact derogate from its philosophical importance in any way? A persisting goal of Jewish scholars was to do battle with influences that seemed harmful to them, and above all, first and foremost to defend themselves against their attackers, as in Mendelssohn's case. It is for this reason that Jewish philosophical literature devotes a good deal of space to polemics. Rosenzweig was correct when he said: "...with all our distate for apologetics, the apologetical method remains the legitimate one for (Jewish) thought itself."(46) Nevertheless, this is an inadequate definition, for two reasons: On the one hand, many works in Jewish philosophy, especially in modern times, lack any apologetic aspects. On the other hand, those polemical elements that abound in Jewish philosophy (as they do in general philosophy) are not always directed against an external foe. Quite often they are purposely turned inward, against other Jewish thinkers: The polemics on Maimonides in the 13th century offer a good example. The fact still remains, to cite Rosenzweig once again, that "... only systematic thought is free to choose its subjects; whoever engages in apologetics is dependent on an outside source - on his opponent."(47) Without doubt this factor played an important part in determining the theoretical paths taken by Jewish thought, even though, as has been noted, it was not characteristic of Jewish philosophy as a whole. [Only the apologetic dimension of Jewish philosophy is considered here, not apologetic literature and activity in Judaism in its entirety. Books like <u>Jewish Apologetics</u> (1906) by the Viennese rabbi Moritz Guedemann, which undertook to refute the anti-Semitic charges, one by one, are not relevant for Jewish philosophy. Guedemann and other Jewish scholars regarded apologetics as a scientific occupation or as a public service. To this end, for example, the Central Organization of German Jewry (<u>Zentralverein</u>), the largest Jewish organization in Germany till the Nazis came into power, maintained a special department for apologetics.]

The foregoing comments furnish an explanation for the polemical style, which left its imprint on Jewish philosophy, and became inseparable from it.

Philo may have been exception in that, rather naively, he sought to bring harmony between the Jewish religion and Greek philosophy, eschewing polemics. One need but glance at the works of Rabbi David Kimhi, Hasdai Crescas, Rabbi Judah Arieh of Modena or Abraham Geiger in denigration of Christianity. This tendency to polemics diminished in intensity among modern Jewish philosophers, like Buber and Rosenzweig; however, even Rosenzweig's teachings, which were remarkably tolerant of Christianity - unlike any other work of Jewish philosophy prior to his time - contained a polemical dimension on the general philosophical level, directed against traditional Christian philosophy and theology. But this controvery had no particular Jewish significance.

XII. Jewish Philosophy is Philosophy that is Bound Up with the Fate of the Jewish People.

Can the ties to the fate of the Jewish nation, to its condition and its problems be of such significance for the works of Jewish philosophers as to turn them into a "Jewish philosophy?"(48) This would seem to be an acceptable characterization, since its adoption would obviate many of the difficulties encountered up until now. This definition is apt also for Jewish thinking in our day, when secular and national tendencies are on the ascendant in Jewish life. It does not constrict the discussion to a philosophical consideration of the Jewish religion, as did the other definitions. However, were we to judge Jewish philosophers of other ages by the criterion suggested here, certain problems would arise requiring one's attention.

Medieval Jewish philosophy, at least up to the time of Judah Halevy, never took an interest in the Jewish people as a Peculiar People, Israel the Chosen People, its bond to the Land of Israel, and the like. There is no doubt that these moments were preserved as a part of the Jewish religious beliefs, but they had become routine and required no theoretical consideration. Hence they were not dealt with on the philosophical or theological level. Jewish philosophers of the period centered their attention on the problems that engaged the attention of the general community of philosophers and theologians, especially the Islamic ones, such as the renewal of the universe or its antiquity, God's existence, His essence and His attributes, Providence, Free Will, Miracles and Prophecy. It may be, as Eliezer Schweid thinks, that this dealing in general problems of religious philosophy, that are devoid of any distinct Jewish tinge, reflected the desire of the Jewish writers to become an integral part in the general intellectual arena of their day, and to become rooted in the Diaspora and its culture.(49) The same tendency may be noted in Mendelssohn's works, in the modern era, during the period of the Enlightenment. However, from the Kuzari onward, matters changed. From them on, the Jewish philosophers' attention also turned to questions of uniquely Jewish moment.

Yet, in this connection the question of gradation arises. According to the criteria of the definition, certain philosophical doctrines may be described as more Jewish and others as less Jewish. Weltsch (50) has already described Maimonides's philosophy as being "more Jewish" than that of Spinoza. Following this logic, the philosophy of Judah Abarbanel, even though it is part and parcel of Italian Renaissance philosophy, is to be regarded as "more Jewish" than the philosophy of Ibn Gabirol, upon whom Abarbanel drew a great deal: Abarbanel in his Dialoghi d'Amore also took up, among other subjects, problems that clearly belonged to Jewish religious thought - whereas Ibn Gabirol's The Fountain of Life at first glance gives no inkling even as to the Jewish identity of the author. Sometimes this distinction may be made with respect to different works by the same author. The teachings of the "old" Hermann Cohen are a good deal "more Jewish" than those of the "young" Cohen. To go a step further, The Theologico-Political Treatise by Spinoza, who was excommunicated by the Jewish community, is a philosophical work that is "more Jewish" than The Fountain of Life of Ibn Gabirol, who had deep roots in Judaism. In fact, if we characterize philosophy as Jewish if it involves "ties to the fate of the Jewish Nation, to its condition and its problems," as suggested in this section, then Spinoza's Theologico-Political Treatise is a much more Jewish book than most of the essays of the medieval Jewish philosophers. This points up the weaknesses of the present definition. Indeed, Spinoza's philosophy cannot be cut off from its Jewish roots, but to declare it "more Jewish" than Ibn Gabirol's philosophical meditations, or those of Maimonides and their like, would certainly make of the definition something that could not be seriously entertained. According to this definition, even Marx's essay "On the Jewish Problem" could be considered a part of Jewish philosophy, because it concerns itself with certain aspects of the Jewish situation from a philosophical standpoint. (Once again, the unconscious psychological motives that moved Marx to write this essay are beyond the purview of this book.) If we proceed along this line, how is one to evaluate Sartre's essay, "Reflections on the Jewish Question"?

Nevertheless, despite the difficulties, or perhaps taking them into account, the present definition seems to bring us a good deal closer to understanding the unique essence of Jewish philosophy. Clearly, no definition using one particular criterion will exhaust the essence of the problem. Yet, a certain number of philosophical problems have a clear and distinct Jewish aspect, such as the philosophical question (not the one of faith) of the Election of Israel. Most Jewish thinkers, from Philo's day to the present, have dealt with it (although only since the time of Judah Halevy has it come to occupy a more central position in Jewish philosophy). Other such problems are the philosophical aspects of the significance of the Dispersion and the special place of the Land of Israel; the concept of the Commandments and the reasons behind them, and others. (Some of these questions will be discussed in Part Five below.) These are subjects that affect Judaism in its entirety. For example, it is certainly not difficult to enumerate, one by one, the essential differences between the viewpoints of Judaism and Christianity; between the concept of the Unity of the Godhead as opposed to the Divine Trinity; the incorporeal perception, as opposed to the corporeal one; the negation of the cult of the individual person and the cult of saints, as opposed to their affirmation; and the derogating of the importance of miracles, in contradistinction to making them the basis of faith. (An example may be found in the well-known Talmudic story of the debate between Rabbi Eliezer and the Sages. The latter refused to accept supernatural phenomena as arguments in determining the Halakha.(51))

Further differences that can be cited are: free will as against original sin; personal salvation as against salvation through Jesus; the Jewish negation of abstinence and monasticism, and the denial that they are religious ideals. Other areas touched upon are: a positive attitude toward the body; a balanced attitude to property, in contradistinction to poverty as an ideal (a goal that the institutionalized Church was very far from realizing); the Torah (i.e., the Law) versus faith; the idea of a Chosen People as opposed to a Chosen Church; the different attitude to Jesus and his Evangel, and many more. Are there, in all these perceptions that have been enumerated, any which are characteristic of Judaism and not of Christianity, so that they may serve as identifying marks to demarcate a Jewish philosophical position? Despite the instinctive leaning, as it were, to reply in the affirmative, it would seem that it is still difficult to give an unequivocal theoretical answer to the question.

CHAPTER TWENTY

AN ATTEMPT AT SUMMARY -
JEWISH PHILOSOPHY as the PHILOSOPHY of JUDAISM

It would appear that every characteristic examined and discussed in the preceding chapter is in some sense or other flawed. Every attempt to formulate a precise and unambiguous definition that would give the characteristics of a philosophy that could be termed "Jewish" is doomed to complete failure. The reasons for which the teachings of X may be accepted as "Jewish philosophy" do not necessarily hold for a characterization of Y's thought as Jewish philosophy. The criteria by which <u>The Guide of the Perplexed</u> may be judged as Jewish philosophy are not exactly those by which <u>The Fountain of Life</u>, <u>Jerusalem</u> or <u>The Star of Redemption</u> are appraised. It is far easier and more accurate to ascribe a philosophical work by a Jewish thinker to the domain of Jewish philosophy, if the subject discussed is of Jewish concern. From this standpoint, <u>The Fountain of Life</u> by Ibn Gabirol belongs to Jewish philosophy. Neither the fact that a work has been written by a Jew, nor that the author has ties with the fate of the Jewish people are determinative. What makes a work belong to Jewish philosophy is that it gives expression to creativity in the area of the religious and national culture of Judaism throughout the generations. (Clarification and details follow.) This was one of the reasons - perhaps even the main one - that caused Julius Guttmann to entitle his book <u>The Philosophy of Judaism</u>. (In the English translation the title is <u>Philosophies of Judaism</u> (1964), which renders the problem still more conspicuous.) In this fashion Guttmann sought to avoid the difficulties with the term "Jewish philosophy" that have been discussed above. But that raised another problem which we encountered above: Is the "Philosophy of Judaism" something like the "Philosophy of Mathematics" or the "Philosophy of Science," or the "Philosophy of Art"? What distinguishes the "philosopher of mathematics" from the mathematician, the "philosopher of history" from the historian, the "philosopher of science" from the scientist, and so on? In other words, what sets apart the activity of a philosopher from that of a researcher, when both work in the same field? Specifically, what distinguishes a "philosopher of Judaism" from the research worker in the Jewish sciences? At the end of Part Two, in connection with Geiger's view of Jewish theology, it was made clear that there is no clear-cut distinction in this field.

On the other hand, are we to classify Montaigne, Descartes, Voltaire and so on as "Philosophers of Frenchism", Hobbes, Locke, Berkeley and Hume as "Philosophers of Englishism" or Leibniz, Kant, Fichte, Schelling and Hegel as "Philosophers of Germanism," and so on? The very terms are absurd. Why doesn't the term "Philosophy of Judaism," even though we are aware of the problems involved, evoke a similar reaction of absurdity? It would seem that we almost instinctively sense the meaning of the phrase, and only the philosophizing itself about this subject brings up the theoretical difficulties in the terms "Jewish philosophy" or "a philosophy of Judaism." In other words, the two terms become problematical as soon as we attempt to clarify what the special common denominator is that makes Jewish philosophers unique, and whether there really is one.

The little word "of" is not as innocent as it sounds. It has an ambiguity and a problematic nature of its own. When one speaks about "the philosophy of Buber," one refers to the philosophical ideas that Buber entertained. The subject is not Buber, rather his thought. Those who deal critically with Buber's philosophy will direct their attention not to Buber, but to his philosophy. However, when we speak of "the philosophy of science" or of "the philosophy of art," then we engage in a philosophic investigation of science or of art. Despite the similar language structure, which in both cases employs the word "of," we find that in the first instance the subject under investigation is philosophy, whereas in the second instance the subject is something else. What, then, according to this distinction - one that is clearly not trivial - is the "philosophy of Judaism"? I believe that it is closer in meaning to the second instance, even though this interpretation was not entirely satisfactory when first raised in this investigation. Leon Roth, whose comments on the subject of "Jewish philosophy" have already been mentioned, also tends to this kind of interpretation:

> Jewish philosophy, or rather the Philosophy of Judaism, is the thinking and rethinking of the fundamental ideas involved in Judaism, and the attempt to see them fundamentally, that is in coherent relation one with another so that they form one intelligible whole.(52)

Thus, the term "the philosophy of Judaism" resembles "the philosophy of science." As in the latter instance the subject is "science" and "the philosophy of science" examines the general foundations of the sciences, so in the former instance the subject is Judaism, and "the philosophy of Judaism" investigates the general foundations that are uniquely Jewish. That special tinge, which made various Jewish philosophers become philosophers of Judaism, was not especially conspicuous when they were considering the concepts of God, of the universe and of man, subjects with which all philosophers deal. But it did stand out when they came to discuss the nature of Judaism and the problems that were uniquely bound up with its status and fate. Without trying to assign rank or grades, it may thus be said that Judah Halevy, in this respect, was more of a Jewish philosopher than were Maimonides, Abraham Ibn Ezra or Ibn Gabirol. Such an evaluation is reinforced by Luzzatto's rating Rashi and Judah Halevy above Maimonides and Ibn Ezra. It loses some of its force as a consequence of his firmly negative attitude toward Spinoza.

Some of the Jewish scholars, at the beginning of this century, who were aware of these terminological difficulties, attempted to circumvent them in different ways. David Neumark called his most important book, written in Hebrew, The History of Philosophy in Israel (1921-29). Similarly, and even before him, Simon Bernfeld ornately named his book, published in 1897, The Knowledge of God, and gave it the sub-title The History of Religious Philosophy in Israel.(53) The name of the book, which was more journalistic than philosophical in content, gives convincing evidence of the author's intention.

In fact, all the books mentioned above deal more or less with the same philosophers, beginning with Philo (very few writers, like Israel Efros, went back to the Bible). Yet, each had a different ideological approach, and so each reflected different perceptions and emphases in regard to the meaning of Jewish philosophy and the areas that it covered. Leon Roth attempted to grade the following books dealing with the history of Jewish philosophy in accordance with the weight given to the subject of Jewishness in the title:

a) Neumark, in calling his book The History of Philosophy in Israel, laid less stress on the Jewish-philosophical element.

b) S. Munk, I. Husik and others dealt with the History of Jewish Philosophy, mostly concentrating on a certain period, such as the Middle Ages.

c) Jewish scholars in 19th century Germany tended, as has been remarked, to speak about the History of the Religious Philosophy of Judaism.

Bernfeld regarded the Knowledge of God as a characteristic of Jewish philosophy.

e) Finally, Julius Guttmann saw in Judaism the subject on which Jewish philosophers center their endeavors, and so he deals in his book with the Philosophy of Judaism.(54)

From this last standpoint, the definition of Jewish philosophy is, then, finally dependent on the personal evaluation of the person engaged in this field, and one can make no absolute judgments. Guttmann, in speaking of the "Philosophy of Judaism," seems most reasonable. Nevertheless this should not prevent us from being clearly aware of the theoretical difficulties, some of which have already been discussed. The main problem, as has been stated, is that there exists no basic content that might serve as a common denominator for all Jewish philosophers, nor is there a basic form that might serve the same purpose. That is to say, there is no definition whatsoever of Jewish philosophy that holds for all Jewish thinkers, or that can serve as a general criterion for belonging to the world of Jewish philosophy. Someone has suggested the formula, "the confluence of Judaism and philosophy,"(55) but this too, is inadequate. When the writer who made this suggestion explains that "The Jewish Philosopher ... on the one hand, is a man, and, as such, he is a philosopher ... but, on the other hand, the philosopher who is firmly imbedded in Judaism relies on the Torah, which he regards as the word of God"(56) - then, in effect, this comes to an almost literal acceptance of Gersonides's position that philosophy and the Torah are two things apart (v. supra). In this manner, the term " Jewish philosophy" once again loses all meaning. What remains is merely philosophy, in the best of circumstances engaged in by a believing Jew, who in like manner may occupy himself with biochemistry or neurophysiology. S. Rosenberg's conclusion that "... the result of this meeting ... of the impudent man with the man who accepts the Torah is Jewish philosophy"(57) may perhaps be valid from the genetical point of view, i.e., existentially. Jewish philosophy over the generations did indeed come into being as the result of such a confrontation (more on this subject below), but nothing in the above formulation tells us what is unique about this Jewish philosophy. The opposite is true: All that we are left with is the trivial conclusion that the Jewish philosopher is a philosopher in his capacity of being a man, while as a Jew he is a Jew - the kind of tautology that recalls a paraphrase of a favorite saying with the men of the Enlightenment: Be a philosopher in the world, and a Jew in your home.

This matter requires further clarification. No one doubts that a Jewish philosopher is entitled to being called a philosopher, if his thought contributes to philosophy, which, as has been said, is a general discipline, not belonging to any specific nation or religion. Thus, Jews who have excelled in the field of philosophy have done so as philosophers and not as Jews. The philosophies of Philo, Sa'adia Gaon, Ibn Gabirol, Maimonides, Judah Abarbanel, Mendelssohn, Hermann Cohen, Rosenzweig and Buber (it is no accident that these recurring names are those of the lions of Jewish philosophy; Spinoza's name has been omitted here because his philosophy, from the standpoint of the question being considered, is a problem in itself) fall within the scope of philosophy because they deal with philosophical problems, project their influence beyond the bounds of Judaism, and are not restricted to the confines of the Jewish people alone. Consequently, as philosophers all these thinkers are of universal importance, some being better known than others. Nevertheless, we, as Jews, have a special interest in them not only because they are Jews (this, too, is a reason that one should not reject in principle), but because we have a feeling, without being able to present a systematic line of thinking in its support, that their philosophy has a Jewish dimension as well. This is exactly the question under discussion in these pages. From the standpoint of Jewish philosophy, not only does the philosophy of Rosenzweig and Buber elicit more interest than, let us say, that of Gabriel Marcel, their contemporary, who also was a religious existentialist, but it also evokes in us, from the Jewish aspect, more interest than the philosophy of Bergson, who was both a philosopher and a Jew. From the point of view of their weight as philosophies, certainly the work of Marcel and Bergson is in no way inferior to that of Rosenzweig and Buber, as long as the criteria for evaluation are solely philosophical, as indeed they must be. But the question still remains: Why are the philosophies of Rosenzweig and Buber classified without question as Jewish philosophy, and that of Bergson is not necessarily so? As to the first two, there is no one who disputes their being Jewish philosophers, whereas on Bergson there is a difference of opinion, as we have seen. But if we adopt Rosenberg's formula, as set forth above, a Jewish philosopher is a philosopher as a man, and a Jew only as he faces the Torah. Consequently, one's ties to Judaism ought to be irrelevant to one's being a philosopher. Buber and Rosenzweig and Bergson were all philosophers according to this canon, and different degrees of their ties to Judaism are of no moment. Nevertheless, Rosenberg would not hesitate to describe the first two as Jewish philosophers, but would certainly deny such an appellation to Bergson. Yet, he would have difficulty in explaining such a distinction on the basis of his formulation.

It is not the mere encounter of Judaism and philosophy that gives birth to "Jewish philosophy," but the encounter that is, in fact, a confrontation.

That is what happened, first and foremost, in medieval Jewish philosophy. Undoubtedly, the Jewish philosophers felt that here were two completely different systems, neither derivable from the other, yet there is no need for either to lose standing on account of the other. As Emil Fackenheim put it:

> (They) accepted, first, the existence of two independent sources of truth, of which one was human reason and the other a divine revelation, embodied in the Sacred Jewish Scriptures. On the basis of this fundamental assumption, they accepted these additional ones: that reason and revelation cover at least in part the same ground; that there is at least some apparent conflict between them; and that the conflict is apparent only - that it can be resolved without violence to either reason or Judaism. Without the first and third of these additional assumptions, there would have been no possibility of a Jewish philosophy, and without the second, no necessity for it.(58)

The attempts to clarify these assumptions, especially the middle one, constitute some of the important identification marks of "Jewish philosophy," a discipline of thought that is both philosophical and Jewish, without one aspect overshadowing the other.

PART FOUR: FUNDAMENTAL PROBLEMS IN JEWISH PHILOSOPHY

CHAPTER TWENTY-ONE

SOME BASIC PROBLEMS in DIDACTICS

Inquiry into Jewish philosophy has given rise to a number of didactic questions of principle, which should be considered:

1. The teachings of a philosopher must be understood in the context of his period. This postulate is as valid for general philosophy as it is for Jewish philosophy. Nevertheless, the point is emphasized here because Jewish philosophers throughout the ages, while using the same sources in conducting their investigations - the Bible, the Talmud, etc. - related to them and interpreted them quite differently, each in accordance with the philosophical influences current in his time and with the historical, social and cultural circumstances that furnished the intellectual background for his thought.

2. The thought of the various philosophers should be dealt with not from a mere scholarly or "antiquarian" point of view, but rather should an attempt be made to clarify its significance for problems that continue to beset the contemporary Jewish and philosophical scene. Even though one ought not discuss a philosopher outside the context of his period (v. supra), yet the special interest we display in his teaching is dependent on the degree of its relevance to the philosophy of our time. The approach should be first of all systematically philosophical, not merely historical. This, of course, holds for general philosophy as well. The ties between philosophy and its history, from this standpoint, have already been discussed in Part One. Yet in this context another problem arises. A modern scholar is much better equipped to analyze and understand in depth a philosophy that is distant from him in time than was a contemporary or near-contemporary of the philosophy under consideration. This holds not only for philosophy. The scientific trustworthiness of a modern investigator of the Bible or the Talmud, to take an example from the subject matter being discussed, is undoubtedly greater than that of the traditional commentators. The relatively recent scientific inquiries on Jewish philosophies and philosophers of the past have contributed a great deal to our understanding. Suffice it to mention the research of Harry A. Wolfson on Philo, Crescas, Spinoza, the Kalaam et al., or the work of Shlomo Pines on medieval Jewish and Arab philosophy.

3. Here a problem emerges that has already been alluded to several times: Is newer, more modern thinking, necessarily superior, from the standpoint of philosophical achievement, to that of earlier philosophers? Of course, our knowledge, both general and philosophical, has grown steadily, since it encompasses the achievements of the past, but have we come any closer, to a significant degree, to the longed-for truth (as Nicholas of Cusa and Hegel believed, v. supra, Part One)? I believe that there is no place here for simplistic comparisons. Every period in the history of Jewish thought produced thinkers of unusual intellectual stature, and it is senseless to try to grade them. Clear

distinctions should be drawn between various philosophers and between various periods. This problem, as well, is not unique to Jewish philosophy - by its very nature, it belongs to the general sphere. Classical Greek philosophy was the cradle of Western philosophy not only chronologically - it was the source from which Western philosophy developed from a spiritual and ideational point of view. Similarly, medieval Jewish philosophy was the matrix of Jewish thought of later generations. A.N. Whitehead once remarked that all Western philosophy was but "marginal comments on Plato." Incidentally, a similar observation was made long before him by the medieval Jewish philosopher, Moshe Narboni, who claimed that the entire content of philosophy came from "one shepherd," meaning Aristotle,(1) i.e., that all philosophy was but "marginal comments" to Aristotle's doctrines, as interpreted by Averroes, whose fervent follower Narboni was. Without taking sides as to the validity of the foregoing determinations, one can also regard Jewish philosophy throughout the ages to some extent as nothing more than "marginal comments" on Maimonides and Yehuda Halevi. Yet we must beware of too simplistic a parallel. Jewish philosophical activity was not limited only to a continuation of and a confrontation with the early Jewish philosophers - it also reflected the general philosophical influences of every period. Jewish philosophy does not operate in a hermetically closed world. It may therefore be said (even though every such assertion is somewhat schematic) that on the diachronic level there is in Jewish philosophy a perpetuation and an internal continuity, though there is no lack of a strain of criticism of earlier views; but on the synchronic level the main importance rests with the external influences of contemporary general philosophical thought and with the intellectual confrontation with it.

4. Just as there has always been a bond - sometimes stronger and sometimes weaker - between philosophy and the sciences, there exists a bond between Jewish philosophy and other Jewish studies. This was well understood by the scholars of the "Science of Judaism" (Wissenschaft des Judentums) of the preceding century. Krochmal, Geiger (cf. the chapter on his theological conception at the end of Part Two), Formstecher, Hirsch and Steinheim - all regarded the Science of Judaism as a foundation on which there would rise a philosophy of Judaism. This leads to an important conclusion as to the method of teaching and study of Jewish philosophy. Just as the general philosopher must have a knowledge of the natural and social sciences (cf. the chapter, "Philosophy and Science," in Part One), so must the Jewish philosopher be acquainted with the various branches of Jewish studies, not only with the traditional sources.

5. Lastly, there remains a didactic problem that is primarily concerned with methodology. In Jewish philosophy, one unconsciously pays more attention to the philosophers than to the problems they deal with. This means that the main subjects of Jewish philosophy are the philosophical doctrines of the various thinkers, such as the philosophy of Philo, of Maimonides, or Rosenzweig, and the like. The subjects are not logic, epistemology, ethics, aesthetics and so on, even though the Jewish philosophers wrote on most of these philosophical subjects. In the

ever-growing number of recent books and anthologies on "Jewish ethics" one will, generally speaking, fail to find systematic studies of the subject, such as in the parallel general philosophical literature. They usually deal with moral problems as they were reflected in the Bible, the Talmud, the Midrashim, or the teachings of one Jewish philosopher or another. The reason for this phenomenon is simple: morals are morals; there is no unique Jewish ethics, as there is no unique Jewish logic or Jewish epistemology. However, the Jewish sources and the Jewish philosophers do deal with problems of ethics, which in their very nature have a general philosophical meaning. The same holds true for the other systematic subjects with which general philosophy deals. Any consideration of these subjects from a Jewish point of view merely shifts the discussion to a different course of treatment.

Nevertheless, it is inconceivable that Jewish philosophy should confine itself to a description of the teachings of individual philosophers. [Rosenberg, in the symposium mentioned above, defined this approach as "Philosophography"](2). The main purpose of any study of philosophy is to get to a point where one philosophizes, i.e., clarifies the theoretical and practical problems for their own sake, and does not confine oneself merely to studying the ideas of one philosopher or another on the given problem and to expressing one's opinion on these ideas. In this matter Jewish philosophy is faced with grave problems, the solutions for which are being sought actively. Clearly, the study of Jewish philosophy - in the spirit of the Hegelian identity of philosophy and its history - must be inseparably bound up with the theoretical study of the ever-recurring problems in the world of Judaism and contemporary Jewry.

As a philosophy, it must clearly touch upon both. The subjects of inquiry for Jewish philosophy are not only the "traditional" topics, with which Jewish philosophy has grappled in all periods, e.g., the Election of Israel, the reasons for the Commandments, the meaning of Exile, the status of the Land of Israel, the Torah, the Halakha and the like. The actuality of these traditional topics has not diminished; however such problems as Israel and the Nations, the relations of religion and State, religion and secularism in modern Judaism, the ties between the State of Israel and the Dispersion (problems of "the center" and the "periphery" in the terminology of Ahad Ha'am) are even more immediate today. These are the main subjects for inquiry - with the emphasis on the word "inquiry" - while present-day Jewish philosophy must continue to draw, and does draw, a great deal of inspiration from the sources of the past, as well.

On the other hand, one must never forget that what is valid for general philosophy applies to Jewish philosophy as well. Philosophy - though conscious of problems of the day - is in its essence abstract thought. It must indeed maintain its "involvement" (v. supra. Part One), not in a simplistic, pragmatic way, but by doing the job that belongs to philosophy. Its inquiries may, of course, serve in the future as a guideline for practical life as well.

Parenthetically one might note that the Sabbatical Year, instituted in ancient times to fall every seven years, was established not merely for the reasons set forth in the sources, or for agricultural purposes, such as permitting the land to rest and recuperate - it affected other spheres as well, e.g., the remission of debts, et al. Possibly the Sabbatical Year had another hidden intent as well, such as to teach man that from time to time he should put aside his worldly endeavors and devote himself to matters of universal significance, to contemplation and to matters of the mind. What Aristotle stated to be the aim of philosophy (v. supra), Judaism turned in this way into a commandment, binding on all, a kind of recurring spiritual "refresher course." This, of course, is only a hypothesis and exegesis - the realities of life certainly would not permit us to live in accordance with the above precept, even if we wished to. However, the idea itself, not necessarily in the form dictated by the Halakha, is worth considering as to its applicability to modern life. Apart from the significance of the seventh day of rest as a social achievement, the main purpose of the Sabbath was that it be devoted to the worship of God, i.e., that on that day one should devote all one's thought and attention to the ties between man and God, to metaphysical problems, to the exclusion of all other endeavors.

It is a matter of regret that philosophy has never achieved the status of a guide for human behavior, as Plato had intended. There is no one other than the philosopher for whom the Biblical phrases, "a man is not a prophet in his own city," or "a voice crying in the wilderness," are better suited. Few philosophers, whether in Israel or the world, have lived to see their doctrines and their messages adopted by their societies. The greatness of the giants of philosophy, and perhaps of other disciplines as well, lies, inter alia, in the fact that through their foresight they have anticipated their contemporaries. It was in this spirit that Hugo Bergmann commented on Spinoza, despite the reservations he held as to his doctrines, that, in reality, Spinoza was Kant's contemporary.(3) Perhaps it is also no accident that, when Rosenzweig spoke about the "possibility of living the miracle," he based it on the prophetic ability of foreseeing the future.(4)

CHAPTER TWENTY-TWO

THE SOURCES of INSPIRATION of JEWISH PHILOSOPHY

As has already become clear in the previous Part, the main inspiration for Jewish philosophy came from outside sources, namely from general philosophy. Julius Guttmann began his book <u>The Philosophies of Judaism</u> with the following words:

> The Jewish people did not begin to philosophize because of an irresistible urge to do so. They received philosophy from outside sources, and the history of Jewish philosophy is a history of the successive absorptions of foreign ideas which were then transformed according to specific Jewish points of view.(5)

The Sages had already written graphically, "God enlarge Japhet, and he shall dwell in the tents of Shem; (this means) that the words of Japhet shall be in the tents of Shem."(6) In other words, the wisdom of Greece, which was of the seed of Japhet, will dwell in the tents of Israel, which was of the seed of Shem. Later commentators used this quotation in different ways and for contradictory purposes, but it itself undubitably reflects a favorable view of mutual relations between Jewish and Greek philosophy. True, as will be seen below, generally speaking the Sages, especially the Palestinian <u>Tannaim</u> (Jewish sages from the time of Hillel to the end of the Mishna), were very reserved in their attitude to the study of Greek philosophy.

The source of Western philosophy is to be found in Greece, and not in Israel. Eastern philosophy, that of India and China, does not pertain to the issues discussed here, even though sometimes there are some very remarkable parallels - Hillel's dictum, "Do not do unto thy fellow-being that which is hateful to thee," appears word for word in the teachings of Confucius, who preceded him by several hundred years. Nevertheless one cannot assume that there were reciprocal influences between Jewish and eastern philosophy. Persian Zoroastrianism may have had some influence on early Jewish thought. For a certain historical period the Jewish people lived under the political rule of the Persian kingdom, and this must have had some spiritual and intellectual consequences. But there is an essential opposition between Persian dualism and Jewish monotheism, and, furthermore, the degree to which Zoroastrian doctrine belongs to philosophy is open to question. When Buber dealt with the problem of Good and Evil, he made a few interesting comparisons between the Persian religion and some of the Psalms, however the philosophical lesson that was implied in these comparisons was essentially Buber's own.(7)

Yet it is important to stress that the existence of external inspirations and influences does in no way affect the originality of the philosophy that absorbs them. To the contrary: the quality of the absorption is evidence of the spiritual power of the absorber and of his ability to deal with the matter absorbed. It may well be that Mosaic law was influenced by the laws of Hammurabi, which antedated it, or that both had a common ancient source. (There are scholars today who are inclined to cast some doubt on the connection between the two codes of law.) Yet, there is nothing in the similarity between the various laws [e.g., "an eye for an eye," or "an ox that has gored" (7a)] that negates the originality of the laws of the Torah that, because of different historical and social circumstances, developed in a more humane form, e.g., the laws about slavery. (On the other hand, Hammurabi's laws were sometimes more "progressive," as for example, the laws relating to matrimony.) At any rate, external influence and originality are not mutually exclusive. The greatness of any idea, a fortiori of a philosophical one, lies in the fact that it is not linked to a specific socio-historical reality, and with the passage of time it acquires universal significance. Therefore there is nothing disreputable in borrowing from the spiritual achievements of another culture to help overcome the contradictions and the confusions that beset man in his spiritual life. Every thinking individual contends with problems, and from a purely human standpoint the spiritual problems and difficulties of the different peoples and cultures have a great deal in common, because the human race and the human spirit are one.

Despite this basic unity, there were those who tried to show that Western thought rests on two distinct fundamental concepts: the Idea, which was derived from Greece, and the Commandment, which stemmed from Israel.(8) The Idea is achieved, as Plato thought, by recollection and observation, whereas the Commandment is based, according to tradition, on a revealed Divine law that is achieved by hearing. [It is of interest to note that J.G. Herder, largely influenced by Biblical sources, emphasized in his essay on the development of language the importance of the vocal and auditory elements.(9)] In such fashion, in the course of man's spiritual development, there came into being, on the one hand, a trend associated with observing and remembering and, on the other, a trend based on doing and hearing. "We shall do, and we shall hear." The process of integrating these two trends began in Hellenistic Jewish thought, reached its peak in the ideas of Maimonides, and was completed in the works of Spinoza and Mendelssohn.(10)

The problem, then, is not whether Jewish philosophy has been influenced by external factors, for better or for worse. It is, rather, when and how that body of thought, which we are accustomed to characterize as Jewish philosophy, began to take shape. This question is open to controversy.

CHAPTER TWENTY-THREE

IS THERE JEWISH PHILOSOPHY in the BIBLE?

No one will question that there was Jewish philosophy in the Hellenistic period, the Middle Ages and the modern era, whatever its content may have been; but whether or not there was a Jewish philosophy in ancient times is debatable. Israel Efros was among the few who tended to see the budding of a Jewish philosophy in the Bible.(11) However, in order to prevent a double misunderstanding, the following must be emphasized: 1) There is no question that philosophical subjects are to be found in the Bible. The question is whether they constitute Jewish philosophy. 2) In this investigation reference is not made to interpretative attempts to uncover concealed philosophical significance in Biblical descriptions and stories, as was done by Maimonides and others. (The subject will be elaborated on below.) These exegetical writings are not Biblical philosophy - they are the philosophical hermeneutics of later medieval thinkers, and they are a part of the thought of the medieval, not the Biblical, times. (In some cases, hermeneutics of this sort is also found in earlier periods. An example is the claim that the Song of Songs symbolizes the love of God for the Jewish people.) The question of whether an early Jewish philosophy existed arises mainly in connection with those Biblical books or passages that deal explicitly with philosophical subjects, such as the Book of Job, Ecclesiastes, Proverbs, parts of the Prophetic books, and a few other scattered chapters. Sayings such as "He who is righteous suffers evil, and he who is wicked enjoys good fortune", "The preminence of man above beast is nought", "To know good and evil", "Thou shalt love thy neighbor as thyself", and others like them are without doubt expressions of philosophical problems. The question in point, however, is whether they concern Jewish philosophy.

There are scholars who believe that in Ecclesiastes there is clear evidence of the influence of Greek philosophy. There are some who claim to see in it a Jewish reflection of the Platonic dialogue, Philebus. The confrontation in Ecclesiastes between "wisdom" and "madness" is supposed to reproduce the confrontation between Sophia (wisdom) or Phronesis (practical wisdom) and Hedone (pleasure) in Philebus. However, Plato chooses "wisdom", while the conclusion of Ecclesiastes is that they both are "vanity."(12) These are general philosophical problems. There does not seem to be much validity to the view of Leibowitz, that the pessimistic ideas expressed by Ecclesiastes, such as "The preeminence of man above the beast is nought," are a true expression of Judaism, since they emphasize the uniqueness and supremacy of God, to whom all are subject.(13) The Jewish religious way of life does seek to turn every human act into a means of communication between man and God, into worship of the Creator. But that does not constitute a philosophical doctrine.

The Greek and Biblical ways of philosophizing are certainly not identical, but the problems are often similar. One might ask why it is that Greek and Biblical thought, though they deal with common subjects, nevertheless arrive at different solutions. One might conclude from this that the views and the opinions expressed in the Bible characterize Jewish philosophy. In consequence, Greek philosophy could be defined as rationalistic, and Jewish philosophy - non-rationalistic, because it pins all of its hope on God. For example, the Book of Job, philosophically speaking, clearly formulates a religio-philosophical problem - he who is righteous suffers evil - without any attempt to obscure or paint the facts in pretty colors. But after Job and his friends have completely argued the problem, the outcome is a return to faith. God, the Creator of the universe, is beyond any critical or rational argument, beyond comprehension by the human intellect. Here, the difference is very clear between Greek "scientific" philosophy - which is based on observation, analysis, search for cause and effect and the like - and Job's philosophy, according to which reason cannot find the desired solution. The problem of justice - again a very important philosophical concept - is the main subject of both Plato's Republic and the Book of Job. But does Job's conclusion, that the human intellect is incapable of comprehending God's purposes and deeds, necessarily make it Jewish? On the one hand, it stands in direct contradiction to all we know about medieval and modern Jewish philosophy, and on the other hand this conclusion is familiar to us from general philosophy, from the views of Pascal, Kierkegaard, and others.

There are no philosophical elements in Biblical thought that might be characterized as being uniquely Jewish, and that can therefore be regarded as Jewish philosophy. A great number of philosophical problems are touched upon in the Book of Books of the Jewish people, but they do not contain any uniquely Jewish moment. Most of the philosophical ideas and their implications in the Bible are of moral and humanistic significance, but by that token they are universal and apply to humanity as a whole. Symptomatically one can note the fact, for example, that explicit Divine prohibition of murder is to be found in Biblical verses addressed to Noah,(14) that is, before the Torah was given to the people of Israel. The Sages of the Talmud and the Midrash refer to some of these commandments as "commandments for the children of Noah," i.e., universal ones. The fact that the other two monotheistic religions accepted the Bible as Holy Script reinforces the conclusion that from an ideological perspective it expressed general views and not specifically Jewish ones. (It should be understood that our concern here is with the philosophical aspects. and not with the other aspects which made the Bible a great and unique national creation of the Jewish People). In short, the philosophical ideas found in the Bible are of a general nature. There is no "Jewish morality," there is only "morality." (v. supra). It is written, "And thou shalt love thy neighbor as thyself," and not "Thou shalt love thy Jewish neighbor as thyself." Furthermore, when a distinction is made between a Hebrew and a non-Hebrew slave, "a Canaanite slave," one can perhaps explain it by the sociological and historical circumstances prevailing at the time, but the Biblical distinction cannot be justified by present-day moral standards. The basic immorality of slavery is not at issue here; the fact that the Bible speaks ill of slavery, and commands that the (Hebrew) slave be set free at the end of seven years "... because you were a slave in the land of Egypt," was a social achievement (reached only later by Greek philosophy) whose significance is universal. It is a source of pride that the Jewish People were the first to enunciate that commandment. Or take another matter: without going into specialized technical problems of Biblical interpretation, no one could argue that the verse "From an alien thou mayest take interest, but from thy brother thou shalt not take interest"(15) is an expression of "Jewish morality," except for Jew-baiters and anti-Semites of all ages.

We conclude, then, that a unique Jewish ethic does not exist. However, one cannot ignore the very important fact that the early Jewish sources - the Torah and the Oral Law - include a humanist and universal content of moral value that is a part of the spiritual foundation of Judaism, just as such content is to be found in the heritage of Greek philosophy, in Western culture and in other cultures. One can legitimately speak of the humanist values to be found in the Bible, the oldest and holiest Jewish "document," in which - as far as is known - some of the universal values were articulated for the first time in history. However, none of the ethical subjects in the Bible - and ethics is one of the most important branches in philosophy - have a unique Jewish tinge. They are general philosophical ideas. Spinoza, too, thought that Judaism was the first - even before Aristotle - to raise the philosophical problem of the good man as opposed to the good citizen, but can one claim that this problem is uniquely Jewish? The Bible is not a book on philosophy, nor a book on ethics. Just as there are moral ideas in the Bible whose value has been acknowledged throughout the ages, so there are also many matters that reflect the times, and can no longer be regarded as acceptable today. The commandment, said to be divine, to wipe out the seven peoples of Canaan, including women and children, not only is contrary to our basic philosophical conception, but raises problems on the religio-philosophical plane as well. Could such a commandment come from the mouth of God? Could God, who is eternal, who exists outside the dimension of time, be subject to the cruel ways of a certain historical period? This knotty problem is relevant, of course, for only a person of faith. A secular Biblical scholar will have no trouble in understanding that in the Bible are described historical events and concepts, characteristic of ancient peoples, including the People of Israel. These ideas and events were ascribed to God, in order to lend them greater weight and authority, or perhaps even to justify them. In all likelihood those harsh commandments were not carried out literally, as may be learned from various passages in the Bible.

Moreover, it is these very descriptions that highlight the contribution of early Judaism, in the field of ethics which went beyond the conventions of its time and anticipated that of other nations. (v. supra concerning slavery, etc.) Even the concept of "an eye for an eye," which in our day seems so barbaric - before the Sages redefined it in terms of monetary payment - does not necessarily correspond to the barbaric customs then in vogue among other peoples. Its purpose, in the view of some scholars, was to prevent unbridled acts of revenge, as described in the incident of Dinah and the vengeful murder of the people of Sichem. The words of Nathan the Prophet to David, after the murder of Uriyah the Hittite, also undoubtedly speak of a punishment that goes far beyond the nature of the crime: "And now, the sword shall not depart from thy house forever: for the reason that thou hast despised me, and hast taken the wife of Uriyah, the Hittite, to be thy wife."(16) This is not the position espoused by the laws of the Torah. The Biblical Encyclopedia points out that the punishment of measure for measure is meant primarily for the criminal himself and does not apply to the members of the family (in contradiction to the Laws of Hammurabi.)(17) It is of interest to note that one of the reasons given in the Talmudic tractate Baba Kama (from the early period of the Palestinian Amoraim) for abrogating the injunction an "eye for an eye" in its literal sense was that taking out an eye for an eye may lead to a fatal disproportion of punishment to the crime. It could be that, in taking out the eye in recompense, one may cause death.(18) However, these are all philosophical, legal and moral problems that have a general character, that apply to man as man.

Viewed philosophically, one may find in the Bible ideas of varying trends. The God of the Prophets is not identical with the God of Hagiography, the God of Isaiah is not like the God of Ecclesiastes or of Job. Indeed, there is one central world outlook that characterizes the unique Biblical perception, as opposed to that of idolatry, namely monotheism, which is without doubt the religio-philosophical view of ancient Judaism. But is this uniquely "Jewish philosophy"?

To summarize the subject of "Ancient Jewish philosophy": There is some philosophy in the Bible. To a certain extent one may perhaps speak even of "Biblical philosophy", though the difficulties besetting this expression are too numerous to permit its use. All the philosophical ideas mentioned appear in the Bible and in the thought of the Sages without order and system, without a terminology worthy of its name, without a suitable system for argumentation. Therefore, it may be preferable to speak of Biblical and Rabbinic Theology, not "philosophy," even though in using the very term "theology" we have run into difficulty. (vide end of Part Two.) But certainly the Bible contains no teachings that can be described as "Jewish philosophy" on the basis of the criteria set forth in previous paragraphs that discussed the significance and essence of the subject. Jewish philosophy, i.e., philosophy that has uniquely Jewish motivations and content, arose only as a result of the meeting and the clash with Greek philosophy. One cannot ignore the fact that Jewish philosophers of all times have emphasized their bond to the Torah and the Oral Law, not to mention the citations they brought from other Jewish sources, beginning with Sa'adia Gaon and Maimonides and ending with Hermann Cohen and the Jewish philosophers of our day. Incidentally, quotations from the Bible encompass a broader field than those of the Sages, which are essentially legalistic in their nature. Only of late has more attention been paid to Midrashic literature. However, one must not forget, that most of the quotations from the Bible and the literature of the Sages acquire philosophical significance only when philosophers advert to them. It is the philosophical point of view that uncovers the philosophical possibilities inherent in the Bible. The hermeneutic dimension is determinative here. When Maimonides discusses Providence, he attributes a much greater philosophical significance to the Book of Job than was to be found in the original.(19) Every one of Job's companions becomes a representative of one of the philosophical views on Providence, which Maimonides had discussed in previous chapters. It was difficult for Jewish philosophers, especially those of the medieval period, to make peace with the fact that the Torah, which is the expression of God's Word, does not excel in philosophical depth. They so wanted the Torah to be philosophically important that they discovered in it philosophical messages, as it were, by reading between the lines. (More of this - in later chapters.) But all of this does not add up to a philosophy of the Bible - it is the philosophy of thinkers of a later day.

However, it should be stated in all fairness that, even discounting these hermeneutic elements, which are often arbitrary and very forced, the Biblical scholars who discussed philosophical subjects to be found in the Bible - Divine Providence, freedom and responsibility, social ethics and the like - could not have done so had they not been familiar with the problems from later philosophical literature. One will find in the Bible verses dealing with Divine Providence only after having become acquainted with the philosophical problems of determinism and predestination. One will discuss the social content of the Bible only after one understands the complexity of social problems as analyzed in progressive and socialist thought. In short, philosophical problem are found in the Bible, but they are found in potentia. It is the philosopher who discovers them there, because the philosophical, ethical and social problems were known to him previously from another source.

As to the thought of the Sages, one should assume that they had some knowledge of Greek philosophy, but most of the investigators are agreed that they lacked systematic, formal, philosophical training.(20) They do not mention Greek philosophers by name, except for Epicurus. However, he became for them an archetype of the out-and-out atheist, and not necessarily a representative of the ideas of the Greek philosopher, Epicurus. [Even Maimonides, in the discussion of Providence in The Guide of the Perplexed, mentions the philosophy of "Epicurus" (Part 3, Chapter 17) and rejects it in toto. He argues, in his commentary to the Mishna, in the introduction to Chapter Halak (Sanhedrin, Chapter 11) that " Epicurus" is an Aramaic word, derived from a word meaning "lawlessness"; it is used to designate all those who are opposed to religious faith, and it is against them that he promulgated his Thirteen Principles of Faith.]

Wolfson claimed: "In the entire Greek vocabulary that is embodied in the Midrash, Mishnah and Talmud there is not a single technical philosophical term."(21) However, this seems to be an exaggeration. (The term philosophin was commented on at the beginning of this book.) As in the case of the Bible, the philosophical significance of the writings of the Sages was emphasized only in the works of Jewish thinkers from the Middle Ages on. It is doubtful whether the Sages were aware of all the weighty philosophical implications contained in the saying, "Everything is in the hand of Heaven except the fear of Heaven,"(22) and many other aphorisms, with which Jewish philosophers were later to become enamored. (On the attitude of the Sages to philosophy, see below.)

It was in the thought of the Sages that the major concepts of the Jewish religion were first formulated - such as the incorporeality of God and creation ex nihilo - as they came to do battle with the ancient mythic world outlook. Even though these concepts were not yet philosophy, nevertheless there was already in them, because of their abstract nature, a great proximity to philosophical thought. One might perhaps say that the common denominator for ancient Jewish thought and Greek philosophy was the struggle against the mythological picture of the world. Perhaps it would not be an exaggeration to say that it was this common denominator that gave rise later on to the reciprocal ties between Jewish and general thought. It may be well to stress this point at this juncture. The inspiration for Jewish philosophy came later from external sources, but Judaism also influenced general thought. (More about that later.)

Jewish philosophers of the Hellenistic and medieval periods were aware of the fact that Jewish sacred texts were not philosophical writings. In order to compensate themselves for a certain feeling of inferiority vis-a-vis Greek philosophy, which was then in its flower, they spread about a theory in Alexandria, which was to be repeated by medieval Jewish philosophers, that Greek philosophy had borrowed from Hebrew philosophical sources, but that the original texts had been lost. According to this, the Greek philosophers were the disciples of Moses, Plato - that of the Prophets and so on. One of the stories related that Plato had met Jeremiah in Egypt, and had received from him the concept of monotheism, contained in the Torah. Traces of these notions are still to be found in the writings of Judah Halevy,(23) who hypothesized that the basic principles of all the sciences were handed over by the Hebrews to the Babylonians, were later passed on to the Persians, and from them finally, to the Greeks and Romans. Maimonides writes in the same vein: "Consider accordingly that these strange but correct notions attained by the speculation of the most sublime of those who have philosophized are found scattered in the Midrashim."(24) Further along, in the same chapter, Maimonides comments: "Know that many sciences devoted to establishing the truth that have existed in our religious community have perished because of the length of time that has passed, (and) because of our being dominated by the pagan nations..."(25) The medieval Jewish philosophers could not believe that the ancient Hebrews, who lived on their land and there gave birth to their great spiritual creations, should not have been the equals of other nations in achieving wisdom. Thus the notions came up that the Sages, concomitantly with the creation of the Halakha had developed philosophy, whose contents had come into the hands of other peoples of the world, especially the Greeks.

CHAPTER TWENTY-FOUR

MEDIEVAL and MODERN INFLUENCES on JEWISH PHILOSOPHY

Nowadays it is more or less assumed that "Jewish philosophy" began in the Hellenistic period. Guttmann was in agreement with this point of view. True, he began his <u>Philosophies of Judaism</u> with a short survey of "bodies of thought in the Bible," but he commenced his actual discussion of Jewish philosophy with the Greek influences on Judaism. This, to him, was the first chapter in the history of Jewish philosophy.

Indeed, a debate is still going on as to the Jewish Nature of the philosophy of Philo of Alexandria. There are still scholars who tend to see in him a man who held firm to his Judaism, but who, as a philosopher, belonged to general philosophy. Even though Plotinus does not mention his name, Philo today is regarded as the most important source of inspiration for Neo-Platonism.(26) His influence on early Christian thought is well known. Latterly one finds scholars, such as Wolfson, who ascribe to him a considerable role in the development of the Arab "Kalam." Nevertheless, almost all recent studies of his philosophy emphasize his ties to Judaism. Although Krochmal was critical of Philo's non-historical interpretation of the Bible,(27) he polemicized against the contemporary Christian scholars of Philo - August Ferdinand Daehne and, especially, August Neander.(27a) As opposed to their views he argued that Philo had strong bonds with Judaism. David Neumark, in his volume <u>The History of Philosophy in Israel</u>, was one of the first modern scholars in Jewish philosophy who emphasized the considerable influence that Philo had on Jewish thought. Alexander Altmann, came to the interesting conclusion that it was because of Philo that the Stoic tradition of placing man at the center of the philosophical concern was strongly preserved in Jewish thought. This notion, of course, requires further study. The Neo-Platonic and Aristotelian traditions had considerable influence both on Christian philosophy and on medieval Jewish philosophy, whereas

> The humanist element, as represented by the Stoic tradition which the Renaissance rediscovered from the Latin West, had been at the bottom of medieval Jewish philosophy right from its inception.(28)

Altmann briefly surveys the vicissitudes of Philo's term "logos," which he identifies with the Stoic "logos," as it passed, by way of Jewish philosophers with pantheistic leanings - Ibn Gabirol, Abraham Ben Ezra, Hasdai Crescas, the mystics of Gerona - on to the Renaissance philosophy and to Spinoza. Important studies on Philo, which throw light on the Jewish aspects of his teachings, have been written by Wolfson, Joshua Amir, Norman Bentwich, and others.(29) It is thus fair to state that Jewish - Hellenistic philosophy represents the first steps in Jewish philosophy. Its inspiration came from outside sources - Plato, Pythagoras, the Stoa - but it adapted these sources in accordance with Jewish criteria, and its main goal was to prove to Jew and non-Jew alike that Judaism was a philosophy that had a conception of an incorporeal God and held to a rational ethic. Plato's ideal Republic was embedded, according to Philo, in the Mosaic Law. It is not only possible for harmony to reign between Jewish religious thought and Greek philosophy, but this harmony actually exists.

Nine hundred years passed without any conspicuous Jewish philosophical activity, until the Middle Ages, which witnessed the beginning of the second chapter in the history of Jewish philosophy, mainly in the Islamic zone of cultural influence. This relatively short period, from the 9th to the 15th century, constituted, as all agree, the most important phase of Jewish philosophy. Here, as well, the impulse to philosophic activity came from Greek philosophy, as interpreted by the Arab philosophers, which determined the subjects, the method, and even the terminology.

On this subject it would be well to emphasize a point considered previously. There were modern scholars, mostly non-Jewish, who tried to differentiate between Christian philosophy, on the one hand, and Jewish (and Islamic), on the other, by claiming that Christian Scholastics were engaged in dealing with philosophical problems that are still relevant, whereas Jewish philosophy is essentially only of historical value. They regarded Maimonides and Averroes as being important for general philosophy because they were the harbingers of Thomas Aquinas, and nothing more. In their view, the mission of Jewish and Arab philosophy ended with the appearance and crystallization of Christian Scholastic philosophy. It is only from the latter that strands lead to subsequent developments in philosophy. This perception seems to be completely erroneous. Not our special ties to Jewish thought, but a balanced historio-philosophical view makes it necessary to regard medieval Jewish philosophy not as a harbinger of, or a parallel to, Christian philosophy, from which alone the problem of modern thought derive. On the contrary, Jewish philosophy dealt independently with problems, that have meaning for modern Jewish and general philosophy as well. The study and investigation of medieval Jewish philosophy do not, in any way, constitute an antiquarian occupation, as scholars were deceiving themselves into thinking by their tendentious views.(30)

One cannot ignore the fact that for hundreds of years Western scientific and cultural hegemony lay in the Moslem regions, with the Jews taking an active part in it. Thereafter they played an important role in transmitting the scientific and philosophical achievements of the Arabs to Christian Europe.(30a) However, the important point for the present discussion is that Jewish scholars were not only participants in those processes, but, simultaneously, created an original philosophical type of thought, whose worth continues to this day (even though today we do not philosophize the way they did, as noted in Part One). The rational nature of Jewish philosophy in medieval times was not only a product of Arab thought of the period, but largely flowed from the rational nature of the Jewish religion.

The third chapter - if one is to exclude Biblical thought - in the history of Jewish philosophy is Jewish thought in the modern era. This chapter continues to the present day. Again the inspiration is external, but, unlike the previous two chapters, it does not flow from a single source. Chronologically speaking, there were four major sources of influence: a) Renaissance philosophy, especially the later trends in the 16th and 17th centuries; b) The philosophy of Enlightenment and Deism in the 18th century; c) Classical German Idealism in the 19th century; d) Existentialist philosophy in the 20th century. This, by its very nature, is a schematic description. The great increase in the numbers of trends and movements in philosophy from the beginning of the modern era to the present day has left its impression on Jewish philosophy of the various periods.

In general, one may conclude that Jewish philosophy gained momentum three times in history as a result of a meeting with a "revolt of reason" in the general arena. On these three occasions it came into contact with an intellectual and spiritual atmosphere, in which undisputed primacy was given to the activity and the capability of human reason. The first challenge came from Hellenistic philosophy, and its conspicuous effect on Jewish philosophy was the philosophy of Philo of Alexandria. The second challenge came from Arab culture, and its most conspicuous effect was the philosophy of Maimonides. The third challenge came from the European Enlightenment in the West: Here the most conspicuous result was the philosophy of Mendelssohn. The following chapters will concern themselves with the problems that arose in the medieval and modern eras of Jewish philosophy and gave it its unique status within general philosophy.

CHAPTER TWENTY FIVE

EXTRA-PHILOSOPHICAL MOTIVES for PHILOSOPHIZING, in JEWISH PHILOSOPHY in PARTICULAR

In order to clarify the nature of the challenge that general philosophy presented to Jewish philosophy, due consideration should also be given to the function of a principal factor of a more general nature. In the discussion of Greek and Arab influences on Jewish philosophy, in the previous chapter, attention was paid to subjects of content that were central to Jewish thought as a result of these influences. However, there is also a good deal of interest in the question whether, among the factors that derive from man's basic relationship to the universe and motivate him to philosophize, there is one overriding factor that motivates Jewish thinkers to philosophize. The question may also be formulated as follows: Is there among the extra-philosophical factors that lead a man to philosophize one that is unique to Judaism, and because of which a Jewish sage or modern scholar might be unwilling to limit himself to the traditional interpretation of the Bible or the Talmud? It seems to me that the answer to this question is in the affirmative.

There have been philosophers who rejected the views of earlier thinkers. Their motivation for so doing lay mainly in their dissatisfaction with the views of their predecessors, and did not necessarily stem from a need to tackle problems encountered in their own environment. For example, G.E. Moore, one of the important English analytical philosophers of this century, made the banal remark that it was not problems of the world that moved him to engage in philosophy, but rather an aspiration to deal with the opinions expressed by other philosophers.

> I do not think that the world or the sciences would ever have suggested to me any philosophical problems. What has suggested philosophical problems to me is things which other philosophers have said about the world or the sciences.(31)

There is no reason to assume that this view is acceptable to many philosophers. Even Moore himself could not doubt, on grounds of simple logic, that there once existed a philosopher who had no predecessor, whose words could have moved him to philosophical endeavors. It is exactly on this point that the greatness of the first Greek philosophers was manifested. It was their audacious leap from the pre-philosophical, mythological world to the world of the reflective thought of philosophy that made them great.

What, then, might have been the main motives of the first philosophers who engaged in philosophical activity? More generally, what are the factors that are likely to motivate a person to philosophize (mot merely to argue with another philosopher)? Schematically, three such main factors can be suggested. They are: wonder, doubt and confusion.

Greek philosophers believed the prime motivation to be wonder, which arouses curiosity. So Plato said: "For wonder is the feeling of a philosopher, and philosophy begins with wonder."(32) It is not our concern to note here the mythological garb that Plato gave to this assumption by speaking of wonder as the gift of the Gods. The principle itself is of interest. Similarly Aristotle noted: "For it is owing to their wonder that men both now begin and at first began to philosophize."(33) While Plato stressed wonder as the prime motif, Aristotle emphasized that it is a constant urge that exists and is valid for "today, as well." Furthermore, he goes on to say: "So, if it were to escape ignorance that men engaged in philosophy, plainly they were pursuing science for the sake of knowledge, and not for any practical purpose."(34) Thus Aristotle underlined the fact that wonder is a result of a lack of knowledge: People wonder at phenomena that they do not understand. For this reason, wonder brings about the aspiration to pass from ignorance to knowledge. Yet, this kind of aspiration exists only for the satisfying of intellectual curiosity, and not for the satisfaction of real needs. Here we have observation as the highest purpose of philosophy, already discussed in Part One of this volume.

Aristotle's view differs from that of the Bible, which emerges, inter alia, from the Story of the Garden of Eden. Aristotle dealt with the connection between knowledge and wonder, whereas the Bible story brings out the connection between knowledge and freedom. It is possible to regard the eating of the fruit of knowledge as a refusal to come to terms with an existing situation, as a wilfull violation of discipline, that leads to the beginning of knowledge. Therefore human freedom involves rebellion against authority. But this is only the first step to freedom, and it is incumbent on man to struggle and strive for the achievement of real freedom and of more complete knowledge. Christian dogmatics explained the act for which Adam and Eve were driven from the Garden of Eden as "original sin." The rejection of authority, disobedience, an aspiration for independent thought are regarded as sin. Yet, another possible moral lesson, more Jewish perhaps, holds that from this point on it is incumbent on man to build his universe by his own power. "In the sweat of thy face shalt thou eat bread."(35) There is here an emphasis on the active element of work and deed. Parenthetically, the Biblical account of the snake tempting man hints at the possibility that sin was brought to man by external forces and was not initially part of his nature. Of course, there are a number of other possible allegorical interpretations of this story. Man was not yet ready for conceptual knowledge, and so his safety was dependent on conventions and obedience. The injunction against eating of the tree of knowledge was meant, as it were, to protect the holy traditions from untimely incursion by an imperfect rationalization. [Whether the apple has some special symbolic meaning as an expression of free choice, since it appears in several myths and stories that deal with the problem of choice and freedom, is an interesting question. In addition to the story of the Garden of Eden, one comes across the apple at the beginning of the Iliad, when Paris was to choose the fairest of the three Goddesses (Venus, Juno, Minerva), and also in the story of the Swiss freedom fighter Wilhelm Tell, who shot the apple of his own son's head. But this recurrence of the apple may be merely accidental.] However, whereas Plato and Aristotle explicitly referred to wonder as the cause of philosophizing, yet, in the case of the Bible, such interpretations were offered later, some even in modern times. It is highly doubtful whether the writer of the Biblical text had in mind all these interesting and instructive conclusions, that may be inferred from the one story.

Later philosophers returned to the concept of Greek philosophy that wonder is the source of philosophizing. Francis Bacon argued that wonder was the seed of knowledge. Later Schopenhauer noted that man wonders not only at natural phenomena, but at his very existence, and that it is from this wonderment, which grows as man faces the phenomena of suffering and death, that "the metaphysical need of man"(36) is born. In the same spirit, Leibniz, then Schelling, and in their footsteps Heidegger wondered at the existence not only of the "is", but of the "is not." Why is there not only "being" but also "nothingness"? Modern scientists, as well, have returned to the motif of wonder from time to time. J.C. Maxwell described as one of his earliest childhood memories "lying on the grass, looking at the sun and wondering." Albert Einstein remarked:

> ...whoever is devoid of the capacity to wonder, whoever remains unmoved, whoever cannot contemplate, or know the deep shudder of the soul in enchantment, might just as well be dead, for he has already closed his eyes on life.

In the same connection Einstein states that the knowledge that there are things beyond human understanding is the true religion, whereas the traditional image of God is unacceptable to him.

> The mystery of life's eternity, the awareness and feeling that I have of the wonders of the edifice of being, the modest aspiration to achieve a very minute portion of the supreme wisdom that is revealed in nature, suffice for me.

Freud commented that this oceanic feeling of wonder is the common source of religious mysticism, or pure science, and of art for art's sake.(37)

The philosophers and scientists mentioned above understood wonder as the source of philosophizing. There were philosophers, however, who sought to understand the meaning of wonder itself from the point of view of its philosophical significance. Descartes regarded it as one of the emotions that takes man out of his lethargy and concentrates his attention on the unusual. Spinoza continued this line of thought: Wonder is involved with an object that contains something unusual, which does not exist in other objects or images. Descartes emphasized the rarity of the subject, and Spinoza pointed out its lack of an associative connection.

> Wonder is the thought of any thing on which the mind stays fixed because the particular thought has no connection with any others.(38)

Kant attempted to define "wonder" as the incompatibility between our anticipation and the real image that is revealed to us.

> Now <u>astonishment</u> is a shock that the mind receives from a <u>representation</u> and the rule given through it being incompatible with the mind's existing fund of root principle, and that accordingly makes one doubt one's own eyesight or question one's judgment.(39)

Doubt, or the casting of doubt as a factor in philosophizing, appeared for the first time in philosophical thought in Descartes's doctrine. There were sceptics in philosophy before him, beginning with the "Sceptics" of post-Aristotelian Greek philosophy. In the case of most of his predecessors, scepticism was the subject of their philosophical thought, and not necessarily the factor that motivated them to philosophize. Even a religious man is at times beset by doubts, but he tries to overcome them by praying to God and asking Him for help in regaining his tranquillity and certainty. The religious man seeks to flee from doubt, whereas Descartes intentionally turned to doubt - he tried to reach certainty <u>by means</u> of doubt. He therefore decided systematically to cast doubt on all the conscious faculties - senses, images, thought - that were unable to furnish knowledge that was "certain and distinct". His words on the subject deserve to be quoted in full:

> But since then I desired to attend only to the search for truth, I thought it necessary that I do exactly the opposite, and that I reject as absolutely false everything in which I could imagine the least doubt, so as to see whether, after this process, anything in my set of beliefs remains that is entirely undubitable. Thus, since our senses sometimes deceive us, I decided to suppose that nothing was exactly as our senses would have us imagine. And since there are men who err in reasoning, even in the simplest matter of geometry, and commit paralogisms, judging that I was just as prone to err as the next man, I rejected as false all the reasonings that I had previously taken for demonstrations. And finally, taking into account the fact that the same thoughts we have when we are awake can also come to us when we are asleep, without any of the latter thoughts being true, I resolved to pretend that everything that ever entered my mind was no more true than the illusions of my dreams. But immediately afterwards I noticed that during the time I wanted thus to think that everything was false, it was necessary that I, who thought thus, be something. And noticing this truth - <u>I think</u>

therefore I am - was so firm and so certain that the most extravagant suppositions of the sceptics were unable to shake it, I judged that I could accept it without scruple as the first principle of the philosophy I was seeking.(40)

Descartes' point of departure is the principle that one should never accept anything as true, until one is certain of its truth. However, our concern here is not with the philosophical problem of the Cartesian <u>cogito</u>, but with Descartes's methodological approach, that one must rely on no authority that antecedes thought. Socrates, Plato and Aristotle sought the truth of being, while Descartes looked for the certainty of truth. For him, doubt was both a methodological instrument that guides the philosopher in his search for certainty and truth, and the motivation for his philosophizing. Kant, however, regarded doubt as a kind of second thought on the justification of an expectation that had proved false (see above), i.e., when the mind had failed to achieve certainty. Rotenstreich, in dealing with the concepts of wonder and doubt in Kant, sums up as follows: "Wonder is a reaction, whereas doubt is a critical judgment."(41)

Hegel also made use of the concepts of wonder and doubt,(42) but he went on to the third source of philosophizing - confusion. Philosophy must begin with confusion, a confusion that results from casting total doubt on all early previously accepted assumptions. Only then does the possibility arise of conceptually building everything anew.(43) Hegel, then, like Aristotle, not only established the motive for philosophy, but also its goal. Wonder and doubt are the preliminary, pre-philosophical factors that cause confusion. The goal is to dispel the confusion and reach a state where man will no longer need to resort to wonder and doubt. Confusion is vital for philosophy, especially in the learning stage. The purpose of philosophy is to dispel that confusion.

To sum up: Aristotle, Descartes, Spinoza and Kant spoke about the strangeness of the phenomenon, whereas Hegel spoke about the pre-philosophical stage of confusion, wherein a distinction exists between the knower and the known, between man and his world. This disjunction results in wonder and doubt. Philosophy is meant to bridge the gap. When one reaches the sought for identity of the knower and the known, and everything is perceived by the mind, then wonder and doubt vanish. Thus Hegel does not continue the line of Kant, the agnostic of the preceding generation, but that of Descartes and Spinoza. Like them, he regards wonder and doubt as the initial stages of philosophy, whose goal lies in achieving certain knowledge that is clear and distinct. All three are bent on reaching a certainty that will dispel all doubt. But while Aristotle, Descartes, Spinoza, Kant and Schopenhauer dealt with objects and images that evoked wonder, Hegel turned his philosophical attention primarily to methaphysical hypotheses, that evoked wonder and caused confusion. What they all had in common was the idea that wonder, doubt and confusion constitute fruitful and desirable states in philosophy that move man to think and to meditate. [I have been aided in this discussion of wonder, doubt and confusion by N. Rotenstreich's analysis of the sources of philosophy in his book, <u>The Scope of Philosophy</u>.(44)]

Schematically, this short discussion of wonder, doubt and confusion may be summed up as follows: Wonder refers to the phenomenon itself; doubt refers to the truth of the phenomenon; and confusion refers to two truths, and sometimes more, which require one either to choose one over the other, or to try to harmonize them. Without any doubt, of the three factors, confusion is the one that is most characteristic of Jewish philosophy. It is one of its unique features. Maimonides, in the introduction to The Guide of the Perplexed, said:

> Its purpose (i.e., of this Treatise) is to give indications to a religious man for whom the validity of our Law has become established in his soul and has become actual in his belief - such a man being perfect in his religion and character, and having studied the sciences of the philosophers and come to know what they signify. The human intellect having drawn him on and led him to dwell within its provinces, he must have felt distressed by the externals (i.e., the literal meaning of the text) of the Law ... Hence he would remain in a state of perplexity and confusion.(45)

This is not a problem that is limited solely to Jewish philosophy - it concerns general philosophy as well. However, it is very characteristic of Jewish philosophy, both medieval and modern. The confusion resulting from the clash between religious and philosophical truths, that causes philosophers to increase their efforts to overcome the clash, is one of the distinguishing features - if not unique, at least, characteristic - of Jewish philosophy. The problem can appear in various forms. The best-known version is that of the twofold truth, or the problem of two independent sources for the one truth. In medieval philosophy, the intellect was the arbiter whose authority was accepted in matters concerning truth or falsity, and the Jewish sages, including the Halakhists, were forced to reckon with this view. Consequently Jewish philosophy set as its main task to justify the religious content of Judaism - as reflected in Holy Writ - at the bar of the human intellect. The goal was to verify the principles of Judaism by the use of logic. There were two possible aspects to this matter:

a) Rational confirmation of the content of the Jewish religion.

b) The harmonizing, or even, the identification of philosophical and religious truth.

Religious truth appears through Divine Revelation and rests on Holy Writ - the Torah and the Oral Laws. Philosophical truth, on the other hand, is achieved by reason assisted by evidence of the senses and the validity of the inferences and syllogisms of logic. [Until Kant's day "intellect" and "reason" were synonymous. In the present study the later distinction between the two - which reserves "intellect" for the empirical world and "reason" for the world beyond experience - is not adhered to.]

One of the basic premises of medieval philosophy, and later of the Age of Enlightenment, that served as a most important fundamental point of departure, was that Revelation and Reason are not necessarily contradictory, since both stem from God, the sole source of truth. Of course, this premise ignored the fact that the representatives of scientific truth and those of religious truth have in mind two different things in their perception of truth. As was made clear in Part Two, the first truth is phrased in sentences, propositions and concepts, whereas the second is based on religious faith, and is essentially a matter of works and their consequences. The characteristic usage of the term "truth" as we find it in the Bible, is instructive: "... ride prosperously because of truth" (Psalm 45:5); "... Thou hast done truth" (Nehemiah 9:33); "Truth shall spring out of the earth" (Psalm 85:12); "The works of his hands are verity and judgment" (Psalm 111:7); "... truth is fallen in the street" (Isaiah 59:14); "... hath executed true judgment" (Ezekiel 18:8); "Buy the truth, and sell it not" (Proverbs 23:23); "Hezekiah ... wrought that which was good and right and truth" (Chronicles II 31:20).(46) Here is to be found one of the typical differences between Greek philosophy and the Biblical tradition, between observation and doing. (The description of its metamorphoses in philosophical thought, following Plato and Aristotle, were discussed in Part One.) Greek philosophy favors thought, whereas the Biblical perception gives primacy to doing.

The concept of the identity of scientific and religious truth received its clearest expression in the Neo-Platonist trends of the Middle Ages. The implications became clear in Renaissance philosophy. The truths of Revelation and of Reason are one, since supreme reason is inspired by the Godhead. The act of knowing, itself, acquired religious significance. The knowledge of God meant the adherence of the human soul to its Divine source. These perceptions stress the analogy to sexual activity, which was to play an important part in future mystical schools of thought, general and Jewish. In this matter, the Neo-Platonic and the Aristotelian traditions were in agreement: The adherence to God constituted the highest stage of perfect knowledge. Here one may find the beginning of the trend that will lead - via Judah Abarbanel - to the Spinozistic "intellectual love of God."

CHAPTER TWENTY SIX

CHRISTIAN DOGMA and JUDAIC LAW

There remains an additional area of great importance in the relations between religious faith and science in medieval philosophy. The rationalist trend, which held that reason and revelation constituted two sources of knowledge of equal validity, was much more prominent in Jewish and Arab philosophy than in Christian. Scholasticism is not of one piece. Generally speaking, Islam and Judaism granted autonomy to scientific knowledge side by side with revealed faith. The two were considered compatible: they were not contradictory. The roots of the difference between Christianity and Judaism were to be found in their different attitudes to Holy Writ. For the former, Holy Writ was the authority for a dogmatic revealed theology (the terms "dogma" and "dogmatic" in this context are not meant to be pejorative, as in present-day usage). Whereas for Judaism (and for Islam) it was primarily a legal interpretation of the Torah, that had been given in revelation. In Judaism, unlike Christianity, philosophy did not become an integral part of holy doctrine. This perhaps explains why Jewish (and Islamic) philosophy came to a halt at the end of the Middle Ages, and were not to be renewed until the 19th century.

A Christian theologian, then as now, had to have a thorough philosophical training. On the other hand it was possible for a learned Jew to be thoroughly familiar with Jewish Law without having had any philosophical training. Compare, for example, Maimonides and Thomas Aquinas, who are generally regarded as being very close in their thoughts. The Guide of the Perplexed, Maimonides's great philosophical work, never served as a religio-spiritual authority in Judaism, unlike Thomas's Summa Contra Gentiles (his most important philosophical essay) in Christianity. In seeking a similarity between the two philosophers from the philosophical point of view of their respective religious authority (a dangerous comparison), one may regard the place held by the Mishneh Torah in Judaism as the equivalent of the Summa in Christianity. The Rabbis preferred the name Yad Hahazaka ("The Strong Hand" - the letters of "Yad," when used as numerals, add up to fourteen, a reference of the fourteen sections of the book), rather than the more pretentious Mishneh Torah, but, be that as it may, the fact remains that the authority of the greatest Christian theologian is to be found on the philosophical and doctrinal levels - whereas the authority of the greatest medieval Jewish thinker is on the halakhic level. Neither Maimonides's philosophy nor his Thirteen Principles ever became dogma in Judaism. It was on the basis of this differentiation between Jewish religious tradition and the dogmatic basis of Christianity, which rests on philosophy, that Spinoza somewhat vexatiously spoke of the "Jews who despised philosophy."(47) Spinoza, however, was in error. To a certain extent, this process gave to Jewish thought something of an advantage over Christian philosophy. It was more flexible, freer; it was not subject to binding theological dogmas, as was the case in Christian philosophy. Furthermore, philosophy was not relegated to the status of a "handmaiden" to theology, as it was in the eyes of the Christian scholastics. [Perhaps a hint that philosophy was theology's handmaiden, or more precisely the Torah's handmaiden, may be found in the letter that Maimonides sent to the

Sages of Lunel in Southern France: the Torah is "... a doe of love, and the wife of my youth, to whose love I have abandoned myself, and what is more, many foreign women became her enemies - Moabites, Ammonites, Edomites, Sidonites, Hittites - but Lord knows they were only brought to be her scent-makers, cooks and bakers, to show off her beauty to nations and to their leaders, for she is very beautiful."(48)] Even though Aristotle is regarded as the source of philosophical authority for the two (or three) branches of medieval philosophy - Christian, Islamic and Jewish - nevertheless he never attained in Jewish thought the authority that he enjoyed in Christianity.

It was on this basis that it became customary to refer to the two sources of Western culture - Jerusalem and Athens, the world of the Bible and its interpreters, and the world of philosophy. A further distinction was made: The Jewish tradition, beginning with the Bible, emphasized one's way of life, while the other, stemming from Athens, emphasized theoretical subjects. This held true not only because of the higher status which Greek philosophy assigned to observation, but for the practical dimension as well, which was also perceived in a theoretical way.

The act of interpreting, which was always inseparable from Jewish thought, was a sophisticated sort of ruse to avoid submission to a binding, authoritative view rooted in the past, which in turn, was nothing more than an interpretation of a still earlier viewpoint. It was in this fashion that Jewish philosophy succeeded in accommodating itself to current thoughts. This also had its influence on the viability of a Jewish ethic and its quality. A religious perception that places its emphasis on human behavior, and not on dogmatic principles of faith, naturally devotes its major attention to the kind of relations that should exist between man and his fellows. Ethical problems were dealt with in early sources, but mostly from their legal and practical aspects, and not in a very systematic manner. In Judaism there was no ethic of the kind that existed among Greek philosophers. Certain ethical influences were perhaps discernible as early as the Bible - in the books of Proverbs and Ecclesiastes - but, what in Greece constituted a theoretical ethics, appears in the Bible as ethical guidelines for day-by-day living, resting on divine ordinances. The Book of Proverbs alone among the books of the Bible emphasizes autonomy rather than heteronomy. The goal of the proverbs is to prove to man that it is worth his while to tread the straight and narrow path for reasons of practical wisdom. Whereas the Ten Commandments state flatly, "Thou shalt not commit adultery," the Book of Proverbs speaks of the dangers that beset man as a result of adultery and harlotry.(49)

Judah Halevy was alone among Jewish medieval philosophers in his intuitive capacity to grasp the unique significance of the Jewish moment in religious thought. At the beginning of The Kuzari the angel says to the king: "Your intention is proper, but your behavior is not." This implies that intention alone does not suffice - even an idol worshipper may have good intentions. According to Judah Halevy, the distinction among religions is to be found in the realm of deeds, in the ways of the worship of God. It is here that his views clearly represent the Jewish heritage. The true religious experience is not to be found in principles of faith of one kind or another - on this point Maimonides would demur - but rather in man's relation to God, and this relation is expressed primarily by the observance of the practical commandments. Philosophical consideration <u>per se</u> is not invalid, but it has no place in the religious sphere, where primacy, in almost every instance, belongs to the deed. What appears in extreme and unequivocal form in the thinking of Judah Halevy, appears later, with varying degrees of emphasis, among other Jewish philosophers, including Maimonides, who, on the surface, might be regarded as representing the contrary view. One must not forget that ethics, as other problems in philosophy of the Middle Ages (and of the modern era), were discussed to a very large extent on the basis of an affinity to Biblical and Talmudic commentaries. Maimonides dealt with ethics chiefly in connection with his <u>Halakhic</u> work. His introduction to the Tractate <u>Aboth</u>, the <u>Eight Chapters</u>, is a self-sufficient essay in ethics. The same may be said of the chapters <u>Hilkhot Deot</u> and <u>Hilkhot Teshuva</u> in the <u>Sefer Hamada</u>, which is part of the <u>Mishneh Torah</u>. It was thus no mere chance that Maimonides dealt with Jewish uniqueness - the People of Israel, the Land of Israel - not in <u>The Guide of the Perplexed</u>, but in his <u>Halakhic</u> essays. These subjects belong to the practical realm. In <u>The Guide of the Perplexed</u> he actually discussed only one major problem that was clearly Jewish - the question of the uniqueness of Israel's Torah. Likewise, Bahya Ibn Paquda, in his <u>Duties of the Heart</u>, not only sought to guide the Jew in matters of religion and morals, but also to develop a systematic ethic that would combine general philosophical ideas with the ethical precepts of the Torah and the Talmud. In this way he emphasized the importance of man's inner <u>intent</u>, which comes from the heart, and is not fixed <u>ab initio</u> in the 613 commandments. Nevertheless, he too was of the opinion that the domain of practice was the most important of all.

CHAPTER TWENTY SEVEN

THE DOCTRINE OF THE TWO TRUTHS - THE VERSION OF SA'ADJA GA'ON

The notion that no contradiction can exist between scientific and religious truth, between Reason and Revelation, gave rise to two medieval Jewish philosophical traditions that were not mutually contradictory, but each placed its emphasis on a different aspect. The first tradition began with the philosophy of Sa'adja Ga'on, and is known as the <u>Doctrine of the Two Truths</u>. The other tradition, whose most renowned proponent was Maimonides, was based on the <u>twofold meaning of Holy Writ</u> - revealed as opposed to hidden truth. This tradition had far-reaching consequences for Jewish thought in later periods.

The "Doctrine of the Two Truths" sought to counter the argument that philosophy and the Bible present two alternative conceptions, and that we are required to choose between them, as it were, because each claimed to possess the sole key to truth. This doctrine held that the truth attained through reason and that given by Revelation constitute in fact one Divine truth. The same God who revealed the Torah on Mount Sinai created man, the possessor of human reason; consequently, no substantive differences between the two can exist. The task of the philosopher is to explain why the two courses - that of reason and that of Revelation - are not only both legitimate, but are both necessary - neither one is sufficient. A person is required to coordinate the elements supplied by faith with those of reason, as being two sources leading to the one full truth. But at this point two questions arise: If reason leads to truth, why is Revelation necessary? Contrariwise, if faith in Revelation leads to truth, what necessity can there be for the ratiocinating mind? Sa'adja's answer was that revelation is necessary since the capacity to reason belongs to the few, whereas religion is available to all; furthermore, religion is necessary for those who are not yet capable of attaining religious truth by inquiry, e.g., children. In addition, human reason is not capable of grasping all the truths and to reach ultimate certainty, and consequently, revelation is indispensable. Sa'adja's well-known distinction between "intellectual commandments" and "ceremonial commandments" also calls for revelation, because the latter commandments are not deducible through reason. They are not irrational, they have their causes, but what determines them is the readiness to fulfill the Divine Will. Without revealed faith they would not be observed. One would neither put on phylacteries nor observe the rules of <u>kashrut</u> were he not commanded to do so by the Lord. One could not uncover the reasons for these commandments by way of reason, as one could in the case of the intellectual commandments. Yet reason is necessary for apologetic purposes - "Know what thou shalt answer to the unbeliever." A Jew must be able to enter into a theoretical debate with the enemies of Judaism (v. <u>supra</u>: apologetics as one of the characteristics of Jewish thought), and with deviant sects and heretics within Judaism. Sa'adja himself carried on a disputation with Hivi al-Balhi and the Karaites, and the polemical element is very decisive in his <u>Beliefs and Opinions</u>. He emphasizes this in his introduction:

> When we shall look into and investigate, we will receive complete clarification in every section as He has let us know through His Prophets. And He has assured us that heretics will not be able to argue against our Torah, nor will doubters have proof against our Faith ... We shall study and we shall investigate to elucidate all that our God has made known to us, in science and in knowledge.(50)

From another aspect, reason is required for the theoretical persuasion of one's self concerning the validity of the contents of faith. The latter theme subsequently became a major element in the teachings of the Jewish philosophers, and a most important support of Maimonides's. The theoretical understanding of religious values and the perception of the Godhead by philosophical means became a duty and a religious commandment.

According to Sa'adja, the two sources, Reason and Revelation, are of equal validity. In the introduction to his Beliefs and Opinions - the title of the book itself discloses the author's intention of converting "beliefs" into "opinions" - the main emphasis is on revelation, whereas the body of the book stresses scientific study. The rational, theoretical analysis becomes a sine qua non for a proper comprehension of the Torah and of the Oral Law. Sa'adja Gaon and other supporters of his version of the "two truths" thus emphasized the philosophically equal importance of both paths, the rational and the revelational. On the other hand, those who held with the view of the Double Meaning, without negating revelation as the most basic element in the Jewish religious outlook, philosophically sought to stress the rationalistic aspect. True religiosity is philosophical religiosity, i.e., a religiosity that is dependent on reason. Intellectual attachment to God constitutes the longed-for goal. Consequently, philosophy alone is the authoritative interpreter of religious truth, which, in its time, had been given by Revelation. Furthermore, both Sa'adja Gaon and Maimonides, and certainly a philosopher like Ibn Paquda, would never doubt that, with sufficient time, interest, and ability, a man would be able, by the use of his own reason and by relying on the natural sciences and on logic, to arrive at most of the laws, judgments and commandments that were handed down by the Torah by way of Revelation.

The Doctrine of the Two Truths became known to the Christian Scholastics in the 13th century, but was used for opposite purposes. Siger de Brabant made the determination that what is true theologically does not necessarily follow from a philosophic point of view, and vice versa. In the spirit of Averroes, Siger de Brabant sought to guarantee the independence of philosophy from Church dogmas, as Gersonides did at a later stage. This viewpoint received unequivocal expression in the teachings of Spinoza.

CHAPTER TWENTY EIGHT

THE TWO MEANINGS of the TORAH - EXOTERIC AND ESOTERIC - MAIMONIDES'S VERSION

According to Maimonides, the Torah contains utterances that are intended for the masses, but are simultaneously philosophical propositions. A given text contains two types of propositions at one and the same time: propositions of the first type have exoteric meaning, are intended for the masses, and serve as a guide to religious ethics of a day-by-day nature, while propositions of the second type have esoteric meaning and are intended for the elite, for philosophers. When these are fully understood, truth is arrived at.

> The Sage has said: 'A word fitly spoken is like apples of gold in settings of silver' (Prov. 25:11). Hear now an elucidation of the thought that he has set forth. The term 'maskiyyoth' (settings) denotes filigree traceries; I mean to say traceries in which there are apertures with very small eyelets, like the handiwork of silversmiths. They are so called because a glance penetrates through them; for in the (Aramaic) translation of the Bible the Hebrew term 'va-yashqeph' - meaning, he glanced - is translated 'va-istekhe' (a verbal form deriving from the same root as the word 'maskiyyoth', Gen. 26:8, footnote by Pines). The Sage accordingly said that a saying uttered with a view to two meanings is like an apple of gold overlaid with silver filigree work having very small holes. Now see how marvellously this diction describes a well-constructed parable. For he says that in a saying that has two meanings - he means an external and an internal one - the external meaning ought to be as beautiful as silver, while its internal meaning ought to be more beautiful than the external one, the former being in comparison to the latter as gold is to silver. Its external meaning also ought to contain in it something that indicates to someone considering it what is to be found in its internal meaning, as happens in the case of an apple of gold overlaid with silver filigree-work having very small holes. When looked at from a distance or with imperfect attention, it is deemed to be an apple of silver; but when a keen-sighted observer looks at it with full attention, its interior becomes clear to him and he knows that it is of gold. The parables of the prophets, peace be on them, are similar. Their external meaning contains wisdom that is useful in many respects, among which is the welfare of human societies, as is shown by the external meaning of 'Proverbs' and of similar sayings. Their internal meaning, on the other hand, contains wisdom that is useful for beliefs concerned with the truth as it is.(51)

The main problem that occupied Maimonides in this context was that the first propositions, the apparent ones - sentences that could be understood literally - were not identical with and often even contradictory to, the other propositions, the hidden ones, that are interpreted exegetically. For this reason, he believes that the Torah was an <u>esoteric creation</u> that calls for <u>allegorical</u> interpretation. Biblical <u>texts have a double meaning</u> - apparent and hidden. The concept in itself is not new. Philo in his <u>De Opificio Mundi</u> had already adopted a similar type of interpretation, when, influenced by Platonic philosophy, he described the three Patriarchs and Joseph as the archtypes for the Law. In his opinion, the understanding of Holy Writ implies the turning of its ideas which are expressed in secret language into open ideas. This is accomplished by use of allegorical interpretation, which brings into the open what is hidden underground. [A similar methodological perception is nowadays to be found in structuralist hermeneutics, when it deals with criticism of literary texts. This is not the proper place to enlarge on the subject]. However, whereas the philosophical hermeneutics of Hellenistic Jewish thought was primarily free play of the imagination, Maimonides's hermeneutics had more "scientific" foundations. It was based on <u>homonymology</u>, i.e., the attribution of double meanings to words or sentences. This was expressed very clearly by Maimonides in the opening sentence of <u>The Guide of the Perplexed</u>.

> The first purpose of this Treatise is to explain the meaning of certain terms occurring in the books of prophecy. Some of these terms are equivocal ... others are derivative terms ... Others are amphibolous terms ...(52)

Of course, allegorical interpretation is of no use to the simple-minded believers. It is meant for the intelligent believers, those who have had a taste of philosophy. They are confused by the apparent contradictions between the Biblical text and the teaching of reason. By resorting to an allegorical interpretation of the text Maimonides argued that the contradictions cannot be anything other than intentional. Since the author of the Torah was God - the Torah is God's word - who by His very nature is incapable of error, He cannot err by contradiction. He cannot state propositions that are opposed to reason. Only one answer is possible: The Divine Author inserted those contradictions on purpose, in order to prevent spiritual harm to the believer who lacks philosophical understanding. The other believers, those with a philosophical background, who are by nature capable of comprehending these difficult subjects, only need a suitable guide to lead them out of the maze. This task Maimonides took upon himself - the task of being a "Guide of the Perplexed."

Emphasizing the homonymy, the common name, of Biblical concepts or propositions that are contrary to reason and science, is a method that does not void or negate the text itself. It affords the religious philosopher a great deal of latitude in his interpretation, which is often quite arbitrary. Thus, when it was remarked above that Maimonides's system was more "scientific" than Philo's, the term was put in question marks, since this method of interpretation is still antithetical to the scientific method. When a scientist formulates a theory that is meant to explain a certain phenomenon, it is valid only so long as it is supported and confirmed by the facts. Once it is refuted by the facts, it has to be replaced by another. But when a religious thinker or theologian interprets a verse in Scripture to make it compatible with the known facts, he adopts a different strategy. When the facts that come from experience and reason refute a Scriptural text, he does not negate the text, as would a scientist in the case of an exploded theory. He will invent, indeed "invent," a new interpretation for the given text, to make it compatible with the facts as his reason grasps them. In the eyes of the theologian, the text always remains true. No Jewish philosopher, either of the medieval or modern era, would consent to the proposition, raised by Spinoza, that there are verses in the Torah that make false statements. Maimonides's use of the metaphor and the allegory enabled him to lay the foundations of a most important religious philosophy. Its value is beyond doubt, it exists in its own right, yet it is in no way a scientific interpretation of the Torah.

Maimonides, for example, interpreted the story of Jacob's Ladder in the spirit of Plato's Allegory of the Cave: It became a ladder to knowledge, which the philosophers (the Prophets) first ascend and then descend, thus using their intellectual achievements to help the rest of mankind.(53) This interpretation offers an attractive, even inspiring moral lesson, but it is not scientifically valid. In the same fashion Maimonides explained the parable of the harlot in Chapter 7 of Proverbs as an allegory of the relations between matter and form;(54) "The Account of the Beginning" (ma'aseh bereshith; literally: the Work of the Beginning) as an allegorical description of the problems discussed in Aristotle's Physics, and "The Account of the Chariot" (ma'aseh merkaba; literally: the Work of the Chariot)(54a) as an allegorical description of Aristotle's Metaphysics. By illuminating the hidden with allegorical meaning, he sought to transmit to the knowledgeable reader the true message of what is written in the Torah. Only people of strong faith, who have also had a taste of philosophy, are able to grasp its true meaning. Most medieval Jewish philosophers continued the above speculative method, in one form or another. Even Salomon Maimon, the contemporary of Mendelssohn and Kant, adopted this method, when he interpreted the first part of The Guide of the Perplexed, in his Giv'at Hamoreh, in accordance with Leibnizian philosophy. He interpreted the story of Jacob's Ladder, for example, as referring to induction and deduction.(55)

There was point in elaborating on this theme, because the problem of the amphibology between the exoteric and esoteric is not confined to Biblical interpretation alone - the system became an inseparable part of medieval Jewish philosophy. Thus, Maimonides employed this method, which had served him in interpreting the Bible, on his own writings as well. More accurately, just as the Divine Author included intentional contradictions in the Torah for the spiritual well-being of the simple believers, so did Maimonides in The Guide of the Perplexed. The Bible, as he grasped and interpreted it, served him as a model for his own writing. To him "The Account of the Beginning" and "The Account of the Chariot" are the most important secrets of the Torah, and their proper illumination is one of the major goals of the Guide. However, since these are secrets that are not to be revealed to the general public, their interpretation in The Guide of the

Perplexed must be carried out esoterically, so that they should be comprehensible only to those who are properly trained to grasp them.

On the surface, Maimonides merely continued the line of thought of the Sages. They, too, permitted only the select few to deal with "The Account of the Chariot," i.e., with divine matters.(56) Recall the well known story of the four Sages who entered the Pardess (grove): only Rabbi Akiba emerged unharmed. One of the Sages, Elisha ben Abuyah, even became a gentile: he "cut down the saplings," i.e., denied the faith.(57) However Maimonides did not arrive at the anti-philosophical conclusion of the Sages. They believed that one should abandon philosophy and concentrate exclusively on the Halakha. Rabbi Akiba, as it were, was unharmed because he left the Pardess, and stopped dealing with speculations pertaining to the Godhead. It was not by chance that he decreed that anyone who reads non-sacred books would have no part in the next world.(58) Philosophical inquiry into these two subjects - "The Account of the Beginning" and "The Account of the Chariot" - was regarded as dangerous to the traditional teachings of Judaism, and therefore the Sages ruled that the first subject might be taught at most to two people, and the second - only to one. Furthermore, the students must be of superlative character and ability. However, pursuant to the needs of the time, especially in view of the intellectual struggle against early Christianity, these two subjects became a matter of general concern as early as the days of the Amoraim, especially in Palestine. Thereafter these deliberations began to appear in Jewish mystical literature - "The Literature of the Chariot." Even Maimonides reiterated the words of the Sages, that "The Account of the Chariot" is not to be taught to anyone, unless he is wise and reliable, and then he may only be entrusted with the chapter headings, and for this reason he, too, was unwilling to offer "anything beyond the chapter headings."(59) Nevertheless, in this matter his opinion was contrary to that of the Sages. It is a fact that he did not hesitate to deal with these subjects in his book, which, in the nature of things, was bound to find its way into the hands of a wider public. It is philosophical religiosity that assures the greatest degree of Divine Providence, but it can be attained only by the intellectual elite. To the masses it may very well cause harm, as happened to Rabbi Akiba's three colleagues.

Parenthetically one may mention that the idea that philosophy is dangerous and may prove harmful also appears in Plato's writings. In the dialogue Gorgias, Callicles, the opponent of Socrates, argues that philosophy is suitable for a young man, but if an older man takes it seriously, he will bring ruin upon himself. Thus he and his friend had decided in their youth to engage in philosophizing only up to a point, but not to indulge in it excessively, lest they suffer harm at its hands. True, the harm referred to in this context was only ridicule and uselessness. The philosopher will not succeed in life. Plato, speaking through Socrates, of course rejected this view, and so his conclusion was contrary to that of the Sages.(60) It is impossible to know whether Maimonides had read Gorgias, but his position in this matter was close to Plato's. He certainly could not accept the view of Callicles that philosophy is suitable only for an inexperienced young man, and not for a mature person.

Therefore, in order to prevent possible harm to simple folk, Maimonides inserted intentional contradictions, which were intended to hide from the masses and to reveal to individuals the deep hidden significance of the Word of the Lord, as he interpreted it. This explains the unordered way the subjects are dealt with in The Guide of the Perplexed. This hypothesis cannot in any way be ascribed to later scholars - even though Leo Strauss was among the first to devote full attention to it (61) - since Maimonides presented his program to the reader at the very beginning of his book. It was not by chance that he had adopted the following verses as his motto: "Cause me to know the way wherein I should walk, for unto Thee I have lifted my soul." (Psalms 143:8) "Unto you, O men, I call, and my voice is to the sons of men." (Proverbs, 8:14); "Incline thine ear and hear the words of the wise, and apply thy heart unto my knowledge." (Proverbs, 22:17)(62) (By the way, the second verse highlights the fact that in Maimonides's time a distinction was made between "men" and ordinary human beings.) Maimonides was well aware that his book, like everything else that is distributed to the broad public, would fall into the hands of not only "men," for whom it was intended, but also into the hands of ordinary human beings, whom he wished to protect from misunderstanding the subjects dealt with. Their requirements could be met by the reading of "The Words of the Sages," whereas the intelligent reader, who gives his entire attention to what he is reading, the man Maimonides means to address is expected to give his attention to his, i.e., Maimonides's opinion, which lies hidden behind the words of the Sages. To remove all doubts from the reader, Maimonides added the following few lines to the aforementioned motto:

> It is not the purpose of this Treatise to make its totality understandable to the vulgar or to beginners in speculation, nor to teach those who have not engaged in any study other than the Science of the Law - I mean the legalistic study of the Law. For the purpose of this Treatise and of all those like it is the science of Law in its true sense. Or rather its purpose is to give indications to a religious man ... having studied the sciences of the philosophers and come to know what they signify.(63)

All these problems could have arisen only in a milieu of spiritual ferment and intensive scientific investigation. Thus it was no accident that Jewish philosophy flourished in a region where Arab culture was dominant. Only there could Jewish philosophy have been made aware that the anthropomorphic images of the Godhead, because of their theoretical absurdity, constituted a hindrance, or even a danger, to true religiosity. In other regions, where no such intellectual ferment existed, the Biblical anthropomorphisms did not create any problem, and the Biblical verses were accepted literally, without any second thoughts. However, if a faith based on anthropomorphisms is regarded as a perversion of true religion, then it is harmful to everyone, whether philosopher or layman.

In Maimonides's view, a belief in God's corporeality borders on actual heresy; it is therefore imperative that the matter be clarified for the ordinary people as well:

> For just as it behooves to bring up children in the belief and to proclaim to the multitude, that God, may He be magnified and honored, is one ... so it behooves that they should be made to accept on traditional authority the belief that God is not a body; and that there is absolutely no likeness in any respect whatever between Him and the things created by Him; that His existence has no likeness to theirs; nor His life to the life of those among them who are alive ...(64)

And Maimonides continues

> On the other hand, the negation of the doctrine of the corporeality of God and the denial of His having a likeness to created things and of His being subject to affections are matters that ought to be made clear and explained to everyone according to his capacity and ought to be inculcated in virtue of traditional authority upon children, women, stupid ones, and those of a defective natural disposition.(65)

Consequently, Maimonides demanded even of simple believers a minimal rational comprehension of the Godhead. Not enough attention has been paid to this aspect of his doctrine. It is true, that the idea of the incorporeality of God involves a considerable intellectual effort, which not every person is capable of, and therefore there is a danger that an abstract perception of the Godhead might possibly cause believers to lose their faith. This, of course, was something that Maimonides sought to prevent; consequently he occasionally appears to be of two minds on the subject, and not only because he seeks to hide his true beliefs.

This kind of vacillation can already be found in the sources. In the Talmud there are differing, and even contradictory, views as to God's corporeality, and many anthropomorphic descriptions of the Deity are to be found in it. According to Maimonides, such beliefs are to be regarded as idolatry, but he certainly would give them a metaphorical interpretation. One might perhaps argue, that the Jewish conception of the Godhead calls for a personal God, but not necessarily for one possessed of human traits. This is not the place to enter into a deep discussion of the theoretical problem of the quiddity of the Godhead, which is only defined in negative terms, such as "without end," "incorporeal," and so on. How does such an "existent" differ from a "non-existent"? How can attributes of activity, which are after all no less anthropomorphic than attributes of essence, apply to an existent that is expressly non-anthropomorphic and whose deeds are not human? The argument by analogy which is based on the hypothesis of a "name in common," according to which the "will" of God is unlike the human will, does not solve the problem of principle involved. If the will of God is not a will, as we understand the concept, then we have said nothing about

God. All this is to illustrate the unavoidable philosophical difficulties in this matter.

To a certain extent these difficulties played a role in the development of Buber's dialogical philosophy. Buber's personal conception of God as an "eternal Thou" and of man as an "I" who can engage Him in dialogue without having to ask about His quiddity, enables man to avoid anthropomorphism, which stems from relating to God, in the third person, as a "He," as a "Creator of the Universe," etc. When one perceives the Deity as a "He," even if one denies Him corporeality, He is nevertheless imagined on the model of human activities. Such a God is nothing but a product of the human spirit (as Feuerbach averred in his day). Through his dialogic thought Buber liberated himself from Feuerbachian influences, traces of which were discernible in his earlier writings.

Maimonides's opponents sensed in him a strain of heterodoxy, albeit hidden, and possibly unconscious. They attacked him for that, yet they failed to adequately understand Maimonides's motives for his positive attitude to religion. It would be correct to state that his esotericism pertains to metaphysics, while his exotericism is bound up with his conclusions on the political and ethical levels. Thus in the parable of the "apples of gold among figures of silver" (v. supra), the esoteric meaning, i.e., the hidden metaphysical conclusions, is of the essence for Maimonides, and hence it is compared to gold. But the apparent, exoteric meaning is not treated as valueless - it deals with the social and moral consequences, and is compared to silver. Maimonides was not explicit on the distinction between metaphysics and religion. In consequence there has been a plethora of interpretations, from his day to the present, as to what he "really" meant, even though this position was stated openly and specifically by his contemporary, the Arab philosopher Averroes. To clarify Maimonides's view, it is well worth quoting Averroes directly:

> In general (philosophers) are of the opinion that the (religious) laws are essential political arts, whose principles are based on reason and inspiration, especially with regard to what is common to all the laws... they believe that there is no need to oppose these general principles, when we relate - for example - to the question, either positively or negatively, whether we are obliged to worship God or not. Or to a still greater (question): Does He exist or not? And, in general, since the (various) religions lead to wisdom by a road that is common to all and is obligatory for all of them, and since philosophy leads to the well-being of only one person (or a few) possessed of reason, it is his function to impart wisdom and the laws of religion with an aim of teaching them to the broad masses.(66)

This position, which was expressed by Maimonides obliquely and by implication, is stated later by Spinoza as a conclusion in his

Theologico-Political Treatise. By all indications he arrived at it through Maimonides, though he improved on and refined the concept in his own original fashion.

Basing themselves on this Maimonidean view, namely, that philosophical truth is meant only for the elite and should be transmitted esoterically, some commentators of Maimonides came to the conclusion, that since The Guide of the Perplexed is an esoteric commentary on an esoteric doctrine, a proper commentary on The Guide of the Perplexed must also be esoteric, for similar reasons. Such a commentary was actually written by Joseph Ibn Caspi.(67) This type of commentary, motivated by basic philosophical considerations, is not only characteristic of Maimonides and his followers, but recurs, in one form or another, among the other medieval Jewish philosophers. Nor is it limited to Jewish thinkers alone. It was quite common in the general philosophic and political literature. [Leo Strauss's book, Persecution and the Art of Writing,(68) has gained renown. In it, he examined the teachings of Maimonides,

Judah Halevy, and Spinoza, among others, on the basis of the criteria set forth above.]

CHAPTER TWENTY NINE

THE DIFFERENCE between the ESOTERIC DIMENSION in JEWISH MEDIEVAL PHILOSOPHY and that in the PHILOSOPHY of SPINOZA and the MODERN ERA

There is another basic and important subject that should be considered, which is unique to Jewish philosophy in regard to esoteric writing. The impelling motives of Maimonides and other medieval Jewish philosophers with respect to this were not the same as those of the generality of philosophers or of Spinoza. Maimonides's concern was to insure the religious welfare of the ordinary believers. He and his pupils sought to prevent any ruffling of their spiritual tranquillity. Maimonides was interested in reaching only a select and knowledgeable body of readers. His writing was esoteric because his message was, ab initio, limited to a small group. Undoubtedly under Aristotelian influence he presupposed a distinction between the "masses" and the "sages," between "people" and "men." From the outset philosophy was limited to the "sages" and "men," since the "masses" and "people" were suspicious of it. This was the lesson to be learned from the case of Socrates, and, in its literary form, from the tragic ending of Plato's "Allegory of the Cave," so well remembered by philosophers of every generation.

The later philosophers, on the other hand, primarily those in the general field, sought to enlarge the circle of the learned. They were interested in spreading their doctrines to a large audience. While Maimonides wrote for actual (Jewish) philosophers, Spinoza turned to "potential" philosophers. His aim, especially in the Theologico-Political Treatise was to free men from superstition and prejudice, and to bring them closer to rational thought. He resorted to the esoteric method only in cases of unavoidable necessity, i.e., out of consideration of caution. It was not necessarily a concern for his own welfare and personal safety, though this factor, too, should not be ignored. His chief object was caution vis-a-vis the censor, to insure publication of his work. A certain camouflaging of his true aims was intended to aid in the dissemination of his views. He hoped that the intelligent reader would in any event be able to read between the lines, and the general reader would derive some benefit from whatever he was grasping. The ordinary reader would also feel at home with the spiritual ambiance, since Spinoza made use of the traditional religious vocabulary. These considerations of caution also guided the writings of many other philosophers, both before and after Spinoza, such as Rabelais (Gargantua and Pantagruel), Jonathan Swift (Gulliver's Travels), and Montesquieu (The Persian Letters). In their books the true intent was very much more transparent. One must remember that Spinoza's books and those of his contemporaries were published after the invention of printing, and so could reach a much wider public than those of their predecessors. Furthermore, one must not ignore the historical changes that had occurred in the meantime. Esoteric writing, however, has always been a part of the philosophical endeavor. [Lessing, for instance, looked for esoteric elements in Plato's writings. It is well to recall that certain plays by Camus and Sartre, staged during the Nazi occupation, also employed the same tactic.]

However, it would seem legitimate to determine in schematic fashion - and every schematic statement has exceptions - that Jewish medieval philosophers made more use of the esoteric dimension than did the non-Jewish philosophers mentioned above. They strove, as evidenced by Maimonides's way of writing, for a maximum amount of disguise, in order to engage the attention of a minimum number of scholarly readers; whereas Spinoza - whose Theologico - Political Treatise has relevance for Jewish and general thought alike - and other philosophers strove for a minimum amount of disguise, in order to reach a maximum amount of intellectual and potentially-intellectual readers. The theoretical subjects that occupied the attention of Maimonides and his contemporaries were focused on the philosophical religious domain, whereas the theoretical studies of Spinoza and most of the non-Jewish thinkers were meant to deliver a political message as well - to defend for philosophical reasons freedom of thought and expression, and the like. [It is true that Maimonides too, had hidden socio-political motives, as Strauss and Pines, inter alia, argue. (v. supra)]. Yet the common factor in all esoteric writing, be the weight of the hidden element as against the revealed what it may, is that it stems from the utterance of heterodox opinions. Expressing unpopular views, whether religious or political, gives birth to a special skill in writing, a kind of writing between the lines. This sort of literature is meant for trustworthy readers, especially scholarly ones. It has all the advantages of private communication. It has the further advantage of imparting the basic message to a wider audience. In other words it also has an element of public communication, yet does not place the writer in imminent peril - or so, at least, he hopes. Maimonides, in the main, sought the advantages of private communication, whereas Spinoza sought mainly those of public communication.

Such writing is generally based on the following assumptions: Lazy thinkers are naturally superficial readers, while thoughtful people read with more attention. The latter are generally more trustworthy, and less dangerous for the writer. [D'Alembert, a leader of the "Encyclopedists" on the eve of the French Revolution, once commented on Montesquieu: "What would be obscure for vulgar readers is not so for those whom the author had in mind."(69)].

An intelligent and wary author is certainly superior to the most intelligent censor. This explains how in earlier days many heterodox works came to be published, and only after the passage of some time did the religious and political authorities become aware of their "dangerous" nature. On the one hand, cases in point are the controversy on Maimonides in the 12th and 13th centuries, and, on the other, Spinoza's Theologico - Political Treatise and the storm it raised during his lifetime, which caused him to abandon his plan to publish his Ethics.(70)

Unfortunately, in the history of thought the roster of people who were persecuted for their philosophical opinions is very long. It includes Anaxagoras, Socrates and Aristotle in Greece, Giordano Bruno in the waning days of the Renaissance, and many contemporary philosophers living under totalitarian rule in its various forms. The list is even greater for philosophers, who had to write with special care, for the reason set forth above: Protagoras, Plato, Avicenna, Averroes (the writings of the latter two were burned by the religious authorities in Arab countries), Maimonides, Descartes, [Cf. his remarks at the beginning of Chapter Six of his <u>Discourse on Method</u>, following the Galilei affair.(71)   Cf. also what he called "a Temporary System of Ethics," whose first main premise states: " ... to obey the laws and customs of my country, firmly holding on to the religion in which, by God's grace, I was instructed from childhood, and governing myself in all other things according to the most moderate opinions and those furthest from excess that were commonly accepted in practice by the most sensible of those people with whom I would have to live."(72) Spinoza wrote in a similar vein at the end of his introduction to the <u>Theologico - Political Treatise</u>, and then repeated the sentiments at the end of the work word by word.] Hobbes, Spinoza, Locke, Montesquieu, Voltaire, Rousseau, Lessing, Mendelssohn, Kant [Kant was forbidden to lecture on his original philosophical opinions at his university. Similarly, his comments on the French Revolution were, characteristically, very cautious.] - and the list is by no means complete. Not without reason did the 18th-century jurist William Blackstone state: "<u>Scribere est agere</u>" (to write means to act).(74) General public opinion was not yet ripe for the idea, first raised in Renaissance thought, that what God considered worthy of being created is also worthy of being known and understood.

From another angle, esoteric writing also raises a serious didactic problem, because it is likely to product arbitrary interpretations of the text by later readers and investigators. When an author writes ambiguously, differences of opinion will arise as to his true meaning. Is some contradiction in the author's words a real contradiction discovered by the researcher, or is it perhaps an intentional contradiction by the author? This difficulty, which exists for every philosophical or literary text, increases when one deals with esoteric texts, as is evidenced by the mounds of interpretation that accompany them. Sometimes things can come to such a pass, that later commentators invent in the text a supposedly esoteric meaning and present it as the true meaning of the author. [This is a marked tendency nowadays in literary hermeneutics, which draws its inspiration from certain structuralist and post-structuralist methods that presume to find in a work the true meaning, of which the author himself was unaware.] The standard editions of <u>Guide of the Perplexed</u>, for example, contain four commentaries in the margin of the text, those of Efodi (Profiat Duran), Shem-Tov, Crescas, and Isaac Abarbanel. In addition, there are many books of interpretation, beginning with Falaquera's <u>Guide of the Guide</u> and ending with Salomon Maimon's <u>Hill of the Guide</u>. There are also contemporary essays on the subject. The same phenomenon appears in Kabbalistic literature.   It is on account of all these texts that esoteric writing presents one of the most important, and also most difficult, problems in Jewish medieval and early modern philosophy.

To the above distinction between the esoteric writings of Jewish medieval philosophers and those of the beginning of the modern era a corollary should be added. Early esotericism was an expression of a dualism: The philosopher had two different messages - practical ethics for simple people, and a theoretical epistemology for the chosen elite. In later esotericism, the dualism gradually disappeared: The philosophical message is now only one - the second one is merely a deception and a diversion, lest harm befall the true message. The philosopher no longer turns to two kinds of readers, wise and ignorant, with different approaches. In his eyes all are regarded as potential philosophers. For Maimonides, teaching to the ignorant religious truths beyond their ken was immoral, but from the beginning of the modern era onward it was regarded as immoral for the philosopher's heart and mouth to entertain different notions.

The later perception was characteristic of Jewish thought in the modern era, beginning with Judah Abarbanel's _Dialoghi d'Amore_. Clashes with the censor - both ecclesiastical [Abarbanel's book appeared in the course of 70 years in more than ten editions in Italian and was translated into Spanish and Hebrew, before it was placed on The Index of books forbidden by the Church (v. _supra_).] and political (v. _supra_ in connection with Spinoza) - continued, but this significant change in purpose of philosophizing could no longer be halted. There is no basis for the suggestion of some investigators that Spinoza's _Ethics_ represents his esoteric doctrines, and his _Theologico - Political Treatise_ his exoteric views. The basic philosophical viewpoints that are expressed in both books are identical. In his _Ethics_, the emphasis is placed on metaphysical aspects, which require, by their very nature, a high philosophical level of the reader, and so are understood by fewer people, whereas in his _Theologico - Political Treatise_ the stress is placed on the political aspects and on Biblical criticism, which are more easily comprehensible. There was less need for caution in Spinoza's _Ethics_, which was not published in his lifetime, than there was in the case of _Theologico - Political Treatise_. Both books have an esoteric dimension, but the basic viewpoint in both is the same. It was only Spinoza's different aims in writing these two books that determined the difference in the type of discussion. One may, therefore, sum up by saying that in the new Jewish philosophy, as in the general philosophy of the time, the intent is to express only a single meaning, and the earlier duality of meaning has disappeared.

Finally, the growing shift away from esotericism in medieval Jewish philosophy to greater exotericism in the new era leads to another very important conclusion about the nature of the attitude of Jewish thinkers to the _Halakha_ and the Principles of Faith. Esoteric writing does not usually lead to controversy, especially not of the direct and open kind, neither with the _Halakha_ nor with the binding Principles of Faith. Evidence for the foregoing is provided by Maimonides's great _Halakhic_ work, and especially by the fundamental conception that underlies it. On the other hand, the aim of exoteric writing is, as we have seen, that as many people as possible reap the benefits of reason, abandon illogical beliefs, and rid themselves of prejudices and superstitions. At this point conflict can easily arise, and indeed did arise, between reason and _Halakha_. Philosophical writing that is mainly exoteric usually also evokes rebellion against accepted principles of faith. Evidence for this may be found in Spinoza's views, which challenged the validity of _Halakha_ by identifying it with the laws of the early Jewish kingdom, laws that had become obsolete with the destruction of the Temple and with the loss of independence. A similar outlook may be found in Mendelssohn's teachings that negated the validity of and the need for Principles of Faith, since religious truths were intellectually attainable, in his opinion, by any man, by virtue of his being a rational existent.

Thus, while esoteric writing sought to clarify the contradictions between the conclusions of reason and what was written in Scripture - in the opinion of the followers of this line of thought, these contradictions were imaginary - exoteric writing no longer tried to deny their existence. In the distinction between esotericism and exotericism the relationship of the philosopher to religion also became a matter of basic significance, which had far-reaching influences on modern Jewish philosophy.

CHAPTER THIRTY

REVELATION, PROPHECY and MIRACLES
in JEWISH PHILOSOPHY - TRADITION versus MODERNITY

The foregoing description of the esoteric dimension in medieval Jewish philosophy is based essentially on Maimonides's theoretical assumptions and interpretations. Intrinsically, it attempts to make the truths of Holy Writ compatible with those achieved by reason. Belief in Revelation does not require esoteric writing - it serves anyway as the principal base for all the monotheistic religions in their orthodox garb. The Jewish thinkers entertained no doubts about Revelation, nevertheless most of them attached great importance to the support of reason for their religious faith, and they invested more intellectual effort into the function of reason than into the question of Revelation. Their chief aim was to prove to their readers the necessity of reason. However, one must not completely dismiss the possibility that the foregoing view of the two truths - i.e., that a given verse furnishes one truth for the masses and another for the intellectuals - implies a certain reservation as to the validity of Revelation. Julius Guttmann, for example, raised such doubts - directed mostly to certain developments in Averroes's philosophy regarding

> our uncertainty whether we are to regard this theory (namely the doctrine of 'double truth' - Z.L.) as having been held in all seriousness or merely as a disguised denial of the authority of revelation. The doctrine of the double truth has, to be sure, often been used to conceal freethinking radicalism.(75)

Some scholars had doubts as to Maimonides's belief in Revelation. In any event, the discussions about the relation of revelation to reason - as has been said, mainly because of a desire to defend reason - began because of the external philosophical challenge. During the long period of the formation of the Talmud, while Christian thought was devoting great philosophical effort to clarify the meaning of Revelation, Jewish thought ignored the problem. The Sages were engaged in the formulation of the Halakha, and though they hinted on occasion in a legend or in a Biblical homily, at the relation of revelation to reason, they saw no need to devote a more detailed, systematic discussion to the matter. For them revelation was ab initio a truth that required no proof - it did not constitute a particular problem. And so, in the first centuries of the Common Era, when Christian thinkers were engaged in theological studies, their Jewish counterparts concentrated on Halakhic investigations and in homiletic interpretations of a moral and religious significance. The medieval Jewish philosophers, for more or less the same reasons, had no doubts as to the revealed source of the Torah. They dealt mainly with the narrative parts of the Bible, in order to explain contradictions - imaginary, in their opinion - between the rationalistic method and faith in revelation.

However, it is impossible to disregard, especially in our times, the philosophical difficulties presented by the concept of revelation. To accept revelation means to accept a supposition that is prior to philosophy itself (cf. Geiger's remarks on theology, Chapter Sixteen), whereas philosophical thought is required to abjure all presuppositions. In other words, faith in revelation and the religious perception underlying it are essentially pre-philosophic. That there are today religious philosophers, among them some of the greatest Jewish thinkers, who believe in revelation as a cornerstone of their philosophical thought, after the philosophers of the Enlightenment sought to "sweep it under the rug," calls for a re-evaluation of the problem of revelation. It is impossible to deal with it in its entirety here, and only matters that touch upon aspects relevant to the present discussion will be considered.

The traditional version of revelation is today accepted only by the orthodox elements in Judaism and in other religions (less by Protestant than by Roman Catholic thinkers). Present day philosophers, including religious ones, find it difficult to defend the "classical" arguments for revelation. If at one time philosophers were ready to accept as historical proof the fact that revelation took place on Mount Sinai when God gave the Torah to the people of Israel - since tens of thousands had witnessed the event, related it to their children, who passed it on to their children, and so on throughout the generations - this kind of proof can hardly be regarded as authoritative or valid in our time. This sort of an argument carried weight in the days of Judah Halevy; however, when Mendelssohn, in the days of the Enlightenment, argued that the 600000 eye-witnesses to the giving of the Torah were more to be believed than the three witnesses to the Resurrection of Jesus, it is doubtful whether the contemporary deistic thinkers, to whom Mendelssohn felt a close kinship, gave much weight to his argument. The religious-philosophical question may be stated as follows: If "evidence" is to be based on "seeing," is there any historical proof for the phenomenon of Revelation, as there is proof for historical events, based on the evidence of contemporary observers? The wars of the Maccabees and the subsequent purging of the Temple of the Greek religious rights performed there are accepted as indubitable historical fact. But is the story of the vessel of oil that burnt for eight days an accepted historical fact of the same kind? Why does a modern historian grant more validity to the historical facts described by Josephus Flavius (with all due caution and criticism), than to the "facts" that are recounted in the Bible? The doubts multiply the closer you get to acts of revelation in the early mythic days of the history of the People of Israel. The vulnerable point in traditional belief in revelation is that it does not, and cannot, lean on the evidence of contemporary eye-witnesses or any other objective proof for support. Archaeology, for example, has confirmed many things that are found in the Bible, but its findings include no facts concerning the revelatory acts that the Bible relates. Leo Strauss was correct in remarking that there have been instances of false Revelation and false Prophets, but that there never have been cases of false murder (he was referring to the murder of Julius Caesar) or false wars.(76)

The Jewish Biblical perception posited very clear criteria for the authenticity of revelation. Only a true prophet could be worthy of the grace of Divine Revelation. The Mishna differentiates between a true and false prophet in that the false prophet is "he that prophesies what he has not heard and what has not been told him."(77) Therefore, one who presents himself as a prophet, repeats the words of a true prophet, and even draws the correct logical conclusions from the words of a true prophet, is still regarded by the Sages as a false prophet - even if his prophecy comes true. Only Divine Revelation affords a man the status of a true prophet. Consequently, it is even possible for a true prophet to utter a false prophecy. Jonah prophesied the destruction of Nineveh, but his prophecy was not fulfilled. Nevertheless, it was a true prophecy, because it was supposedly uttered on the basis of Divine Revelation. Thus a vicious circle was created - what is the criterion for the actual occurrence of a revealed act, so that a man may become a true prophet, and not a false one?

Thomas Hobbes has written very clearly and unambiguously on this matter:

> For if a man pretend to me, that God hath spoken to him supernaturally and immediately, and I make doubt of it, I cannot easily perceive what argument he can produce, to oblige me to believe it... To say he hath spoken to him in a dream, is no more than to say he dreamed that God spake to him... So that though God Almighty can speak to a man by dreams, visions, voice and inspiration; yet he obliges no man to believe he hath so done to him that pretends it; who, being a man, may err, and which is more, may lie.(78)

In modern Jewish philosophy this problem was of great concern to Buber. He believed, as stated mainly in his later dialogic writings, that ethical values were absolute, i.e., that they stemmed from the Absolute (God). Were that not so, they could not be regarded as binding. "Only out of a personal relationship with the Absolute can the absoluteness of the ethical coordinates arise, without which there is no complete awareness of self."(79) The bond to the possible Absolute can be maintained only by Revelation. On this point Buber made use of the concept he took from traditional religious philosophy. Yet, how can one know that he is indeed hearing the voice of the Absolute? Buber admits that this is a very difficult question. One might ask further: If, as he argues, revelation, i.e., the bond to the Absolute, is expressed by a kind of sudden internal intuitive understanding - like the "flash of lightning" Maimonides speaks about (v. supra) - every claim to revelation would have equal validity. Again one is left without an authentic criterion. Buber was not prepared to accept an act of revelation as binding only because it had been sanctified by tradition, and had been passed on from generation to generation. According to him, only a revelation directed at an individual person could be regarded as valid. The uniqueness of the act at a given moment in time is that counts. But here again, the question of the authenticity of the revelation itself crops up. Buber argued against Sartre's dictum that only the person himself can determine whether he heard a Divine voice. In Buber's eyes this was "a demagogic phrase."(80) However, do his words "... even when the individual calls an absolute criterion handed down by religious tradition his own, it must be reforged in the fire of the truth of his personal essential relations to the Absolute if it is to win true validity" (81) consist of anything more than a declarative statement by a believing person? What is the theoretical basis for this proclamation of faith? Buber, then, diverges from the conventional religious perception in that he does not believe in revelation that is sanctified by religious tradition, but recognizes only personal revelation that the believing person himself has experienced. Nevertheless, the basic difficulties as to the criteria for the authenticity of revelation persist.

The traditional religious view - both Jewish as general - sought to overcome these difficulties through the explanation that the proof lies in the "miracles," i.e., the supernatural events. It is true that this argument was usually based on "miracles" wrought in ancient, mythic times. In speaking of miracles, we mean not the events that had once been considered miraculous, for which in the interim a reasonable interpretation based on the laws of nature has been found. We mean only those phenomena whose miraculousness could today only be accepted on the basis of faith. Can a Jewish or non-Jewish religious thinker of the modern era - and the emphasis is on the word "thinker" - claim that Balaam's ass really opened its mouth and spoke? At the most he could argue that God had evoked such an image in Balaam's mind. In his eyes, this too could be considered a great miracle. All the miracles that we have encountered in the Torah, the Talmud or the Midrash, came to us by way of tradition. It would be even more accurate to state that belief in miracles was a kind of precondition for the stories about them.

Let us take the example of the renowned "miracle" that occurred to Marie Bernadette Soubirous at Lourdes in the 19th century, and which the Roman Catholic Church, after some hesitation and doubt, recognized as "miraculous." Could one imagine such a "miracle" happening to a Jew, a Moslem, or a Buddhist? Why do Jesus and Mary reveal themselves only to Christians, and not to believers of other religions? Would not such a revelation be "final" proof of the truth of Christianity? The same holds true for the stories of miracles ascribed to Jesus himself, as related in the New Testament. These occurred, as it were, at a specified historical time, unlike the miracles of the Old Testament in the distant past, where history, fiction and myth co-mingle. Yet, as concerns all miracles - whether of the far past or of more recent historical times - belief in them is, in fact, a precondition for the miracles themselves.

But here problems arise for religious philosophy _per se_ as well. If God is the Creator of the world and the Supreme Providence, how is it that every so often He is compelled to intervene in the ordered course of the world? Does this mean that the work of Creation was not perfect? Maimonides tried to explain this matter by assuming that necessity and causality had not functioned before Creation. Therefore God had created the laws of nature, and they are His doing for His everlasting glory. In creating the world and its laws, God pre-determined possible deviations from the law, as occasion required, so that in reality miracles were not a violation of the laws, but were included ab initio in the Divine Plan. God, as it were, had Himself created the possibility of suspension of the laws of nature.(82) Furthermore, miracles can occur only on the particular level. They cannot occur on the general level, i.e., in relation to the species, or to man's fixed nature.(83) Thus, the possibility of miracles is preserved for

Maimonides, though he generally tends to interpret the miracles described in the Bible allegorically. But the basic philosophical difficulty has not disappeared. How could the arbitrary violation of the laws of nature by their Author be explained, especially when the violation was perpetrated for purposes of reward and punishment? If God the Creator is possessed of infinite will and power, why do His creations persistently violate His will? From a philosophical point of view the concept of miracle poses a very great difficulty for the religious thinker. What was for the ordinary believer a matter of miracle and mystery, becomes a problem for the philosopher, including the religious philosopher. The believer can content himself with the adage "Don't seek that which is beyond you," but for the philosopher the encounter with the miracle is a challenge requiring investigation and study.

Rosenzweig, who was conscious of this vulnerability, sought to rescue miracles from the clutches of the 19th century rationalists, who, as it were, were "ashamed" of the concept and excluded it from their religious outlook. He tried to limit the phenomenon to the ability of the prophet to foresee the future.

> The miraculousness of a miracle lies... not in its deviation from the way of nature, which, from the beginning, was established by law, but in its being foretold.(84)

The laws of nature, created by God, are not violated. But, by saying this, all Rosenzweig did was transfer the philosophical problem from one pigeonhole to another, as was the case with previous similar theoretical difficulties, such as distinguishing between a false and a true prophet.

Moreover, today man can also serve as a symbol and expression of God's alienation from Himself, i.e., from His creatures. In the accepted religious understanding, God created man as the crown of Creation. However, man has now reached a situation, where he, himself, is capable of bringing about the total destruction of Creation, or, more specifically, of the planet Earth, the only place in the universe that sustains life, as far as is known to science today. This problem, which was alluded to in Part One in connection with general philosophy, has raised unforeseen questions, which are especially difficult for the religious thinker, and a fortiori for the Jewish religious thinker. Attempts to use arguments by analogy from human life do not solve the problem. If, for example, one can predict the election results in some democratic country with a high degree of probability, this does not mean that every individual citizen did not cast his vote freely. (The philosophical question of free will or determinism is not of concern here.) The forecasts of a sociologist or of a political scientist rely on certain factual data, and not on his being omniscient. But the religious outlook cannot accept a situation where God knows in advance the statistical results of human behavior, yet He does not know in advance the choice of each individual. Here is the point of vulnerability of the proverb of the Sages, "Everything is in the hands of Heaven, except for the fear of Heaven." Beginning with Sa'adja Gaon, all the Jewish philosophers have struggled with the problem, and none has found a satisfactory answer to it. If God is Creator and Provider, human autonomy becomes an impossibility. There is no point in creating miracles for the purpose of influencing man's behavior.

Albert Einstein, who was a man with a religious sense, formulated this problem well:

> Nobody, certainly, will deny that the idea of the existence of an omnipotent, just and omnibeneficient personal God is able to accord man solace, help and guidance; also, by virtue of its simplicity it is accessible to the most undeveloped mind. But, on the other hand, there are decisive weaknesses attached to this idea in itself, which have been painfully felt since the beginning of history. That is, if this being is omnipotent, then every occurrence, including every human thought, and every human feeling and aspiration is also His work; how is it possible to think of holding men responsible for their deeds and thoughts before such an almighty Being? In giving out punishment and rewards He would to a certain extent be passing judgment on Himself.(85)

In short, the two main traditional arguments for the validity of revelation - prophecy and miracles - do not stand up to present-day theoretical criticism. "A miracle can never be proved so as to be the foundation of a system of religion."(86) Thus modern thinkers attempted to replace faith in miracle and in prophecy by an argument that substitutes a more theoretical explanation for the simpler one. The suggestion has been made that the Torah, because of its perfection, could not have been composed by an ordinary mortal, and must be the work of a superhuman existent. The Torah is not a human creation, but a Divine one. This is, in a way, a return to Maimonides's basic assumption. The claim that the Torah has greater specific value than all other literary, legal, and ethical creations, which are the work of man, is after all also a human judgment that rests on human criteria. What, then, is the unique element in the Torah that was beyond man's capacity to conceive and that demanded Divine intervention? Again one is caught up in a vicious circle. This view also negates the revelational base of miracles and prophecy, which is linked inseparably to traditional religious faith. Mendelssohn sought to follow this course when he negated all revelations except one - the giving of the Law to the People of Israel in a one-time revelational event. Even though this accepted explanation stemmed from a sincere desire to defend the uniqueness of Judaism, at a time when from a general spiritual point of view it was possible for Jews to integrate socially and culturally with their milieu, this solution was so artificial and so far-fetched, that it was not acceptable to anyone, not even to Mendelssohn's Jewish pupils and admirers. Some questions arouse immediately: if the revelation of the Law was possible, why was not another revelation just as possible? Why should the revelation of the Law be limited to a particular nation? This idea of the revelation of the Law was caused by an error in the Septuagint translation, wherein the Hebrew word "Torah" was translated by the Greek word for "law". This resulted in misunderstandings for generations since the laws are only a part of the Torah, and certainly only a part of the whole Bible. The

Pharisees, during the period of the Second Temple, had already regarded the living tradition (the Oral Law) as the appropriate complement to the written Torah. Medieval Jewish philosophy continued the Pharisaic tradition and interpreted "the reasons for the Commandments," i.e., the Law, in the spirit of the ethical principles that are implied in the words of the Prophets. Maimonides, too, in using the term "Torah" referred not only to the Pentateuch, but to the Bible in its entirety (The "Account of the Chariot" in the Book of Ezekiel was in his eyes one of the two most important secrets of the Torah).

All attempts to justify revelation either by the traditional, religious perception or by rational arguments do not stand up under theoretical scrutiny. Modern religious thinkers have therefore adopted another tactic - they shifted the term "revelation" from the realm of philosophy to that of faith. In this fashion they sought to preserve the idea of revelation for the community of believers. But in this way they gave rise to a new difficulty, one of whose full significance and implications they were perhaps unaware. For example, the moment one shifts, say, the account of the Revelation at Mount Sinai to the sphere of faith, it follows that there no longer is any historical, objective evidence for this event. Consequently, the ground is removed from under the accepted historical basis of the Covenant between God and His people. Thus, the revelational event is solely dependent on the content of the belief - a position that is opposed to the religious tradition of Judaism. It would follow that the historical evidence, on which Jewish philosophers from Judah Halevy to Mendelssohn and various modern Jewish thinkers relied, is not in the least relevant and the only remaining evidence is metaphysical faith. How then can revelation be real, when it relies solely on belief in the truthfulness of what is written in books composed by man? Certain modern Jewish philosophers, like Rosenzweig, Buber, and, in latter years, Will Herberg in the United States, have responded that revelation occurred to men, who told about it in works that they composed. The Torah is indeed the Word of God, but simultaneously it is a creation written by man.(87)

In opposition to the accepted belief that modern philosophy and science, together with modern historical criticism, have disproved revelation, another idea has of late been presented: There are two spheres that are autonomous, as it were - the sphere of science and the sphere of faith. The same phenomena have different meanings in each sphere. The story of Creation in the Book of Genesis does not contradict the scientific findings that the universe has been coming into being over periods of billions of years, nor is it merely an allegory. The two "theories" are on different levels, and consequently they cannot clash. The rules of logic and science are equally valid for the believer and the non-believer, whereas revelation including its expression in miracles and prophecy, is valid only for the believer (cf. Part Two, supra). Science has indeed succeeded in explaining the great majority of the world's phenomena without resorting to Divine intervention, and whatever is still enveloped in mist is so due to the inadequacy of human reason. However - the proponents of this position continue - science has failed to prove by accepted scientific procedures that God does not exist. This is a question that is beyond the realm of science. This idea may be formulated differently: So long as the assumption that God is beyond human reason has not been refuted, faith in His Revelation will not disappear. On the other hand, one might ask how a being man is not able to conceive of, is able to reveal himself to man? To make use of the view that Karl Popper has adopted in his writings on the philosophy of science, a claim is scientific only on condition that it is in principle given to refutation. This determination may be turned around to say that anything outside the scope of science cannot be refuted. Consequently, belief in revelation necessarily implies the impossibility of its refutation. At this point of cleavage theology parts company with philosophy and science.

CHAPTER THIRTY ONE

REASON and REVELATION – TWO FACULTIES of COGNITION

In one of the preceding chapters the reader was informed of the basic difference between Jewish (and Arab) philosophy, on the one hand, and Christian philosophy, on the other. The former did not become crystallized into obligatory dogmatic formulae as did the latter. However, there is an additional difference between the two, in regard to reason versus revelation. Whereas medieval Jewish and Moslem thought adhered to the twofold truth, in one or another of its variations (those described above were primarily the versions of Sa'adja Gaon and of Maimonides), Christian Scholasticism adopted a different approach. It held that reason and revelation do not relate to the same content, because faith recognizes a realm of supernatural truth to which reason has no access. Consequently, revealed truth includes more than rational truth. It is only in relation to natural truth that they are on the same level, whereas to the highest metaphysical plane, that of truth in mystery, rational truth has no entree. One may diagram the Christian view as follows:

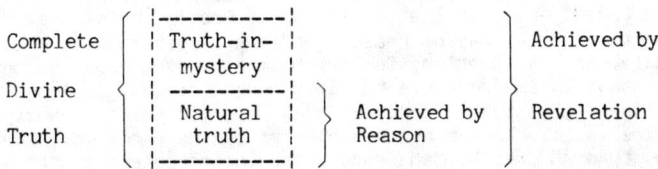

This conception resulted in interesting developments in European philosophy; inter alia, its influence was reflected in Jewish philosophy, especially that of the 19th century. One of the conclusions of Scholasticism was that on the specific level of religion – the sphere of revelation – scientific reasoning is not valid. It is replaced by dogmatic - religious principles or by those of faith. Just as there is a natural realm and a supernatural one – physics and metaphysics in Aristotelian terminology – so is there a rational conception and a super-rational one.(88) Accordingly, the diagram drawn above should be replaced by the following:

```
----------------------
 Supernatural Sphere    -----> Faculty of Knowledge  - Revelation
----------------------
 Natural Sphere         -----> Faculty of Knowledge  - Reason
----------------------
```

This conception seems to fit in easily with the scientific outlook. Just as science does not aspire to know things that are outside of nature, society and history, and it makes no claim to knowledge about the supernatural, so revelation does not claim any knowledge in the natural sphere – it belongs entirely to the supernatural realm. There is a sort of division of functions. Nature and reason are bound together, and so are, in parallel fashion, the supernatural and revelation. Human reason is incapable of comprehending the supernatural, and belief in revelation serves in its stead. Likewise, revelation does not presume to function as a key to the understanding of natural reality. In its time, this position was well expressed in Kant's famous statement: "I have therefore found it necessary to deny knowledge, in order to make room for faith."(89) One must not forget that Kant, the agnostic, himself did not have the faith that he recommended to his readers for its usefulness.

In such a view, knowledge is comparable to a vehicle that can travel only a certain distance on a given road, after which it must be exchanged for one capable of traversing the rest of the route. But, to continue with the analogy, how is one to know whether the continuation of the road indeed leads to the desired goal? Further, how can one know whether the belief in revelation is the proper vehicle for that section of the road, over which no ordinary vehicle could pass? Again, is the road to the destination perforce a straight line, with only its quality changing at a specific point? There are many such questions, which, of course, have here been couched in metaphorical language.

In modern Jewish thought, this view is expressed in a sophisticated form in the religio-philosophical teachings of Ludwig Steinheim.(90) He holds that truth is indeed one, but that it is two-layered. The natural stratum is perceived by thought, by way of reason, and the supernatural one - by belief in revelation. Revelation, in Steinheim's phrase, provides man with "study content" that is inaccessible to him through reason. Actually he continued a line of thought found in Judah Halevy's Kuzari, namely, that beyond sense experience, through which man knows ordinary reality, there is an experience through which man encounters the phenomenona that are not achievable through his senses. It is this kind of experience that makes the prophet unique, by virtue of a gift of knowing that is unavailable to the ordinary man. Steinheim did not speak of sensory and extra-sensory knowledge, but of knowledge based on reason and knowledge beyond reason. He did not regard the second faculty as belonging only to unusual men, but the principle behind the distinction was very similar. Steinheim had in mind a clear purpose, which seemed to him very important from the religious aspect. The doctrine of the two truths of medieval Jewish philosophy seemed to him to be an outlook that post factum derogated from the value of revelation. According to its logic, revelation would seem to be necessary, for the most part, only for people incapable of achieving the sought-for degree of rational knowledge. Such a view makes revelation a surrogate for simple people (v. supra), something similar to Spinoza's "refuge for ignorance." But Steinheim tried to show that Revelation is an independently specific faculty of knowledge, that explicitly affords man such truths that he would never acquire without it. This, then, was the "study content" that reason can never supply. He referred, primarily, to concepts like creation ex nihilo, God's freedom, and man's freedom, afterlife, God's unity and uniqueness. The influence of Kantian philosophy on Steinheim is clear. Nevertheless, it is important to emphasize that his formulation lacks the elements of agnosticism that accompanied Kant's philosophy. The belief in revelation is an inseparable part of his general religio-philosophical view as a theologian. Consequently, according to Steinheim, a theoretical comprehension may exist outside the realm of theoretical knowledge. But such a position is in opposition to the traditional Jewish religious conception, since the term "revelation" becomes a kind of faculty of knowing, operative only for the supernatural and for nothing else. In this manner, Steinheim's theology brings us back precisely to the original meaning of the term - "a knowledge of God."

Sometimes the difference between the natural stratum and the supernatural is also described as a division into the world of nature and the world of Grace.(92) This, however, does not alter the basic nature of the problem.

CHAPTER THIRTY TWO

REVELATION in JUDAISM versus
REVELATION in OTHER RELIGIONS

In Jewish philosophy we encounter an additional problem. Scientific "truth" is general and one. (We shall refrain here from considering the concept per se - it also has its problematical aspects - v. Part One). The laws of nature are equally valid for every place and for every individual, irrespective of philosophy or religion. In contrast, religious "truth" is particular, for each individual and for each religion. In consequence, a twofold problem arises in relation to Revelation:

a) There is the problem of the relation of revealed truth to rational truth: This is a general problem, not confined to Judaism, and it has been discussed in the previous chapters, mainly as reflected in the thought of Jewish philosophers. But it is a problem of a general nature - part of the story of relations between religion and philosophy.

b) There is the question of Revelation in the Jewish religion, in comparison with the other monotheistic faiths - Islam and Christianity. When several religions all claim to be based on revelation, the question arises as to which is the most authentic. No such problem exists with the second basic concept of Judaism - that of Creation - there is only one. In this respect, the philosophical difficulty is reduced to a confrontation between differing views as to the age of the world, but there was no difference of opinion among the monotheistic religions as to the idea that the world was created by God.

This then, is the problem of revelation that is peculiar to Judaism. It has occupied a very important place in Jewish thought, especially during the Middle Ages. It determined, to no small degree, the routes of the philosophical endeavor. The appearance of Islam constituted a great challenge to establishing the truth of the Jewish religion, greater than that of Christianity in its time, a religion that evolved from Judaism. Islam presented the medieval Jewish scholars with the stark problem: Did one divine revelation displace another? As is well known, this claim was made by Christian theology with reference to the appearance of Jesus. But in the case of Islam the matter was a good deal more serious. According to its tenets, the revelation to the prophet Mohammed was God's final one, and thereafter it represented His bounden wish and commandment. Islam, in its monotheism, resembles Judaism more than Christianity. Mohammed was a prophet, not the Son of God. In consequence, Jewish thinkers displayed a more tolerant attitude toward him, as exemplified in the writings of Maimonides; but, on the other hand, the controversy was sharper.

And so, the philosophical problem came down to whether Divine Will was subject to change. This question evoked a spate of theoretical discussions in Jewish philosophy on the problems of Truth and Will. Maimonides defined the subject of his Guide of the Perplexed as "the science of Law in its true sense,"(93) and Ibn Gabirol, in his Source of Life, devoted the main part of his investigation to the concept of "Divine Will." This problem related to two others: God's attributes, and anthropomorphism. Could "Divine Will" be compared to the human one? Thus, the problem that was originally a historical one - the appearance of a new revealed religion - became a metaphysical one.

Jewish thought was distinguished by an internal feeling of a special shared condition - finding itself surrounded by a foreign, frequently hostile, culture, and at the same time united by ties to the Judaeo-religious tradition. What was common to all Jewish philosophy, the existence of the various schools and trends within it notwithstanding, was the expression it gave to the Jewish uniqueness, and the view it took of Judaism as a religion and as an exceptional historical and supra-historical phenomenon.

The foregoing two factors - the external theoretical influences (discussed at length above) and the challenge presented by other revelational religions - caused Jewish philosophy to be defensive and apologetic for a very long period. These factors determined the major subjects it dealt with, e.g., the essence of the Divinity and His attributes, the creation of the universe, the nature of the soul, and the reasons for the Commandments. The view of the medieval Jewish philosophers - it does not apply to the same extent in the case of modern Jewish philosophers - was that dealing in philosophy was a Commandment enjoined by the age (v. supra). It was not only permissible, but obligatory, to make use of the scientific tools of the period to defend the Torah of Israel against its enemies and assailants.

PART FIVE: MEDIEVAL and MODERN JEWISH PHILOSOPHY COMPARED - DIFFERENCES and
CHANGES

CHAPTER THIRTY-THREE

THE CENTRALITY OF MEDIEVAL JEWISH PHILOSOPHY

Between the medieval and modern periods far-reaching changes occurred in the methodology and theory of Jewish philosophy, as was the case with philosophy in general. However, attention must not be diverted from an important aspect that is particularly relevant to Jewish philosophy. Quite naturally, every person tends to regard the problems of his age as more significant than those that engaged earlier generations. However, even though in philosophy it is impossible to ignore the diachronic dimension, it is not determinative, but rather are the dimensions of content and method. In Part One of this book, in comparing philosophy with science and art, it became clear that the rise of modern thought in no way detracts from the philosophical interest in earlier thought. The same, of course, holds true for Jewish philosophy, but here there is an additional factor. Not only does modern Jewish philosophy fail to diminish one's interest in medieval Jewish thought, but the later actually preserves its primacy. Previously, comparison was made between the relationship of modern Jewish philosophy to its medieval Counterpart, and of general philosophy to its classical Greek counterpart. One should add at this point that the centrality of medieval Jewish philosophy vis-a-vis that of other periods is even greater than that of Greek philosophy in the history of general philosophy. Husik definitively and laconically entitled the chapter following his discussion of medieval Jewish philosophy "No Modern Movement."(1) This statement would seem however rather dubious, since one cannot simply ignore all the changes that have taken place in Jewish philosophy since the Golden Age of medieval times.

These changes did not constitute a break. True, a modern philosopher will no longer resort to the terms employed by Maimonides or Judah Halevy, but neither can he permit himself to disregard their ideas (v. Part One, supra). In general philosophy it used to be said that all philosophers are either Platonists or Aristotelians. One may, in like fashion, characterize all modern Jewish philosophers as followers of either Maimonides or Judah Halevy. There is not much point in speaking of the followers of Ibn Gabirol, the Neo-Platonist, since, except for Judah Abarbanel, his main influence made itself felt beyond the bounds of Jewish philosophy. The philosophy of another important Jewish Neo-Platonist, Ibn Paquda, had less impact on Jewish philosophy than on the later moralistic literature, which is different in its nature from accepted Jewish thought, even though several modern scholars have noted his impact on Maimonides. Thus, there is reason to refer, in the main, to the followers of Maimonides and those of Judah Halevy. Salomon Maimon, Krochmal and Hermann Cohen may be regarded as the disciples of Maimonides, while Luzzato, Steinheim, Rosenzweig and Rabbi Kook may be counted among the followers of Judah Halevy.

The special shared quality that characterized Jewish philosophy in the realm of thought (v. supra) served to strengthen the lines of continuity from medieval to modern Jewish philosophy. Nevertheless, certain significant changes did take place, and they deserve consideration.

CHAPTER THIRTY-FOUR

SEGREGATION IN THE GHETTO AND CULTURAL-SPIRITUAL ISOLATION

By force of circumstances, and sometimes also by choice, Jews in the Middle Ages engaged in professions and crafts that enabled them to observe the commandments of their faith, as well as to devote time to study and prayer. Observance of the Jewish religion permitted the maintenance of a more-or-less normal Jewish existence in many countries, even though the Jewish community was subject to frequent disturbances caused by hostile edicts, persecutions, and expulsions. While preserving its national coloration, the Jewish religion was sufficiently universal to permit Jews to fulfill useful functions in the general economic life. In modern times the situation is different. Economic affairs are a good deal more complex, and the Jews, participating more intensively than ever in economic life and in the activities of society as a whole, find themselves beset with great difficulties and complications. Today the observance of the Sabbath and the Holy Days and the proper adherence to the Commandments involve objective hardships. From the time of the Enlightenment and the Emancipation, these have intensified considerably. Among other consequences, this situation has directly affected religious studies and meditation, endeavours for which time could always be found in earlier generations.

In addition, the two-hundred-and-fifty-year transition from the Middle Ages to the Modern Era, a period when Jews were forcibly herded into ghettos, was the time of the greatest degradation in the history of the Exile. Despite all the somewhat nostalgic literary efforts to represent communal life in the ghettos of that time in a rose-colored hue, this segregation, imposed on the Jews against their will, resulted in a significant narrowing of spiritual horizons. The fruitful encounter of Jewish thought with the general culture and philosophy, which characterized earlier eras, especially in Islamic regions, vanished completely. Outside the ghetto walls, the period following the Renaissance was marked by an intellectual and artistic reawakening, but within those walls spiritual activity was limited to matters of interpretation of the Bible, and, more so, of the Talmud.

Of course, the foregoing description is schematic. Exceptions can be cited: the Jewish philosophers and poets in Italy during the Renaissance, from Immanuel Haromi to Rabbi Leone Modena, and the philosophical work of the Maharal (Rabbi Loew of Prague). Nevertheless, generally speaking, the above description reflects the circumstances of Jewish life and, more specifically, of Jewish spiritual life.

The bitter end of Spanish Jewry also brought in its wake an attitude of suspicion and scepticism towards philosophy. The fact that many Jews converted to another religion was ascribed to their involvement in philosophical endeavours. Thus was born a reaction to philosophy, holding that the Jewish sources and the Rabbinic literature were self-sufficient and there was no need to resort to the wisdom of the gentiles (i.e., to Greek philosophy and its continuation). This was in the nature of a return to the mood of Rabbi Akiba and the Sages in their time (v. <u>supra</u>). Thus, though there was general continuity in Jewish thought from generation to generation, the continuity was no longer organic, as was the cause with Jewish philosophy in the Middle Ages. Now it became rather more sporadic.

These processes, especially the compulsory segregation in ghettos, brought about a cultural isolation that was clearly harmful to the Jews, to their spiritual life, and to Jewish philosophy. When, in the wake of Napoleon's armies, the ghetto walls were breached, the young Jew found himself culturally and spiritually far behind his non-Jewish contemporary of equal intellectual potential. (The present discussion does not concern the sectors of population, like the peasant class, whose objective backwardness in any case prevented them from participating in the general culture.) The audacious breakthrough of Moses Mendelssohn, and more especially of Salomon Maimon, into the first rank of the philosophical and intellectual elite of their time was a rare and atypical exception that only serves to confirm the generalization. Thus, it is because of the spiritual "time-out" - among other things - that the nature of modern Jewish philosophy differs so sharply from that of the Middle Ages, even though the problems considered in the two eras are similar.

In Western Europe in the period of the Emancipation, or, rather in the period of the struggle for Emancipation, there was also a problem that had not existed theretofore: How was one to remain a Jew and simultaneously take an active part in the general spiritual and cultural life? This question was first raised clearly in Mendelssohn's Jerusalem, and thereafter it became the major ground for the division of Judaism into different religious streams - a phenomenon that scarcely existed in the Middle Ages (except for the Karaites), but constituted an important element in the subsequent changes in Jewish life. Modern Jewish philosophy is distinct from that of the Middle Ages in that it exhibits a very much more marked religio-ideological pluralism. The medieval trends in Jewish philosophy - Neo-Platonic, Aristotelian, etc. - did not differ as to their conception of the quiddity of Judaism: They were all "orthodox," whereas today Judaism is apprehended very differently by Orthodox, Reform, Conservative, Reconstructionist and secular Jews. There are problems concerning which it is pointless to ask: What is the Jewish position? All that can be done is to ask: What is the Orthodox position? the Reform? the secular? It is sufficient to compare the views of Orthodoxy and reform on the quiddity of Judaism, in order to grasp the vital differences on the subject, differences that were totally inconceivable in the past.

CHAPTER THIRTY-FIVE

FROM DEPENDENCE on AUTHORITY to INDEPENDENT THOUGHT

Until Maimonides's day, Jewish philosophy, from an internal Jewish point of view, was carried on in tranquillity. No Jewish philosopher ever referred to another. Maimonides, in his Guide of the Perplexed, except for references to the sources, cites only Arab and Greek philosophers. Only in his letter to Samuel Ibn Tibbon, the translator of The Guide of the Perplexed into Hebrew, does he mention the book on Palestine (exclusive of Jerusalem) by Izhak Israeli, and the works of Rabbi Joseph the Just. Incidentally, in the same letter, which Maimonides wrote at an advanced age he also mentions, among the Arab philosophers, Averroes, with whom, it would seem, he had been unacquainted when he wrote The Guide of the Perplexed. In his opinion, they were all inferior to al-Farabi, "all of whose works were little but good." In the Sixth Chapter of The Eight Chapters, Maimonides, and, later on, in dealing with the distinction between intellectual and Kabbalistic commandments, hints at Sa'adja Gaon (though he does not mention him by name): "Some of our later sages, who were infected with the unsound principles of the Mutakallimun called these rational laws."

Likewise, in his day, Sa'adja Gaon only polemicized against those who, in his opinion no longer belonged to Judaism, such as Hiwi Al-Balkhi and the Karaites (v. supra). He and Izhak Israeli never refer to each other, even though they were contemporaries. After Maimonides, matters changed in the extreme. A Maimonidean circle was formed; for a time a Maimonidean controversy raged (in the 12th and 13th centuries); and all the post-Maimonideans up to Crescas and Albo necessarily had to relate to their predecessors - either positively or negatively - especially to Maimonides and Judah Halevy. From Spinoza's time on, critical rivalry with earlier Jewish thinkers became an integral part of Jewish philosophic writing.

Polemic is not characteristic of Jewish philosophy alone; it is inseparable from all philosophic activity. Philosophizing, inasmuch as it is a very personal attempt to contend with various problems is of necessity bound up with other people's views. Here, all that was indicated is a shift of the controversy from the external to the internal arena. However, in this connection one must mention another aspect, which is characteristic of modern religious philosophy and common to both Judaism and Christianity: Whereas medieval philosophy directed its attack against the views of other religions, against apostasy and against deviant sects, since the 19th century religious philosophers increasingly attacked irreligious views per se. The main polemical thrust is no longer between different, rival religions, but between the religious approach and the secular one. At present, less emphasis is placed on proving the preferability of the Christian or of the Jewish perception of the Godhead, and more is devoted to fortifying belief in God as opposed to disbelief. This ideational trend is very prominent in present-day American-Jewish philosophy, and of late it has appeared in Israel, as well. (v. supra).

In medieval times, Jewish philosophy relied on two major sources of authority - Aristotle's philosophy and the thought of the Sages. The original thought was accompanied by interpretations, and often it was difficult to distinguish between the two. For medieval Jewish philosophers, the Torah and the Oral Law were, as has been said, God's truth revealed, binding on Israel for all eternity. Therefore, they were not open to critical inquiry, and could only serve as a subject for exegesis. Perhaps only Maimonides, though even he paid lip service to the foregoing determination in the Guide of the Perplexed, may have been an exception in his intellectual daring. He gave clear priority to independent thought over mere interpretations of words of the Sages. In discussing the five views of Providence (v. supra), he openly said:

> The fifth opinion is our opinion, I mean the opinion of our Law. I shall let you know about what has been literally stated in the books of our prophets and is believed by the multitude of our scholars; I shall also inform you of what is believed by some of our latter-day scholars; and I shall also let you know what I myself believe about this.(2)

Here may be discerned the first inklings of a shift of the center of gravity from reliance on the Torah and the sayings of the Sages to original, independent thought. This trend became very much more marked during the Renaissance, from Judah Abarbanel through the Italian Jewish philosophers to Leone Modena. It finds strong expression in the teachings of the Maharal of Prague, which, despite its Kabbalistic character, have a remarkably modern ring (v. supra). From Spinoza onward all the Jewish philosophers have emphasized the philosophical element, while interpretation has been used only as an accompanying illustration. Most modern Jewish philosophers tend to look upon Judaism as a historical phenomenon, whose spiritual creation was the fruit of human thought. Consequently, it includes more permanent elements, which they do not hesitate to define as "eternal," along with elements that are more transient and temporary.

CHAPTER THIRTY SIX

LIBERATION from SUBMISSION to RELIGIOUS COMMANDMENTS and REVELATION in a NEW LIGHT

In medieval times, philosophy was religious in character, and was regarded as the handmaiden of theology. Philosophical inquiry was included in its entirety within the religious conceptual framework. This held for general philosophy, and a fortiori for Jewish philosophy: Because of the special circumstances of life in Exile, the Jewish religion was not only a matter of faith - it also prescribed an entire way of life, encompassing every realm of thought and practice. These processes began as early as in the time of the Second Temple, when a sizeable Jewish Dispersion was already in existence.

In the modern era, Jewish philosophy, like philosophy in general, has liberated itself from submission to the theoretical and practical demands of religion. In Judaism this process was slower than in the general arena, and came rather belatedly, yet it could not be halted. Generally speaking, the ties of the Jewish philosophers to their religion were stronger than those of other philosophers: Spinoza and later Salomon Maimon were two exceptions. Religious problems have continued to concern Jewish philosophers in the modern era, more than they have philosophers in general, for obvious reasons. However the philosophical inquiry into these problems was no longer dictated, or motivated, by religion. Jewish philosophers commencing with Mendelssohn and Naphtali Herz Wessely, through 19th century philosophers, including the orthodox among them (Isaac Bernays, Samson Raphael Hirsch, Samuel David Luzzato) and up to the Jewish philosophers of our time, all treated religion, and primarily the Jewish religion, as philosophers. It is no accident that there were very few Rabbis among them. (Even Rabbi Nahman Krochmal never functioned as one). Modern Jewish philosophy has been the work of "secular" individuals ("secular" with respect to their formal status, not necessarily with respect to their outlook). Rabbis, save for a few from the Reform Movement, displayed little interest in the philosophical aspect of Judaism. In this matter, again, a certain change has occurred in the 20th century, when, for the most part, rabbis in the Western countries were required to have an academic background. Abraham Geiger and Manuel Joel (one of the first to point out the influence of Hasdai Crescas on Spinoza) in the 19th century, and Leo Baeck of Germany in the 20th century, together with Andre Neher of France (now of Jerusalem), and many present-day Jewish philosophers in the United States, all were, or are, engaged in their philosophical studies as philosophers, and not as rabbis or commentators. Independence of thought has replaced subordination. Even though most modern Jewish philosophy is religious philosophy, it is not a theology that is "authorized." Beginning with Renaissance Jewish philosophy there has been a reversion, on a higher level than theretofore, to a consideration of general questions, that concerned Greek and, later, European philosophy. However, it has been accompanied by an intensive interest in matters uniquely Jewish. Judah Abarbanel's Dialoghi d'Amore is a classic example of the opening of the new era. (The importance of this work as a landmark in modern Jewish philosophy has been pointed out several times in this volume.) Nor should one ignore the fact that what medieval Jewish philosophers were able to do within the confines of the Jewish religion, some modern ones were compelled to do beyond those confines. Maimonides remained "within"; Spinoza found himself "outside."

The attitude to the problem of Revelation has also changed. Difficulties arose that were virtually non-existent for medieval philosophers. The problem of revelation has been dealt with extensively in Part Four, and all that remains is to emphasize one additional aspect. As has already been pointed out, not a single medieval Jewish philosopher ever cast doubt on revelation as an objective historical fact, not different in essence from any other historical fact, established and verified by the same criteria, such as eye-witness accounts transmitted from generation to generation. The truth of a particular revelation rested on the authority of the witnesses to the historical occurrence. This was Judah Halevy's main argument. Its traces may also be found in the thinking of a rationalist philosopher like Mendelssohn. Could all the 600,000 eye-witnesses present at the giving of the Law at Mount Sinai have been wrong? However, today this view is unacceptable, not only to philosophers, but to religious thinkers as well. The modern view is that it is not the authority that renders the revelation valid, but the faith. Revelation is not an objective occurrence, but a subjective relationship of a man who has faith. Only he who is prepared ab initio to listen to the voice of God, is capable of hearing Him. (v. supra). The very listening is an act of faith. Jewish philosophy - and this holds true of any religious philosophy - is based on a presupposition of faith. But, while in medieval Jewish philosophy Revelation was regarded as objective in its nature, today, for the most part, it is regarded as subjective.

Thus, when, in the heat of controversy, orthodoxy is described as an expression of a medieval outlook, this is not merely a pejorative statement, as many would have it; it also is a statement of fact that orthodox thought is acting as the "Guardians of the Walls," namely it cleaves to a position, which was characteristic of the Middle Ages, and has been abandoned by modern Jewish religious philosophers.

CHAPTER THIRTY SEVEN

NEW SUBJECTS for STUDY: POLITICAL SCIENCE and PHILOSOPHY of HISTORY - THEIR SIGNIFICANCE FOR JEWISH THOUGHT

The main subjects that occupied medieval Jewish philosophy were Theology, i.e., the problems of God's reality, His essence, and His attributes; Ethics, especially everything that was bound up with the fulfillment of the Commandments, including "Commandments of the Heart"; and Epistemology, which dealt, first and foremost, with the weighty subject of reason as opposed to revelation (v. supra). All these subjects were dealt with from the specific standpoint of Jewish religious uniqueness. Occasionally, as already mentioned, the approach was apologetic. In the modern era Jewish thought continued to deal with all these problems. In addition, two new philosophical branches were added - Political Science and the Philosophy of History, which previously had not attracted the philosophers' attention. The political significance of Maimonidean teachings, an aspect which has been discussed or hinted at by a few modern scholars, including the moral lesson to be drawn from the story of "Jacob's Ladder," was marginal (v. supra.) In no way was it comparable to the importance that problems of political philosophy had for Spinoza and Mendelssohn, for example. It was mainly the political, social and legal status of Jews in their countries of residence that led modern Jewish scholars to take up political philosophy. In a similar fashion, interest in problems of the philosophy of history was connected with the national uniqueness of Jews in the Diaspora. The Maharal and his disciple David Gans, on the one hand, and Spinoza, on the other, sought to clarify the continued national existence of the Jews in the Diaspora, and to understand the uniqueness of Judaism in a Christian country and environment. The outstanding historiosophic work in this area is Krochmal's Guide of the Perplexed of our Times, which already reflects the romantic approach to the problems of political philosophy. The other scholars of the Jewish Science Movement in Germany, beginning from the small society formed at the end of the second decade of the 19th century and ending with the great German - Jewish philosophers, also found that they could not avoid dealing with the historical status of Judaism. It was no mere coincidence that modern Jewish historiography had its beginnings in this period. In fact, Heinrich Graetz preluded his historiographical oeuvre with a historical and philosophical essay, in the Hegelian spirit, entitled "The Construction of Jewish History."(3) He wrote a few additional essays in a similar vein. As compared to the traditional questions that had previously engaged Jewish thought, the importance of such studies increased considerably in the 19th and 20th centuries.

Jewish scholarship tended to emphasize the historical consciousness that had characterized Judaism ever since its earliest days. In this connection, the memory of the exodus from Egypt was stressed as one of the recurrent themes in the Bible. But beginning with Hellenistic Jewish philosophy attention shifted almost completely from actual historical events - except for the works of Josephus Flavius - to the idea of Divine intervention and salvation. In the days of Philo, the Day of Atonement, an event of no historical significance, had become the holiest day in the Jewish calendar. In the celebration of Hanukah, the miracle of the small vessel of oil overshadowed the victories of the Hasmoneans. A contemporary Jewish-American thinker has already asked the question: What kind of historical consciousness pervades Judaism if the Talmud fails to mention Judah Maccabee even once?(4) Various scholars, among them Gedalia Alon in Israel, have considered this matter at length. Nor does the Talmud deal with the destruction of the Second Temple - all it has to say about this tragic event in Jewish history is to be found in a number of parables and legends, whose main purpose is to deliver a religious or moral lesson (e.g., the dispute betweem Kamtza and Bar Kamtza), bereft of historical significance. The destruction, according to the Talmud, was brought on by fraternal hatred and other sins.

When Maimonides sought to give some sort of historical reason for the destruction of the Second Temple, he offered an actual political explanation, but his intention was to transmit a religious message as well. "Our fathers ... did not learn the art of war, nor the art of conquest of lands," because they believed in the nonsensical teachings of astrology, that the position of the stars determines everything (his reply to the wise men of Marsilia). The sin of idolatry was a thorn in his flesh. In the Tractate Avot it is written: "Exile comes upon the world because of idolatry and incest and the shedding of blood."(5) When Solomon Ibn Verga, in the 16th century, dealt with this subject in his book, The Tribe of Judah, his religious interpretation overshadowed the historical to an even greater extent. So long as the Children of Israel behaved uprightly and well, God fought their battles, and so they did not need to learn the art of war. But when they sinned, God ceased to do battle on their behalf, and since they had never learned to do battle, "they fell like sheep without a shepherd." From a historical point of view, of course, both opinions are absolutely groundless. There was no polemical intent in bringing up the two examples; they merely point up the fact that in ancient and medieval Jewish thought "historical" interpretation served religious ends and was devoid of any real historical comprehension.

In this matter, as well, the turnabout that occurred in modern Jewish philosophy was dramatic. This is not to say that the speculative elements vanished; however the historical dimension of the Jewish People and Judaism now received much more adequate expression. Every one of the Jewish thinkers, beginning with the Enlightenment and Krochmal up to the founding fathers of Socialist Zionism, interpreted Jewish existence on the basis of historical factors that they regarded as decisive. There were those, like Spinoza, who tried to show that the existence of the Jewish People in the Diaspora, which seemed to contravene the laws of history, was in reality governed by the same historical laws that hold for all other peoples.(6) Contrariwise, there were others, such as Krochmal and Rosenzweig, who attempted to prove that the ordinary laws of history that are valid for all other nations do not hold for the Jewish People and are inapplicable to its history: Judaism exists outside the spheres of history. It is dependent on "the Absolute spiritual", as Krochmal phrased it, or on "the goal," in the words of Rosenzweig. Therein lies its uniqueness. However, all were in agreement that understanding Jewish history was essential for the conduct and planning of Jewish life in the present and the future (cf. Geiger's perception of Jewish history and Judaic studies as a part of Jewish theology.)

Jacob Agus has suggested that the common denominator for Jewish philosophers in their perception of modern Jewish history consists of their seeing it as a history of "monotheism and martyrdom."(7) Yet every modern scholar is subject, to a degree, to the influence of some general philosophical outlook, which gives his perspective a special individual hue. In the teachings of Krochmal, the influences of Herder, Kant and Hegel are recognizable; in Samuel Hirsch - those of Hegel; in Formstecher - those of Schelling; in Steinheim - those of Kant and Schelling, while Geiger was essentially an eclectic; Rabbi Isaac Bernays adopted the ideas of Hamann, whereas his disciple S.R. Hirsch was a follower of Herder; the teachings of Hermann Cohen not only reveal Kantian and Hegelian influences, but also those of the philosophy of culture that prevailed in Germany at the end of the 19th and the beginning of the 20th centuries; the philosophies of Buber and Rosenzweig contain elements of Existentialism; in all other writers, the spirit of the times ("Zeitgeist") can be discerned, in one way or another, in the formation of their particular historiosophical views. An analysis of these philosophies will show the following presuppositions to be common to almost all of them, with varying emphases:

1. The essential "kernel" of Judaism is embedded in ethical monotheism, completely antithetical to the idolatrous religions of nature.

2. The Commandments were intended to safeguard the ethical-monotheistic idea, and Jewish isolationism mirrored the contrast between monotheism and polytheism.

3. True, Christianity adopted the Jewish monotheistic concept. However, it coupled it with idolatrous ways of thought and worship. Christianity meant religious and spiritual progress for the idol worshippers, but a decline vis-a-vis Judaism. Consequently, Judaism rejected it.

4. The dispersion of the Jews in the world was not an expression of Divine wrath (because of their sins, as it were.) It was, rather, a demonstration of Divine grace, since the Jews were entrusted with the mission of spreading the idea of pure ethical monotheism among the nations of the world. Some Jewish philosophers, such as Samuel Hirsch, regarded Christianity as the emmissary of Judaism, as its compromises with pagan practices of worship rendered it better suited to the task of bringing the nations closer to monotheism, and, in the final phase, to the vision of Judaism.

Therefore, these thinkers negated the Zionist idea. Hermann Cohen did it using extreme language, whereas Rosenzweig displayed disdainful indifference. They regarded Zionism as a retreat from the special task imposed on Judaism and as an attempt to avoid fulfilling its mission among the nations. Most important, they rejected the Zionist attempt to return Judaism - which in their eyes was essentially a-historical - to a historical existence.

These basic ideas were common to the overwhelming majority of Jewish thinkers of the 19th and the beginning of the 20th centuries. Reference is specially made to Jewish philosophy, which was then concentrated in the German cultural zone, and, to an extent, in Italy and France as well. Eastern European Jewry, which made up the great majority of the Jewish People, took virtually no part in these philosophical currents. Its religio-spiritual life was conducted on another level, that of Hasidism, the "Opposition" to it (by the Mitnagdim) and Enlightenment. This shared set of ideas characterized most of the Jewish thinkers in the German cultural realm, irrespective of whether their foundation was reason, (Krochmal, Samuel Hirsch, Hermann Cohen), or revelation (Steinheim, Rosenzweig). From the point of view of Jewish studies, the 19th century belonged to German Jewry, for understandable historical and intellectual reasons. In the 20th century, the center of gravity of Jewish studies shifted to the United States and to Israel. It is quite clear why Jewish scholarship in Israel tends to stress the national aspects of Judaism, whereas in the United States the religious aspect is in the forefront. Of late, in Israel as well the tendency to emphasize the religious dimension in Jewish Studies has come to the fore. This is not the place to consider the causes of, or to evaluate, this phenomenon.

The picture would be incomplete, if account were not taken of other historiosophic trends, such as the nationalist view of Moses Hess, Ahad Ha'am and other Zionist thinkers. However, this new thinking was largely nourished by extra-philosophical roots. Generally speaking it was given its main expression by publicists who lacked a solid philosophical foundation. The influences of Darwin and Spencer on Ahad Ha'am are not sufficient reason to modify this picture. Zionist thinkers, including the Socialist Zionists among them, have had a limited impact on Jewish philosophy.

CHAPTER THIRTY EIGHT

THE SHIFT in CONTENT: from ELECTION to MISSION

In the modern era Jewish philosophy not only encountered new problems that theretofore had received but little attention, but traditional questions had changed in nature and acquired new significance. Thus, the traditional idea of the Election of Israel was replaced by that of the Mission of Israel. No one will dispute that the belief that "Thou hast chosen us from among all the nations," together with the belief in the coming of the Messiah and the religious way of life, were the most important unifying factors for Judaism in its confrontation with a hostile world. These beliefs gave Jews a sense of superiority. Despite all the persecutions, pogroms, derision and discrimination that fell to their lot, they felt superior to "them," because they believed in a one and only God, who had given them the Torah and had chosen them as "a kingdom of priests and a holy nation." They believed that they were superior to other peoples because of their ability to read and write, their higher morality in regard to family life, their greater attention to rules of hygiene, etc. This tendency to self-praise was, of course, not unique to the Jewish people: The ancient Greeks displayed it as well. Herodotus, in describing his travels in Asia, was inspired by pride in being a Greek, a member of the Greek people, a nation endowed with higher intellectual skills than any other. Aristotle had a similar feeling when he defined all non-Greeks as "barbarians," incapable of caring for themselves, because of their intellectual inferiority, and therefore by "nature" suited to be slaves. He advised his pupil, Alexander, when he set out on his road to conquest, to treat the Persians as vegetation and beasts. It is to the credit of his pupil that he paid no heed to his teacher's advice.

This feeling of spiritual superiority faithfully attended Judaism throughout the ages - though it never led to arrogant boasting - but it began to erode in the modern age. The expression of the "Chosen People" acquired a somewhat discordant ring. Other peoples, as well, began to regard themselves as "Chosen" - Dostoyevski believed the Russians to be the Chosen People. Ultra-reactionary views, such as first came to light primarily in Germany from the previous century on through the Nazi period, caused terms such as a "Chosen People," a "Chosen Race" or even a "Chosen Class" to become offensive. Whenever one regards oneself, or one's people, or some other group as "chosen" by a supreme Providence or by History, he is inevitably in danger of entertaining an unjustified feeling of superiority. It is as if he, endowed with unique attributes not available to his fellow man, is required to save everyone else, or, what is infinitely worse, to rule over everyone else. There are today many Jews in the Diaspora, irrespective of the religious trend in Judaism to which they belong, who would find it difficult to accept that God "chose" them specially to worship Him and to fulfill His mission. For them, the concept of Election is an anachronism, an idea that is obsolete and irrelevant to modern life.

Even in ancient times, several thinkers recognized the vulnerability of the concept of Election. In the first century, the pagan philosopher Celsus commented with ironic hostility on Judaism and Christianity:

> Jews and Christians appear to me like a host of bats, or ants who come out of their hiding places, or like frogs who sit in a swamp, or like worms who hold a meeting in the corner of a manure pile and say to one another: 'To us God proclaims and reveals everything. He does not trouble himself with the rest of the world; we are the only beings with whom he has dealings ... To us is subjected everything: the earth, the water, the air, the stars. Because it has happened that some among us have sinned, God himself will come or will send his own Son in order to destroy the wicked with fire and to give us a share in eternal life.'(8)

Despite the poisonous language, the inaccuracies and the misconceptions, the words of Celsus indicate the discomfiture, on the philosophical level, occasioned by a phrase like "the Chosen People."

Modern Jewish philosophers have clearly sensed the problematical nature of the "ideology" of Election in its traditional form. Spinoza devoted a chapter entitled "Of the vocation of the Hebrews,"(9) to proving that any claim of Election, based on the intellectual or moral superiority of a certain nature, is philosopically indefensible. At the end of that chapter he also discussed the possibility of re-establishing political independence for the People of Israel, and used the sentence "God may a second time elect them."(10) But he hastened to emphasize that what he meant was that the laws of nature (and of history) that apply to every people hold for the Jewish People as well. He repudiated any claim to superiority of one nation over another. The possibility of re-establishing a Jewish State exists not on account of "divine election" but because of the laws of general history. Mendelssohn, like Spinoza, dissociated himself from the notion of election. Even though his view that the Law was revealed solely to the Jewish People lends a certain credibility to the traditional doctrine of Election, Mendelssohn refrained from using the term of "Chosen People," and tried to place the main emphasis on the aspect of "mission." The Jewish thinkers of the 19th century supported this view. The mission of Israel, as Moses Hess, the Zionist, was fond of saying, was to replace the concept of Election, and even though the latter term was laden with emotional content, it was no longer acceptable to modern Jewish philosophers. The mission is fulfilled through the propagation of the moral tidings of the Bible, especially as expressed by the Prophets, and the conclusions in the area of social action to be drawn from them. The particularistic element that characterized the concept "the Election of Israel" gave way to the universal element, expressed in the phrase "the Mission of Israel."

At first glance one might ask: Does a change in terminology express a change in ideational content? Is it not merely a case of the same lady disguised in a new cloak? Is not the view that Israel carries a purpose, a special mission, merely a repetition of the concept of Election in a more refined garb? In reply, some scholars have maintained that Judaism was not chosen a priori for the fulfillment of this mission. However, the fact that, because of unique historical circumstances, it was the first to accept ethical monotheism makes Judaism uniquely qualified to engage in spreading the concept. Parenthetically it should be noted that in the Bible itself it was already stated that God did not choose Israel for its superior qualities, but for other reasons.

> The Lord did not set his love upon you, nor choose you, because ye were more in number than any people; for ye were the fewest of all people. But because the Lord loved you, and because he would keep the oath which he had sworn unto your fathers.

And in a similar vein:

> Not for thy righteousness, or for the uprightness of thine heart dost thou got to possess their land; but for the wickedness of these nations the Lord thy God doth drive them out from before thee, and that he may perform the word which the Lord sware unto thy fathers, Abraham, Isaac and Jacob. Understand therefore, that the Lord thy God giveth thee not this good land to possess it for thy righteousness, for thou art a stiffnecked people.(12)

In this respect Spinoza's view, even though it has a somewhat provocative ring, is consonant with the spirit of the Biblical text.

One may say that the concept of the "Chosen People" constituted a sort of ideological self-compensation for the difficult and inferior status of the People of Israel in the Diaspora. Buber once said that the important thing "is not whether we feel or do not feel that we are chosen ..." but "that our role in history actually has been unique."(13)   In summation, as to the concept of "Thou hast chosen us," a distinction must be made between two kinds of matters:

It is true that the concept of Election is unacceptable in the light of scientific and philosophical criticism, and is a contravention of the humanistic view that sees every man and every nation as an embodiment of equal value of one humanity and one human spirit. Yet the foregoing is not in contradiction to appreciating the important function which the concept of Election has played in the development of cohesiveness and self-confidence of the People of Israel in times when they were the objects of ubiquitous hatred and persecution. Just as the secular Jew is able to recognize and value the unique place and function of faith in the 2000-year history of the Dispersion, and is capable of respecting religion without himself accepting the beliefs or obeying the Commandments, so too, in the case of the concept of Election. Without identifying with its ideational content, which is incompatible with a consistent humanistic viewpoint, one may regard with favor the function that it has played in the historical and spiritual circumstances that the people of Israel encountered in the past, and respect the belief in it by previous generations. Nevertheless, this approach does not in any way obviate the need for a critical reexamination based on contemporary philosophical ideas.

One of the most difficult questions for contemporary Jewish thought has been intentionally ignored: How can one continue to cling to the concept of a "Chosen People" after the Holocaust? However, this question is inseparable from the general religio-philosophical context, namely, the problem of Providence and of God's role in history, the theology of the "Death of God," the God who hides His face, and similar ideas. These problems have been of concern, in different ways, to most contemporary Jewish philosophers. Buber treated it in his work, The Eclipse of God; Emil Fackenheim, in his book The Presence of God in History; Richard Rubenstein - in After Auschwitz, Elie Wiesel in his literary and essayistic writings. But this is a separate problem, which does not directly impinge upon the matters of conceptual change that is being considered here.

Nor is this the place for an elaborate clarification of the question, why the traditional view of the People of Israel as a "Chosen People" is again cherished by various circles in our own time. The main roots of this phenomenon are not philosophical, but ideological. One may use by way of analogy the sad witticism that there are non-Jews who reject the historical existence of Jesus, but are convinced that the Jews killed him. Thus in our day one frequently encounters Jews (and even Christians) who reject the existence of God, or of a choosing God, but believe that the People of Israel are a "Chosen People" (for example, the historian Arnold Toynbee, who held to this view not necessarily out of sympathy for Judaism).

Those who believe in the Election of Israel can rely on a very respectable authority. Ahad Ha'am, despite his secular outlook, accepted the idea of the Chosen People, without believing in the existence of a choosing God. In his opinion, the People of Israel excels by its essential "differentness" from all other nations and by its unique ethic that preaches absolute justice (v. supra in connection with the problem presented by this concept). This is its "mission." Based on this premise, Ahad Ha'am valued tradition, with its various beliefs, on the emotional level, but did not identify with its philosophical content. Accordingly, he sought to replace "I believe" with "I feel" in order to buttress his hypothesis of "differentness." In his general philosophical thought, he was of two minds. On the one hand, influenced by Darwin and Spencer, he supported the theory of general evolution, which does not allow for national differentiation, and certainly not for a concept of mission; yet, his own ties to the Jewish heritage led him to the above conclusions.

CHAPTER THIRTY NINE

CHANGES in the CONCEPTION of EXILE

Another instance of a change in conception, to be discussed briefly, is the altered significance of the concept of Exile; Generally speaking, in medieval Jewish thought Exile was regarded as punishment for the sins of Israel. This view, first alluded to in the Bible, became widely accepted by the Apocrypha and in the thought of the Sages.

> And if ye will not for all this hearken unto me, but walk contrary unto me ... And I will scatter you among the heathen, and will draw out a sword after you: and your land shall be desolate, and your cities waste." (Leviticus 26: 27, 33). "Exile comes upon the world because of idolatry and incest and the shedding of blood." (Aboth 5:9 The Babylonian Talmud, Nezikin, Vol. III, op. cit. p.456). "Through the crime of bloodshed the Temple was destroyed and the Shechinah departed from Israel ... As a punishment for incest, idolatry, and non-observance of the Sabbatical and jubilee years exile comes to the world, they (the Jews) are exiled, and others come and dwell in their place..." (Sabbath 33:a, The Babylonian Talmud, op. cit., Moed, Vol. I) "Israel did not go into exile until they had repudiated the Divine Unity, circumcision which had been given to the twentieth generation, the Decalogue and the Pentateuch." (Midrash Rabba, op. cit., vol. VII, Lamentations I, 1, 1, p. 66; Abraham, who first received the commandment of circumcision, belonged to the twentieth generation from Adam.) "And what did His people do that caused Him to expel them from their land? Because they abandoned Him and went to worship other gods" (Aboth of Rabbi Nathan, Version B,A).

One of the fundamental assumptions, or more accurately, one of the fundamental beliefs of medieval thought, was that Israel could atone for its sins by observing the Commandments and could hope that with the coming of the Messiah the punishment of Exile would be abrogated, and all mankind would be redeemed.

In modern Jewish philosophy, especially since the struggle for emancipation, the concept of punishment for Israel's sins was abandoned. True, Exile was perceived by most Jewish religious philosophers at that time as a Divine decree, but for an exalted purpose - the maintenance of the Jewish mission among the nations. The same idea had already appeared in the Midrash, however only in modern Jewish thought did it become the chief one. In the same way that the particularistic "Election of Israel" was converted into the universalistic "Mission of Israel," so was the particularistic idea of Exile as a punishment of one nation replaced by the universalistic concept of preparing for the coming of the Messiah, in the prophetic spirit of moral tidings for all of mankind. The one depends on the other - the change in significance of the concept of "Election" led to the change in significance of the concept of "Exile."

However, at the end of the 19th century, along with the growth of the idea of Jewish nationhood and the rise of Zionism, a change in the opposite direction took place in the conception of the significance of Exile. The new tendency sought to stress once again the idea of Redemption. In its non-Zionist version - as, <u>inter alia</u>, in the philosophy of Rosenzweig, where it received its definitive theoretical formulation - the same idea led to the affirmation of the permanence of the Exile. In its Zionist version, the idea of Redemption was based on the negation of the Exile, because it fostered an abnormal and inauthentic Jewish life. Zionism considered the return to the Homeland, to the Land of Israel, as the road to redemption, which was identified with the renewal of a normal national life. Here we witness something of a dialectical return to the first conception of Exile, but with new significance and content. Most modern Jewish philosophers have noted this relationship between "Exile" and "Redemption," even on the Hebrew linguistic level ("Exile" - "Gola"; "Redemption" - "Ge'ula".) The Maharal, in his <u>Well of Redemption</u>, was one of the first to take this path, albeit his conclusions differed from those of later writers.

This is not the place to linger over the current discussions, which make semantic distinctions between "exile," "dispersion," and "alien lands." These are not philosophical views of the metaphysical significance of Exile in the life of the Jewish people - whether they take a favorable view of Exile or not. However important, they are but ideological debates about the essence of Exile, in particular since the rise of Zionism and, even more so, since the establishment of the State of Israel. The question whether the Jews of the United States live in exile or in dispersion (as, for example, the Jews of Alexandria did in the days of the Second Temple,) occupies Zionist thinking, but belongs to Jewish philosophy only indirectly.

CHAPTER FORTY

CHANGES in the MESSIANIC IDEA

Parallel changes took place with regard to the belief in the Messiah. Medieval Jewish philosophy cast no doubt, at least not openly, on the traditional conception of a personal Messiah, descended from the House of David and destined to be the Redeemer of the People of Israel, who would return them to their ancient homeland. The spreading of the Messianic idea was regarded by medieval Jewish philosophers as one of the ways of hastening the advent of the Messiah. Modern Jewish philosophy forsook the personalistic version of the Messianic idea and regarded the Messianic era as essentially a moral vision that will unite all mankind in a life of justice and righteousness. In the modern era, the early Jewish philosophers showed almost no interest in the Messianic idea. Neither Mendelssohn nor Krochmal dealt with it in their works. Therefore, strangely enough, it came to occupy a central position for Jewish non-Orthodox thinkers, who attempted to interpret the idea in terms of a universal ethical prophecy or to identify it with the Emancipation, which in their eyes was the embodiment of the Messianic era. Jewish religious philosophy in the 19th century, from Samuel Hirsch to Hermann Cohen, regarded Messianism as the spread of the Jewish religion among the nations of the world, which would bring about complete freedom in human relations. (They regarded Christianity as intermediary or preparatory for the realization of this end.) Incidentally, it was Hirsch, one of the founders of the Reform Movement, who, unexpectedly enough, spoke of a symbolical return of the Jews to Jerusalem, where they would establish an ideal state, guided by the spirit of the Prophets, that would radiate its moral message to the entire world.

The Messianic idea was converted into one of Redemption, both personal and communal. It was in this spirit that the Reform Movement replaced the word "Redeemer" by "Redemption" in the prayer of the "Eighteen Benedictions", an amendment that is accepted by all elements in Liberal Judaism to this day. This concept received its most outstanding philosophical expression in Rosenzweig's Star of Redemption, and traces of it can even be found in the Marxist-Utopian thought of Ernst Bloch (who, in his youth, was a regular visitor in Rosenzweig's home). Finally the Messianic idea found its logical realization in Zionism, which justifiably regarded itself as its legitimate heir, though without its religious trappings. This concept appears in many versions in the thought of all modern secular Zionist thinkers. Messianism is perceived as self-realization, rather than as waiting for the Redeemer with folded hands. (David Frischmann, in his day, gave lyrical expression to this idea in his poem, "The Messiah.") A few attempts were also made to bridge the gap between traditional Messianism and modern nationalism (e.g., Buber, A.D. Gordon, Rabbi Kook). However, the traditional conception which was still preserved in medieval thought, now vanished, and persisted only in extreme Orthodox circles.

There are a number of reasons for the change from the traditional viewpoint of "the Messiah" and "the Redeemer" to the new one of "Messianism" and "Redemption". The concept of the personal Messiah was bound up with the belief that when he comes, even if he is delayed, he will bring his people back to their land. In modern times liberal Judaism has rejected this belief, since it implies that the Jews constitute something like a foreign and temporary implantation in the countries of their domicile. Such an idea stood in the way of the struggle for emancipation and civic equality. The American Jewish philosopher Stephen S. Schwarzschild justifiably remarked that it was ironic and paradoxical for the Reform Movement of the 19th century to have rejected the belief in a personal Messiah because it was bound up with the idea of Jewish nationalism - a thorn in its flesh, while on the other hand, ultra-Orthodox circles, such as Agudat Israel and Neturei Karta, rejected Zionism, i.e., the Jewish nationalist standpoint, because of their faith in a personal Messiah. "Reform remained aloof from Zionism because it did not believe in the personal Messiah, the Aggudah remained aloof because it did."(14) In the meantime the two trends have altered their attitude toward Israel, primarily because of the establishment of the State of Israel. However, the basic viewpoint, because of which the concept of the "Messiah" was replaced by "Messianism," remained unchanged. Again, as Schwarzschild aptly commented, "Theoretically, there is no reason why the personal Messiah must mean Jewish nationalism, and the Messianic age must mean 'universalism'."(15) One can claim with equally sound logic that the personal Messiah will redeem humanity, whereas the Messianic era, which one hundred and fifty years ago was identified with Jewish emancipation, equality and civil rights, will be embodied in the national independence of the Jewish people. The tendency to connect the Messianic idea with the national redemption of the People of Israel undoubtedly also stemmed from the fact that the traditional religious perception regarded the Messiah as being a descendent of King David.(16)

Another matter, purely philosophical in meaning, may be appended to that of replacing the concept of the Messiah by Messianism. Jewish philosophers of the 19th century, up to and including Hermann Cohen, found it difficult to accept a belief in a personal God, a fortiori the concept of a personal Messiah. The personalistic perception was for them, as it was for all philosophers of that period, "a terrible stumbling block."(17) It completely contravened the laws of science and the fundamentals of philosophic idealism, which Jewish philosophers sought to adapt to their religious position. Contrariwise, the perception of God as an idea and the Messianic era as an epoch were concepts readily arrived at by abstract reasoning and capable of being integrated into a philosophical system.(18) It was exactly for such reasons that changes in Reform Judaism were introduced into the second benediction of the "Eighteen Benedictions," where the words referring to God as a reviver of the dead were replaced by the words pertaining to "eternal life."(19)

Parenthetically it should be noted that these theoretical difficulties did not escape the attention of the contemporary Jewish philosophers who held to religious existentialist positions, such as Buber, Rosenzweig and Heschel. They adopted the concept of a personal God. It is easier to integrate a faith in a personal God with a philosophical position than a faith in a personal Messiah. Even if the philosophical basis is grounded in faith, not every idea is accepted by faith in equal measure. When Rosenzweig, for example, in his introduction to the second part of The Star of Redemption, tried to preserve the concept of miracle, one that seemed to embarrass modern theologians, he removed from it, as we have seen, all clearly "miraculous" indicia: He tried to present the concept of miracle as the unusual ability of the prophet to see into the future. Without here subjecting such an opinion to critical analysis, one can readily see that it is far more acceptable than that of a personal Messiah. From this aspect, the philosophical change in the understanding of the Messianic idea remains valid to this day for modern Jewish philosophy.

In conclusion, the shift of emphasis from the idea of Election to that of Mission and the changed significance of the concepts of Exile and of the Messianic idea clearly illustrate the fact that many problems that confronted medieval Jewish philosophy still retain their vitality and relevance, even though theoretical attention has shifted to other aspects of these problems. In this respect, the well-known expression which the philosopher A.N. Whitehead used as the name of his book - Adventures of Ideas(20) - is better suited to Jewish philosophy, because of its characteristic "special shared quality," than to general philosophy. Jewish philosophy parallels general philosophy in that they both possess intellectual continuity, even though there was a long hiatus between their medieval and modern periods. However, this continuity in no way is in contradiction of the basic premise that Jewish philosophy in every era reflects the influences of general philosophy.

CHAPTER FORTY ONE

THE CAUSES for the DECLINE of the HISTORICAL APPROACH in PHILOSOPHY as REFLECTED in JEWISH THOUGHT

The term "adventures of ideas," referred to in the previous chapter, has fundamental significance in principle for the understanding of the history of Jewish philosophy: the need to view problems in the context of their historical development. In modern general philosophical literature one can of late discern the contrary tendency - to mimimize the importance of historical aspects, for two reasons:

On the one hand, there has been a decline in the prestige of the historical approach in introductions to philosophy. Until recently the accepted practice was to describe a series of philosophical "systems", each differing from and incompatible with the preceding one, so the impression was created that, in dealing with philosophical views, one assumed ab initio that they do not express truth, since each was disproved by its successor, ad infinitum, as it were. As opposed to this skeptical and pessimistic line, certain philosophers turned to the Hegelian dialectic (considered in the Introduction to this volume), without adopting its pretension to metaphysical absolutism. This system, which was also embraced by the late Israeli philosopher Hugo Bergmann in his introductory chapter to his History of Modern Philosophy, identified philosophy with its history. Not only negation and belittlement characterize the attitude of one philosopher to another of a different trend; on the contrary, what is worthy of acceptance is accepted, and respect and tolerance are exhibited for the achievements of earlier philosophers and their viewpoints.

It is imperative for one who deals with Jewish philosophy, especially for one who deals with its history, to be aware of and sensitive to these aspects. The study of Jewish philosophy, as well, should lead its practitioners to a greater degree of intellectual tolerance. In the past, especially in medieval philosophy, every Jewish philosopher tried to construct a philosophical theory that would be identical with revealed truth, which is one, and one only; but today it should be understood that there is no philosophical teaching - either general or Jewish - that encompasses the entire truth.

A second reason for the loss of esteem of the historical approach in philosophy is that those engaged in it today concern themselves chiefly with the clarification of methodological problems. These problems overshadow the doctrines of the philosophers. The present trend is to arrive at the clarification and illumination of types of philosophy - such as epistemology, linguistic philosophy, philosophy of science, ethics, aesthetics - primarily by employing logical methods, and not necessarily by studying and analyzing the opinions of the philosophers of the past.

This approach, which has now become the main trend of philosophy in the English-speaking world, is not quite suitable to Jewish philosophy. Its bond to ancient sources fulfills a much more important function than it does in general philosophy, and even may be said to constitute an integral part of its essence. In Jewish thought the "statute of limitation" is less important than in general philosophy. Even in the latter, the exaggerated fervor for the solution of problems has resulted at times in an unjustified, excessive disdain for the philosophical thought of earlier ages. Lately a more balanced position has come to the fore in this matter, as evidenced by the series of philosophical books that have appeared recently under the name of "New Studies" in Plato, Aristotle, Kant, and others. In the general field too, a greater awareness is felt today of the relevance of the philosophers of the past to current philosophical problems.

From this standpoint, the Hegelian method, without regard to the dialectic as a general philosophical system, could serve as an adequate guideline for Jewish philosophy, as well. David Neumark, in the introduction to his book, <u>The History of Jewish Philosophy</u>, has written: "The aim of any investigation into the history of philosophy is philosophy itself, philosophical awareness."(21)

NOTES

PART ONE

1. John Burnet, Early Greek Philosophy, Heraclitus, Fragment 49, London, 1958 (1892), p. 137.

2. Phaedros, The Dialogues of Plato, translated by B. Jowett, New York: Random House, 1937, Vol. I, p. 281.

3. ibid., p. 329.

4. Abodah Zarah 54b, The Babylonian Talmud, Seder Nezikim Vol. IV, translated by Rabbi Dr. I. Epstein, p. 278.

5. Midrash Rabba VII, Lamentations, London: The Soncino Press, 1981 (1961), p. 176.

6. Moses Maimonides, The Guide of the Perplexed, translated with an introduction and notes by Shlomo Pines, Chicago: The University of Chicago Press, 1963, p. 10.

7. Rabbi Shem-Tov Falaquera, Reshith-Hochma, Berlin 1902, photomechanic edition Jerusalem 1970, Pt. III, "Plato's philosophy and the arrangement of its parts from the beginning to the end", p. 70 (for the bibliographical details I am grateful to Dr. Abraham Melamed (Haifa University).

8. Lessings Werke, Fuenfter Band, Leipzig und Wien, Biographisches Institut, no date, p. 679; Lessing's words are: "Wenn Gott in seiner Rechten alle Wahrheit und in seiner Linken den einzigen immer regen Trieb nach Wahrheit, obschon mit dem Zusatze mich immer und ewig zu irren, verschlossen hielte, und spraeche zu mir: waehle! Ich fiele ihm mit Demuth in seine Linke und sagte: Vater, gieb! die reine Wahrheit ist ja doch nur fuer dich allein!"

9. Kierkegaard's Concluding Unscientific Postscript, Princeton: Princeton University Press, 1941, p. 97.

10. Immanuel Kant's Critique of Pure Reason, translated by Norman Kemp Smith, London: MacMillan & Co., New York: St. Martin's Press, 1964, p. 657.

11. Rabbi Harlap, Mej-Merom; vide Y. Leibowitz, Lectures on the "Sayings of the Fathers" and "Eight Chapters" of Maimonides (hebrew), Jerusalem/Tel Aviv: Schocken, 1979, pp. 151/2.

12. Bertrand Russell, The Problems of Philosophy, New York-London: H. Holt, ca. 1920, pp. 24-25.

13. Hans Reichenbach, The rise of scientific Philosophy, Berkeley and Los Angeles: University of California Press, 1956, p. 8.

14. Franz Rosenzweig, Der Stern der Erloesung: Frankfurt a.M.: J. Kauffmann-Verlag, 2. Auflage 1930, 2nd part, p. 23.

15. Russell, op. cit., p. 233, emphasized.

16. Compare: Karl Popper, The Logic of Scientific Discovery, 1959; K. Popper, Conjectures and Refutations: The growth of scientific knowledge, 1963; K. Popper, Objective knowledge: An evolutionary approach, 1972; Thomas S. Kuhn, The Structure of Scientific Revolutions, 2nd edition, enlarged, International Encyclopedia of Unified Science, Volume II, Number 2, 1970.

17. Benedict de Spinoza, Theological-Political Treatise (TPT); The Chief Works of Benedict de Spinoza, Volume I, New York: Dover Publications, 1951.

18. Baruch Spinoza, Hebrew Grammar (Compendium Grammatices Linguae Hebreae), edited and translated with an introduction by Rabbi Maurice H. Bloom, New York: Philosophical Library, 1962.

19. Moses Mendelssohn, Jerusalem and other Jewish writings, translated and edited by Alfred Jospe, New York: Schocken Books, 1969, p. 14. In 1983 there has appeared a new translation by Allan Arkush, with an introduction and commentary by Alexander Altmann; Hannover and London: University Press of New England, 1983.

20. B. de Spinoza, Political Treatise, I, 1, The chief works of B. de Spinoza, op. cit., p. 287.

21. The novels of the 19th century Hebrew writer Abraham Mapu or the translations of the Hebrew poet David Frischmann at the turn of the century are at present important only for their historical significance, as a part of the history of modern Hebrew literature. This subject, however, belongs to the area of literary research.

22. Samuel Hugo Bergmann, History of Philosophy from Nicolaus Cusanus to the Age of Enlightenment, Jerusalem: Bialik Institute, 1970, hebrew, p. 11.

23. ibid., p. 17.

24. Rosenzweig, op. cit., 1st part, p. 14.

25. Rosenzweig, op. cit., 1st part, p. 15.

26. Judaism despite Christianity - The "Letters on Christianity and Judaism" between Eugen Rosenstock-Huessy and Franz Rosenzweig, ed. by Eugen Rosenstock-Huessy, New York: Schocken Books, 1971, p. 167.

27. Chronicles II, 1:11.

28. Midrash Rabba X, Ecclesiastes X:20, London: The Soncino Press, 1961, (1931), p. 280.

29. Judah Halevi, The Kuzari, New York: Schocken Books, 1971 (1964), Pt. IV, ch. 9.

30. Compare: Th. Kuhn, The Structure of Scientific Revolutions (note 16) and the controversy in the wake of his book.

31. Ecclesiastes 1:18.

32. Genesis 4:1.

33. Martin Buber, Good and Evil, Two Interpretations, New York: Charles Scribner's Sons, 1953, p. 56.

34. Theaetetus, Dialogues of Plato, op. cit.., vol. II, p. 150.

35. Apology, ibid., vol. 1., pp. 401-423.

36. On Cusanus' "Docta Ignorantia" vide Hugo Bergman, ibid., pp. 23-26

37. Salomon Maimon, Philosophisches Woerterbuch 1791, Gesammelte Werke, Bd. 3, Georg Olms Verlag Hildesheim 1970, p. 186.

38. Exodus 20:4,

39. On the cognitivity of value-judgments there exists a voluminous literature. I have dealt with these problems in my (hebrew) book: Science and Values - on the cognitive status of ethical values, Ramat Gan: Massada Publishing House, 1978.

40. The Kuzari 5:12, op. cit., pp. 265-266, emphasized in the original.

41. Republic, Book VII, The Dialogues of Plato, op. cit., vol. 1, pp. 773-776.

42. Guide of the Perplexed, op. cit., p. 41, emphasized in the original.

43. ibid., Pt. II, ch. 6, pp. 261-262.

44. Numbers 21:21.

45. Aristoteles, Metaphysics Bk. I, ch. 2, 982b21-28; The Basic Works of Aristoteles, ed. by Richard McKeon, New York: Random House, 1941, p. 692.

46. Metaphysics Bk. I, ch. 2, 983a10, ibid., p. 693.

47. Ludwig Wittgenstein, Tractatus Logico-Philosophicus 6.54; London: Routledge & Kegan Paul (New York: The Humanities Press) 1966, p. 151.

48. Russell op. cit., p. 238.

49. ibid., p. 239.

50. Aboth 4:5, The Mishnah, translated by Herbert Danby, London: Oxford University Press, 1938, p. 453.

51. Mendelssohn, op. cit., p. 35.

52. TPT, 1670, title-page.

53. Hegel's Philosophy of Right, translated by T.M. Knox, Oxford: The Clarendon Press, 1942, pp. 12-13.

54. Marx's Theses on Feuerbach; Karl Marx, Selected Works, Vol. 1, New York: International Publishers, no date, p. 473, emphasized in original.

55. Kethubot 17a, The Babylonian Talmud, op. cit., Nashim vol. II, p. 93; the literary translation of "Me'urav" is not "pleasant" but "involved".

56. Vide his "Nethivot Olam", ch. 46; compare: Andre Neher, Le Puits de l'Exile, la theologie dialectique du Maharal de Prague, Ed. Albin Michel Paris 1966, p. 223. (I am obliged to Prof. A. Neher for his personal elucidations on this matter).

57. Hegel's Philosophy of Mind, translated by William Wallace, Oxford: The Clarendon Press, 1971, p. 315. The quotation is from "Metaphysics" XI:7.

58. Russell, op. cit., p. 240.

59. ibid.

60. Bertrand Russell, Wisdom of the West, New York: A Fawcett Premier Book, 1966, p. 20.

61. Claude Levi-Strauss, Overture to le Cru et le Cuit, in Structuralism, ed. by Jacques Ehrmann, New York: Anchor Books 1970, p. 40.

62. Karl R. Popper, The Logic of Scientific Discovery, London: Hutchinson, 1968, pp. 15-16.

63. Rene Descartes, Discourse on Method, Indianapolis/Cambridge: Hackett Publishing Company, 1981, p. 10.

64. Walter Kaufmann, Critique of Religion and Philosophy, New York: Anchor Books 1958, p. 19.

65. Franz Rosenzweig, Das Neue Denken (1925); Kleinere Schriften, Berlin: Schocken Verlag 1937, pp. 375-376.

66. J.P. Sartre, Literary and Philosophical Essays, New York: Criterion Books 1955, p. 142.

67. Russell, Problems of Philosophy, op. cit., pp. 243-244.

68. ibid., p. 244.

69. ibid., p. 249-250.

PART TWO

1. Samuel Hugo Bergmann, Hogim u-ma'aminim (Thinkers and believers), hebrew, Tel Aviv: Dvir Co. Ltd. 1959, p. 12.

2. Nathan Rotenstreich, The Scope of Philosophy, Jerusalem: The Magnes Press, the Hebrew University, 1969, hebrew, p. 210.

3. ibid., p. 211.

4. "lightning flashes", Guide of the Perplexed, op. cit., Pt. I, Introduction, p. 7.

5. Compare Rotenstreich, op. cit., p. 211.

6. Bergmann, Hogim, op. cit., p. 76 in regard of Spinoza's conception of the Godhead.

7. Pensees / The Provincial Letters by Blaise Pascal, The Modern Library, New York 1941, pensee 555, p. 182.

8. Rotenstreich, op. cit., p. 216.

9. Yeshaiah Leibowitz, The Law and the Commandments in our time, hebrew, Tel Aviv: Massada Publishing House, 1954, p. 19.

10. ibid., p. 35, vide also his article "Practical Commandments" in his book: Judaism, the Jewish People and the State of Israel, Jerusalem/Tel Aviv: Schocken, 1978, pp. 13-36 (hebrew).

11. Rene Descartes, Meditations, Hacket, 1981 (vide note 63 above), pp. 68, 77-79, 82.

12. John Hermann Randall, Jr., The role of knowledge in western religion, Boston: Star King Press, 1958, p. 2; vide also Sol Roth, Science and Religion, in: Studies in Torah Judaism ed. by Leon D. Stitskin, New York: Yeshiva University Press, Ktav Publishing House, 1969, p. 527.

13. Sukkah 29a. The Babylonian Talmud, op. cit., Moed Vol. III, p. 130.

14. This summary survey of the relations between Tora and Science according to the Maharal is based on the detailed description by Andre Neher in Le Puits de l'Exile (note 56 above).

15. Andre Neher, David Gans (1541-1613), disciple du Maharal de Prague, assistant de Tycho Brahe et de Jean Kepler, Paris: ed. Klincksieck, 1974.

16. Albert Einstein & Leopold Infeld, The Evolution of Physics, London: The Scientific Book Club, no date, p. 310.

17. Pierre Duhem, The structure of physical theory, Princeton: Princeton University Press, 1954, p. 285; vide also Sol Roth, Science and religion, in: Studies in Torah Judaism, op. cit., pp. 543-552.

18. Bergmann, Hogim, op. cit., p. 19.

19. TPT, op. cit., p. 194.

20. Spinoza, Ethics, Part I, Appendix; Baruch Spinoza, The Ethics and Selected Letters, translated by Samuel Shirley, ed. by Seymour Feldman, Indianapolis: Hacket Publishing Company, 1982, p. 60.

21. TPT, op. cit., pp. 198-199.

22. Bergmann, Hogim, op. cit., pp. 18-19.

23. ibid., p. 20.

24. vide also "Spinoza's God and us", ibid., pp. 71-84.

25. ibid., p. 24.

26. I have dealt with this problem in my Science and Values, op. cit., (note 39 above), pp. 12-14. There, however, the discussion is limited to the first three sentences only, because the subject matter of the book are ethical value judgments.

27. Exodus 20:4; vide above.

28. Ethics, Part IV, prop. 50, op. cit., p. 182.

29. S.D. Luzzatto, Mechkarej Ha-yahaduth, vol. I, Warsaw 1913, p. 11 ff.

30. This issue is treated in my Science and Values; vide also above, note 26.

31. On the relevant problems and possibilities, compare Science and Values, part II.

32. Rosenzweig, Stern, op. cit., 3rd part, p. 162.

33. Jeremiah 10:10.

34. Moses Maimonides, Mishneh Torah, Hilkhot Yesodei ha-Torah 1:4, translated by Hyamson, New York, 1974, p. 34a.

35. Spinoza's Short Treatise on God, Man & His Well-Being, translated and edited by A. Wolf, London, 1910, p. 103, emphasized in the original.

36. F. Rosenzweig, Das Neue Denken (vide note 65 above).

37. ibid.

38. Ludwig Feuerbach, The Essence of Christianity, New York: Harper Torchbooks, Evanston & London, 1957, p. 14.

39. ibid., p. 19.

40. Rosenzweig, Stern, op. cit., 3rd part, p. 162.

41. Feuerbach, ibid., p. 21.

42. ibid., p. 22.

43. Rosenzweig, ibid.

44. Guide of the Perplexed, Pt. I, ch. 50, op. cit., p. 111; "belief" and "affirmation" are of the same Hebrew root.

45. ibid.

46. Jerusalem, op. cit., pp. 61-62, emphasized in the original.

47. Compare: Anthony Flew, God and Philosophy, New York: A Delta Book, 1966, p. 176.

48. Rotenstreich, The Scope of Philosophy, op. cit., p. 226.

49. Proverbs 14:5.

50. Rotenstreich, op. cit., p. 227.

51. Yossef Albo, Ikkarim I:19, translated and edited by Isaac Husik, Philadelphia, 1929, Vol. I, p. 165.

52. Pensee 233, Pensees op. cit., pp. 81-82.

53. Rotenstreich, op. cit., p. 227.

54. "Mu'tazila"; Guide of the Perplexed, Pt. III, ch. 17, op. cit., p. 468.

55. Guide, Pt. I, ch. 50, op. cit., p. 111, vide also above.

56. Jerusalem, op. cit., p. 97, emphasized in the original.

57. Critique of Pure Reason, op. cit., p. 29, emphasized in the original.

58. Immanuel Kant, Religion within the limits of reason alone; New York: Harper Torchbooks, 1960, p. 98

59. Guide of the Perplexed, Pt. III, ch. 17, op. cit., pp. 466-467.

60. G.W.F. Hegel, Vorlesungen ueber die Philosophie der Religion, ed. Georg Lasson, 2 Baende; Hamburg: Felix Meiner Verlag, 1966 (1925).

61. Kaufmann Kohler, Jewish Theology, systematically and historically considered, New York: Macmillan, 1923 (1918); in 1958 Ktav Publishing House, New York, published a new photomechanic edition.

62. F. Rosenzweig, Atheistische Theologie, Kleinere Schriften, op. cit., pp. 278-290.

63. Bertrand Russell, A Free Man's Worship, in: Mysticism and Logic and other Essays, London: George Allen & Unwin Ltd., 1959, pp. 49-53.

64. Eugene G. Borowitz, Liberal Jewish Theology in a time of uncertainty, a holistic approach, CCAR Yearbook for 1977.

65. J. Rosenthal, Hiwi al-Balkhi: A comparative study, 1949.

66. Republic, Book II, The Dialogues of Plato, op. cit., vol. I, p. 643.

67. Yehuda Abarbanel (Leone Ebreo), Dialoghi d'Amore, 2nd dialogue; vide the scientific Hebrew edition by Menachem Dorman, Jerusalem: Bialik Institute, 1983, p. 266.

68. Guide of the Perplexed, Pt. I, ch. 68, op. cit., p. 163.

69. Sinai Ucco, Der Gottesbegriff in der Philosophie Hermann Cohens (1929); a condensed version of that dissertation serves as introduction to the Hebrew edition of Religion and Reason from the sources of Judaism; Jerusalem. Bialik Institute in cooperation with the Leo Baeck Institute, 1971, p. 17.

70. "He (the first man) denied God"; Babylonian Talmud, Sanhedrin 38b, translation of I. Schachter, Soncino Press.

71. Encyclopedia Judaica, Jerusalem: Keter Publishing House, 1971, vol. 15, p. 1106.

72. Abraham Geiger, Einleitung in das Studium der juedischen Theologie, Nachgelassene Schriften, Berlin 1875, Band II, p. 3.

73. ibid., p. 4.

74. ibid., p. 5.

75. Maimonides employs the expression "lightning flash", Guide of the Perplexed, Pt. I, introduction, op. cit., p. 7; vide also above.

76. Among others, this problem was treated by Arthur Koestler in The Act of Creation, New York: The Macmillan Press, 1964.

77. Geiger in a review on S.R. Hirsch's book "Horeb"; Wissenschaftliche Zeitschrift fuer juedische Theologie, 4, Band, p. 377 ff.

78. Eugene G. Borowitz, How can a Jew speak of faith today?, Philadelphia: The Westminster Press, 1968, p. 25.

79. Geiger, Jewish Theology (note 72), op. cit., p. 7.

80. Eugene G. Borowitz, A new Jewish Theology in the making, Philadelphia: The Westminster Press, 1967, p. 52.

81. J.G. Fichte, Erste und Zweite Einleitung in die Wissenschaftslehre; Hamburg: Felix Meiner Verlag, 1961 (1920), p. 21.

82. Ludwig Wittgenstein, op. cit.

83. Herberg described this turning-point in an essay, having a character of spiritual autobiography: Will Herberg, From Marxism to Judaism: Jewish belief as a dynamic of social action, in: Arthur Cohen (ed.), Arguments and Doctrines, New York: Harper and Row, 1970, pp. 98-113.

84. Geiger, op. cit., p. 8.

85. ibid., pp. 27-28.

86. ibid., p. 29.

87. Leviticus, 4:15.

88. Yoma I, ch. 5, The Mishnah, op. cit., p. 163.

89. Berakoth 11a, The Babylonian Talmud, op. cit., Zera'im, p. 60; in the English translation the word "elders" is missing.

90. Kiddushim 32b, The Babylonian Talmud, op. cit., Nashim Vol. IV, p. 159.

91. Aboth 1:1, The Mishnah, op. cit., p. 446.

92. Shabbath 112b, The Babylonian Talmud, op. cit., Moed Vol. I, p. 549.

93. Geiger, Jewish Theology, op. cit., p. 35.

94. Moshe Schwarcz, Jewish Thought and General Culture, Tel Aviv: Schocken, 1976 (Hebrew), p. 116 ff.; E.G. Borowitz, op. cit., p. 63.

PART THREE

1. John Murray Cuddihy, The Ordeal of Civility: Freud, Marx, Levi-Strauss and the Jewish struggle with modernity, New York: Basic Books, 1974.

1a. The formulation of this problem according to the four questions of Isaac Yisraeli I have borrowed from Prof. Shalom Rosenberg; <u>vide</u> his remarks on Jewish Philosophy in: <u>Revelation, Faith, Reason</u>: A collection of Papers, Ramat Gan: Bar Ilan University, 1976, p. 158.

2. vide: Ze'ev Levy, The Impact of Jewish Influences on Spinoza's Philosophy, in: <u>Spinoza Studies - Three Hundred Years in Memoriam</u>, ed. by Ze'ev Levy and Michael Strauss (Hebrew), Haifa: The University of Haifa Press, 1978, pp. 147-165.

3. Vide: Ze'ev Levy, Spinoza's Interpretation of Judaism, A concept and its influence on Jewish thought (Hebrew), 2nd enlarged edition, Tel Aviv: Sifriat-Poalim Publishing House, 1983.

4. Abraham Isaac Hacohen Kook, Eder Hajaquar iqu've hatzon 1908, new edition by the Rav Kook Institute, Jerusalem, 1967, p. 40.

5. Some of these problems were discussed by Prof. Ya'akov Levinger of Tel Aviv University in the symposium on Jewish Philosophy, organized by Bar Ilan University in 1973; <u>vide</u> Revelation, Faith, Reason <u>op. cit.</u>, p. 148.

6. <u>ibid.</u>, p. 149.

7. Encyclopedia Judaica, <u>op. cit.</u>, vol. 13, p. 416.

8. Isaac Husik, A history of medieval Jewish Philosophy, New York: Meridian Books, 1960 (1958), p. 432.

9. Isadore Twersky, Harry Austryn Wolfson (1877-1974), <u>American Jewish Yearbook</u>, 1976, p. 102.

10. Leon D. Stitskin, Jewish Philosophy, A Study in Personalism; Brooklyn: Yeshiva University Press, 1976, p. 8, p. 10.

11. Felix Weltsch, What is Jewish Philosophy?, <u>Iyyun</u>, A Hebrew Philosophical Quarterly, Jerusalem: Hebrew University, Vol. 1, No. 1, 1951.

12. Jossef Klausner, Philosophers and Thinkers (Hebrew), Jerusalem, 1941, p. 70.

13. Alexander Altmann, Judaism and World Philosophy, in: Louis Finkelstein (ed), <u>The Jews, their history, culture and religion</u>, Philadelphia, 1960, vol. II, p. 955.

14. Ssimha Bunim Urbach, The Philosophy of Henri Bergson (Hebrew), Ramat Gan, Bar-Orian Publishing House, 1970.

15. Vide: Ze'ev Levy, Bergson and Judaism, Iyyunim behinuch (Studies in Education), Haifa University, No. 10, February 1976, pp. 17-34 (Hebrew).

16. Stanley Maron, Durkheim and Jewish Tradition, Molad, Vol. V. 29-30, 1974., pp. 626-633, the same: Scientific ideology of assimilation, Shdemoth 57, 1975, pp. 56-60 (Hebrew).

16a. Solomon Ibn-Gabirol, The Fountain of Life, translated by H.E. Wedeck, Introduction by T.E. James, New York, 1962.

16b. The Kingly Crown, translated by Bernard Lewis, London, 1961.

17. J. Klatzkin, Probleme des modernen Judentums, 1918; Krisis und Entscheidung im Judentum, 1921.

18. "Kera'im" (1924), "Zutoth" (1925), "Tehumim" (1928), "Ketavim" (Writings), 1953. An English-language volume of his aphorisms appeared in 1943 under the title In Praise of Wisdom.

19. "Mishnat Rishonim" ("The studies of the first ones"), 1925; "Mishnat Aharonim" ("The studies of the last ones"), 1952.

20. Ought to be mentioned in this connection his four volume Treasure of philosophical terms, 1928-1933, his Anthology of Hebrew Philosophy, 1926, and his biographical index of the authors of Hebrew philosophical books.

21. Revelation, Faith, Reason, op. cit., p. 155.

22. The example is from Sol Roth, Science and Religion, in: Stitskin, Studies in Torah Judaism, op. cit., (2nd part, note 12), p. 532.

23. Randall, op. cit., p. 9; Sol Roth, ibid.,

24. Compare with Kuhn, The Structure of scientific revolutions, op. cit.,

24a. Guide of the Perplexed, Pt. II, ch. 37, op. cit., p. 374.

25. Guide of the Perplexed, Pt. I, introduction, op. cit., p. 7.

26. Hakuzari, I: 71ff., op. cit., p. 55.

27. Talmud Yerushalmi, Berakhot 85b.

28. Midrash Rabba, Vol. XIV, 12, Numbers rabba, op. cit., p. 623.

29. Samson Raphael Hirsch, The Nineteen Letters of Ben-Uziel, translated by B. Drachman, New York, Bloch Publishing Co., second letter (pp. 13-15),

tenth letter (pp. 102-105), eighteenth letter (194 ff.), nineteenth letter (pp. 215-218).

30. Compare with the introductory remarks of the first editor of Gersonides' The wars of the Lord; vide also above, part II, ch. 3.

31. Leon Roth, Is there a Jewish Philosophy? Chapter 1 of Jewish Philosophy and Philosophers, ed. by Raymond Goldwater, London: The Hillel Foundation, 1962, p. 8.

32. ibid.,.

33. Vide Z. Levy, The impact of Jewish influences on Spinoza's philosophy, op. cit.,.

34. In his introduction to the English edition of the Ethics in 1910, quoted by A. Altmann, Judaism and World Philosophy, op. cit., p. 661.

35. I have treated this issue more at length in the above-mentioned paper (note 33).

36. Deuteronomy 16:20.

37. Vide: Martin Buber, The silent question: about Henri Bergson and Simone Weil, Judaism, April, 1952.

38. Abodah Zarah 72a, The Babylonian Talmud, op. cit., Nezikim Vol. I, pp. 352-353.

39. The Autobiography of Solomon Maimon, London: The East and West Library, 1954 (the ten chapters on Maimonides' philosophy are not included in the English edition).

40. Solomon Maimon: Giv'at Hamore. New edition with notes and indexes by S.H. Bergman and N. Rotenstreich, Jerusalem: Publications of the Israel Academy of Sciences and Humanities, 1965.

41. Vide also Levinger, Revelation, Faith, Reason, op. cit., p. 147.

42. ibid., p. 150.

43. Vide also Sermoneta, ibid., pp. 153-154.

44. Leo Baeck, The Essence of Judaism, London: The Macmillan Co., 1936.

45. Kleinere Schriften, op. cit., p. 41.

46. ibid., p. 34.

47. ibid., p. 33.

48. Vide also Weltsch, What is Jewish Philosophy?, op. cit., p. 66.

49. Eliezer Schweid, Homeland and a land of promise (Hebrew), Tel Aviv: Am Oved Publishers, 1979, p. 53.

50. Weltsch, op. cit., p. 67.

51. Baba Mezi'a 59b, The Babylonian Talmud, op. cit., Nezikim Vol. I, pp. 352-3.

52. Leon Roth, Is there a Jewish philosophy?, op. cit., p. 11.

53. Akhiassaf Publishing House, Warsaw 1897, 2 volumes.

54. Leon Roth, ibid.,.

55. Sh. Rosenberg, Revelation, Faith, Reason, op. cit., p. 160.

56. ibid.,.

57. ibid.,.

58. Emil Fackenheim, The revealed morality of Judaism and modern thought, in: Menachem Marc Kellner, Contemporary Jewish Ethics, New York: The Sanhedrin Press, pp. 62-63. The problem of the two truths will be discussed in the next part.

PART FOUR

1. Rosenberg, Revelation, Faith, Reason, op. cit., p. 159.

2. op. cit., p. 158.

3. Samuel Hugo Bergman, Men and Ways - Philosophical Essays, Jerusalem: Bialik Institute, 1967, p. 87 (hebrew).

4. Rosenzweig, Stern, op. cit., 2nd part, p. 9.

5. Julius Guttmann, Philosophies of Judaism, The History of Jewish Philosophy from Biblical Times to F. Rosenzweig, New York: Anchor Books, Doubleday, 1966, p. 3.

6. Megillah 9b, The Babylonian Talmud, op. cit., Moed Vol. IV, p. 50.

7. M. Buber, Good and Evil, op. cit., pp. 3-60.

7a. Exodus 21:29; in the Mishnah: "An ox ... that is accounted an attested danger," Baba Kamma 2:4, The Mishnah, op. cit., p. 333.

8. Compare for instance: Margarete Susman, Der juedische Geist, Berlin: Biko Verlag, 1934, p. 48.

9. J.G. Herder, Abhandlung ueber den Urspruch der Sprache, Halle a.d.S: Verlag Otto Hendel, 1788.

10. M. Susman, op. cit., pp. 55-57.

11. Israel Efros, Ancient Jewish Philosophy (hebrew), Tel Aviv: Dvir Co., 1965.

12. Vide: David Neumark, Essays in Jewish Philosophy, Amsterdam: Philo Press, 1971, p. 14.

13. Leibowitz, Judaism, the Jewish People and the State of Israel, op. cit., p. 310.

14. Genesis 9:5.

15. Deuteronomy 23:21.

16. Samuel II 12:10.

17. Biblical Encyclopedia (hebrew), Jerusalem: Bialik Institute, 1962, Vol. IV, p. 843.

18. Baba Kamma 84a, The Babylonian Talmud, op. cit., Nezikin Vol. I, pp. 477-480.

19. Guide of the Perplexed, op. cit., Pt. III, chapters 22-23.

20. Vide: Saul Lieberman, How much Greek in Jewish Palestine?; in: A. Altmann (ed.) Biblical and other studies, Cambridge: Harvard University Press, 1963, pp. 123-141.

21. Harry Austryn Wolfson, Philo - Foundations of religious philosophy in Judaism, Christianity and Islam; Cambridge: Harvard University Press, 1968, (1947), Vol. I, pp. 91-92.

22. Berakoth 33b, The Babylonian Talmud, op. cit., Zera'im, p. 210.

23. The Kuzari, I: 53, II: 66, op. cit., p. 53, p. 124.

24. Guide of the Perplexed, Pt. I, ch. 70, op. cit., p. 174, emphasized in the original.

25. op. cit., Pt. I, ch. 71, p. 175.

26. Vide: H. Guyot, Les reminiscences de Philo le Juif chez Plotin, Paris, 1906.

27. Nachman Krochmal, More Nebuche ha-z'man. The writings of Nachman Krochmal, edited by S. Rawidowicz, 2nd enlarged edition, Waltham, Mass. 1961, pp. 176 ff. Krochmal calls him by the Hebrew name "Yedid'ya", i.e., "Lover of God" ("Philo" = "lover").

27a. Neander, a Jew whose name originally was David Mendel, converted to Christianity for fundamental religious reasons and became one of the important historians of the Church.

28. A. Altmann, Judaism and World Philosophy, op. cit., p. 984.

29. H.A. Wolfson, Philo, 2 volumes, op. cit.,; Norman Bentwich, Philo-Judaeus of Alexandria, Philadelphia 1940 (1910); E.R. Goodenough, An Introduction to Philo Judaeus, 1962 (1940).

30. Vide also: Leo Strauss, Persecution and the Art of Writing; Glencoe: The Free Press, 1952, p. 8.

30a. For example, Christian philosophers in Europe learned about the Islamic Kalam primarily from the critical description of that school in Maimonides's Guide of the Perplexed.

31. The Philosophy of G.E. Moore, ed. by P.A. Schilpp, New York: The Library of Living Philosophers, 1952, p. 14.

32. Theaetetus; The Dialogues of Plato, op. cit., Vol. II, p. 157.

33. Metaphysics Bk. I, ch. 2, 982b12-13, The Basic Works of Aristotle, op. cit., p. 692.

34. ibid.,.

35. Genesis 3:19.

36. Vide also Rotenstreich, the Scope of Philosophy, op. cit., pp 103-104.

37. These excerpts are quoted in: Arthur Koestler, The Act of Creation, New York: Macmillan Press, 1964, p. 258.

38. Baruch Spinoza, Definition of the Emotions, 4; The Ethics and Selected Letters, op cit. (Part II, note 20), p. 143.

39. Immanuel Kant, The Critique of Judgment, Oxford: Clarendon Press, 1964 (1952), 2nd part, p. 11, emphasized in the original.

40. R. Descartes, Discourse on Method, op. cit., p. 17; vide also Meditations, ibid., p. 54.

41. Rotenstreich, op. cit., p. 106

42. ibid., p. 107.

43. G.W.F. Hegel, Vorlesungen ueber die Geschichte der Philosophie, II, Stuttgart: Saemtliche Werke XVIII, 1928, p. 68.

44. Rotenstreich, ibid., and particularly pp. 101-108.

45. Guide of the Perplexed, Pt. I, Introduction, op. cit., p. 5, my emphasis.

46. Samuel Hugo Bergmann quotes most of these examples in his book: Science and Faith - Seven chapters on their mutual relationship (hebrew); Tel Aviv: Makhbaroth le-sifruth, 1945, p. 89.

47. TPT, op. cit., p. 164.

48. Maimonides' letter to Rabbi Yonathan Hacohen (from Lunel); The Responses of Maimonides, ed. by Abraham Haim Freeman, Jerusalem: Mekitze Nirdamim Publishing House, 1934, pp. LVIII-LIX.

49. Proverbs 6:24-25.

50. Saad'ya Gaon, Sefer ha-emunoth veha-deoth, Leipzig, 1859, pp. 14-15.

51. Guide of the Perplexed, Pt. I, Introduction, op. cit., pp. 11-12.

52. op. cit., p. 5.

53. op. cit., Pt. I, ch. 15, p. 41; vide. also above, Part one, note 42.

54. op. cit., pp. 11-12.

54a. op. cit., p. 6.

55. Solomon Maimon, Givat Hamore, op. cit., p. 27, p. 49.

56. Hagigah 11b-12a, The Babylonian Talmud, op. cit., Moed IV, pp. 60-61., pp. 88-89.

57. Hagigah 14b, op. cit., pp. 90-91, vide., also above, part one.

58. Sanhedrin, XI, 90a, The Babylonian Talmud, op. cit., Nezikin III, pp. 601-602.

59. Guide of the Perplexed, Pt. I, Introduction, op. cit., p. 6, emphasized in the original.

60. Gorgias, The Dialogues of Plato, op. cit., Vol. I, p. 545 , p. 547.

61. Compare among others: L. Strauss, Persecution and the Art of Writing, op. cit.,.

62. Guide of the Perplexed, Pt. I. Introduction, op. cit., p. 5, my emphasis.

63. ibid.,.

64. ibid., Pt. I, ch. 35, pp. 79-80.

65. ibid., p. 81.

66. Quoted by A.L. Motzkin, On the Interpretation of Maimonides (hebrew), Iyyun, Hebrew Philosophical Quarterly, Jerusalem, Vol. 28, No. 2-3, 1978, p. 187.

67. "Pillars of silver" and "Settings of silver"; the author alludes in all his books to his name (Kasspi - "silvery"); the name of the second book also hints at Maimonides' metaphor on "apples of gold in settings of silver" (vide. above).

68. vide. also above.

69. Quoted by L. Strauss, op. cit., p. 29.

70. Letter LXVIII of September 1675; The Correspondence of Spinoza, translated and edited by A. Wolf; London: Frank Cass & Co. Ltd., 1966, pp. 334-335.

71. R. Descartes, Discourse on Method, op. cit., p. 32.

72. op. cit., pp. 12-13.

73. TPT, op. cit., p. 11, p. 265-266.

74. Sir William Blackstone, Commentaries IV, ch. 6.

75. Julius Guttmann, Religion and Science in medieval and modern thought, in: Studies in Jewish Thought, an Anthology of German Jewish Scholarship, ed. by Alfred Jospe, Detroit: A publication of the Leo Baeck Institute, Wayne State University Press, 1981, p. 292.

76. Leo Strauss, The mutual relationship of theology and philosophy (hebrew). Iyyun, Hebrew Philosophical Quarterly, Vol. 5, January 1954, p. 117.

77. Sanhedrin XI: 5, The Mishnah, op. cit., p. 400.

78. Thomas Hobbes, Leviathan, or the matter, forme and power of a Commonwealth, ecclesiastical and civil; Oxford: Basil Blackwell, 1960, Pt. III, CH. XXXII, pp. 243-244.

79. Martin Buber, Eclipse of God, Studies in the relation between religion and philosophy, New York: Harper & Brothers, 1952, p. 129.

80. ibid., p. 92.

81. ibid., p. 129.

82. Guide of the Perplexed, Pt. II, ch. 29, op. cit., p. 345.

83. ibid., Pt. III, ch. 52, p. 529.

84. Rosenzweig, Stern, op. cit., 2nd part, p. 9.

85. Albert Einstein, Out of my later years, London, 1950, pp. 26-27.

86. David Hume, An inquiry concerning human understanding, in: Hume on human nature and the understanding, New York: Collier Books, 1962, p. 133.

87. Will Herberg, Judaism and Modern Man, New York: Meridian Books, 1975, (1951), pp. 246-250.

88. Julius Guttman, Religion and Science, op. cit., (note 75). The paragraph dealing with this issue is, however, omitted from the English translation.

89. I. Kant, Critique of Pure Reason, op. cit., p. 29, emphasized in the original, vide. also above, part two.

90. Ludwig Steinheim, Die Offenbarung nach dem Lehrbegriff der Synagoge, 4 volumes, 1835-1865, Frankfurt a.M./Hamburg-Altona.

91. Compare, among others: Felix Weltsch, Gnade und Freiheit - Untersuchungen zum Problem des schoepferischen Willens in Religion und Ethik; K. Wolff Verlag Muenchen, 1920.

92. Guide of the Perplexed, Pt. I. Introduction, op. cit., p. 5, vide. above.

PART FIVE

1. Isaac Husik, "Jewish Philosophy", Philosophical Essays, 1952, p. 65.

1a. Vide Shlomo Pines, The philosophical sources of the "Guide of the Perplexed", in: Between Jewish and General Thought (hebrew), Jerusalem: Bialik Institute, 1977, pp. 105-106.

1b. "Eight Chapters", ch. VI, in: I. Twersky (ed.) A Maimonides Reader, New York, 1972, p. 378.

2. Guide of the Perplexed, Pt. III, ch. 17, op. cit., p. 469, my emphasis.

3. "The construction of Jewish history"; Heinrich Graetz, Die Konstruktion der juedischen Geschichte; Berlin: Schocken Verlag, 1936.

4. Jacob Bernard Agus, Dialogue and Tradition, The challenges of contemporary Judeo-Christian Thought, London, New York, Toronto: Abelard-Schuman, 1971, p. 215.

5. Aboth, 5:9, The Mishnah, op. cit., p. 456.

6. TPT, op. cit., p. 56.

7. Agus, op. cit., p. 178.

8. Origen, Against Celsus, IV, 23; quoted by Will Herberg, Judaism and modern Man, New York: Schocken Books, 1951, p. 262.

9. TPT, op. cit., ch. III, pp. 43-56.

10. ibid., p. 56.

11. Deuteronomy 7:7-8

12. Deuteronomy 9: 5-6

13. Will Herberg, The "Chosenness" of Israel and the Jew of today, in: Arguments and Doctrines, op. cit., p. 273.

14. Steven S. Schwarzschild, The Personal Messiah, Arguments and Doctrines, op. cit., p. 524.

15. ibid.

16. Vide also Schwarzschild, ibid., p. 525.

17. ibid., p. 533.

18. ibid.,.

19. ibid., p. 534.

20. Alfred North Whitehead, Adventures of Ideas, New York: The Free Press, London: Collier-Macmillan, 1933.

21. David Neumark, Geschichte der juedischen Philosophie des Mittelalters, 1907-1910, p. 5.

INDEX OF NAMES

Abarbanel Isaac — 3 175
Abarbanel Judah — 3 9 15 16 22 23 83 84 108 109 110 114 115 124 130 157 176 195 200 201
Abelard P. — 122
Abner of Burgos — 104
Abraham — 48 209 211
Adam and Eve — 152 211
Agus J. — 80 204
Ahad Ha'am — 109 137 206 210
Akiba, Rabbi — 39 168 197
Albertus Magnus — 110
Albo J. — 71 72 86 199
Alembert J. — 174
Alexander (the Great) — 207
Alexander S. — 107
Alon G. — 204
Altmann A. — 107 147
Amihai Y. — 9
Amir J. — 147
Anaxagoras — 174
Anselm of Canterbury — 72 84 85
Aquinas Thomas — 83 110 148 159
Aristotle — 3 4 14 17 21 25-29 31-33 35 47 75 83 84 89 101 103 110 114 115 120 121 136 138 143 147 152 155 157 160 167 173 174 187 195 198 199 207 218
Augustinus — 63 71
Averroes — 28 136 148 164 171 174 179 199
Avicenna — 174
Bacon F. — 21 153
Baeck L. — 80 94 122 201
Bala'am — 182
Bar-Hillel Y. — 67
Barth K. — 55
Beethoven L. — 9
Bentwich N. — 147
Bergmann H. — 44 47 48 54 55 72 81 91 138 217
Bergson H. — 22 101 107 116 117 130
Berkeley G. — 101 127
Berkowitz E. — 80
Bernays I. — 201 205
Bernfeld S. — 128 129
Bialik Ch. N. — 9
Blackstone W. — 175
Bloch E. — 213
Borochov B. — 99

Borowitz E.   80 89 90 94
Brahe Tycho   52
Brentano F.   91
Brod M.   80 122
Bruno G.   91 108 112 174
Brunschvicg L.   107
Buber   48 55 69 72 78 80 81 91 94
    97 99 109 110 115 117 123
    128 130 139 171 181 185 205
    209 210 213 214

Caesar J.   180
Callicles   168
Calvin J.   78
Camus A   173
Caro J.   11
Celsus   207 208
Chagall M.   57 58
Ciekowsky A.V.   32
Cohen A.A.   80
Cohen H.   5 18 80 85 101 109 111 115
    124 130 144 195 205 206 213
    214
Condillac E.B. de   114
Confucius   36 139
Copernicus N.   14 112
Crescas A.   175
Crescas H.   86 104 114 123 135 147 199
    201

Daehne A.F.   147
Dalton J.   35
Darwin Ch.   51 206 210
David   143 213 214
Derenbourg J.N.   87
Descartes R.   14 35 37 49 70 84 101 116
    127 153-155 175
Dewey J.   101 115
Dostoyewski F.M.   207
Du Bois Reymond E.   19
Duhem P.   53
Duns Scotus   78
Duran Profiat (Efodi)   175
Durkheim E.   107
Efros I.   129 141
Eichmann A.   33
Einstein A.   14 51 52 99 153 184
Eliezer, Rabbi   124
Elisha ben Abuyah   168
Empedocles   113
Epicurus   145
Euclid   119
Fackenheim E.   80 94 131 210
Falaquera Shem-Tov   4 175
(Al)-Farabi   4 28 44 199
Feuerbach L.   32 33 63 64 80 81 171

Fichte J.	32 91 101 127
Flew A.	69
Formstecher S.	80 115 136 205
Freud S.	98 153
Frischmann D.	213 220
Galilei G.	51 112 175
Gans D.	52 203
(El)-Gazali	78 114
Geiger A.	80 87-93 123 127 136 180 201 204 205
Gersonides	54 84 110 114 129 164
Goethe J.W.	9
Goldmann N.	109
Gordon A.D.	213
Graetz H.	203
Guedemann M.	122
Guttmann J.	81 127 129 139 147 179
Guttmann Y.	81
Hacohen I.M.	73
Halevy Judah	9 13 14 16 26 28 48 78 84 101 109 113 121-124 128 136 146 160 172 180 185 188 195 199 202
Hamann J.G.	205
Hammurabi	140 144
Harlap Y.M.	5
Harnack A.	122
Hegel G.W.F.	4-6 9-11 13 32 33 35 43-45 54 56 63 64 79 84 85 94 98 101 108 120 127 135 137 155 203 205 217 218
Heidegger, M.	98 153
Heine H.	104
Hemingway E.	9
Heraclitus	3
Herberg W.	80 91 185 227
Herder J.G.	114 140 205
Herodotus	207
Heschel A.Y.	80 94 99 214
Hess M.	32 104 117 206 208
Hillel (the Elder)	139
Hirsch S.	80 115 136 205 206 213
Hirsch S.R.	114 201 205
Hiwi al-Balkhi	81 163 199
Hobbes Th.	6 101 127 175 181
Homer	9
Hume D.	68 101 127
Husik I.	105 129 195
Husserl E.	44 91 101 107
Ibn Caspi J.	172

Ibn Daud A.	84 86 114
Ibn Ezra A.	81 114 128 147
Ibn Gabirol Sh.	9 14 16 25 101 108 109 114 121 124 127 128 130 147 191 195
Ibn Paquda Bahya	114 161 164 195
Ibn Tibbon S.	199
Ibn Verga S.	204
Immanuel Haromi	197
Isaac	48 209
Isaiah	144
Israeli I.	103 114 199 228
Jacob	48 209
Jacobi F.H.	71
James W.	71
Japhet	139
Jeremiah	146
Jesus	23 71 125 180 182 191 210
Joel M.	201
Jonah	181
Joseph	166
Joseph the Just	199
Josephus Flavius	180 203
Joshuah	93
Jost M.	87
Judah Arieh of Modena	123 197 200
Judah Maccabee	204
Jung C.	98
Kant I.	4 19 21 22 33 36 44 55 65 70 73 75-78 84 85 88 91 101 112 115 120 127 138 154 155 167 175 188 205 218
Kaplan M.M.	80 81 94 114
Kaufmann W.	38
Kepler J.	52
Kierkegaard S.	4 23 55 72 84 142
Kimhi D.	123
(El-) Kindi	103
Klatzkin J.	109 119
Klausner J.	107
Kohler K.	79 80
Konvitz M.	80
Kook A.I.	5 81 104 115 195 213
Krochmal N. (Ranak)	9 56 88 97 101 109 115 136 147 195 201 203-206 213
Kuhn Th. S.	6
Kurzweil B.	81
Lassalle F.	117
Lavater J.K.	71
Lavoisier A.L.	13 14

Lazarus M.	80 115
Leibniz G.W.	68 84 127 153 167
Leibowitz Y.	49 116 141
Leone Ebreo	see Abarbanel Judah
Leone Modena	see Judah Arieh Modena
Lessing G.E.	4 18 44 173 175
Levi ben Gerson	see Gersonides
Levi-Strauss C.	36 107
Locke J.	101 127 175
Loew Judah (Maharal)	28 33 51 52 115 197 200 203 212 224
Lotze R.L.	5
Luther M.	72
Luzzatto S.D.	59 101 114 128 195 201
Maharal	see Loew Judah
Maimon S.	19 84 109 167 175 195 198 201
Maimonides	3-5 9 13-15 21 22 27-28 30 43 44 47 48 52 63 64 67 69 71 75 77 78 84 86-88 94 97 101 109-111 113 114 118-123 128 130 136 140 141 144-146 148 149 156 159-161 163-176 181 183 184 187 191 195 199 200 202-204 228 233 235
Mann Th.	9
Mapu A.	220
Marcel G.	130
Marx K.	30 32 33 104 117 124
Mary	182
Maxwell J.C.	153
Mendelssohn M.	4 7 16 23 30 68 71 76 84 86 89 92 104 109-111 115 119 122 123 130 140 149 167 175 180 184 185 198 201-203 208 213
Midas	48
Mohammed	191
Montaigne M.	127
Montesquieu Ch.	173-175
Moore G.E.	151
Moses	89 93 111-113 148
Munk S.	87 104 108 129
Narboni Moshe	136
Napoleon	198
Neander A.	147 233
Neher Andre	201 224
Neumark D.	128 129 147 218

Neusner J.	80
Newton I.	14 35 51 89
Nicolas of Cusa	18 19 55 135
Nietzsche F.	33
Noah	142
Otto R.	55
Pascal B.	48 55 72 78 84 142
Perelman Ch.	118
Philo	105 109 110 114 115 119 124 129 130 135 136 147 149 166 203
Picasso P.	9
Pines S.	28 135 165 174
Plato	3 9 14 16 17 23 26-28 31 33 83 89 101 115 136 138 140-142 146 147 152 157 166-168 173 174 195 218
Plotinus	113 147
Pope A.	89
Popper K.	6 37 186
Protagoras	174
Pythagoras, Pythagoreans	3 30 147
Rabelais F.	173
Randall J.H.	51
Rappaport Sh. Y.	87
Rashi	114 128
Reichenbach H.	5
Rembrandt van Rijn	9
Rosenberg Sh.	129 130 137
Rosenstock E.	55
Rosenzweig F.	6 10 23 31 33 38 48 55-57 63-65 70 72 78 80 81 84 91 94 97 99 101 109 110 115 122 128 130 136 138 183 185 195 204-206 212-214
Rotenstreich N.	44 45 49 70 71 155
Roth L.	114 115 128 129
Rousseau J.-J.	175
Rubinstein R.	80 210
Rufeisen O. (Brother Daniel)	103
Russell B.	5 6 29 35 36 39 40 91 101
Saadya Gaon	81 83 87 101 103 114 116 130 163 164 183 187 199
Santayana G.	116
Sartre J.-P.	39 103 124 173 181
Savonarola G.	23
Schechter S.	80
Schelling F.W.	84 91 101 127 153 205
Schleiermacher F.	55
Schopenhauer A.	22 108 153 155

Schwarcz M.	81 94
Schwarzschild S.S.	80 214
Schweid E.	123
Sermoneta J.	111
Shakespeare W.	9
Shem	139
Shlonsky A.	9
Siger de Brabant	164
Socrates	16-19 25 27 31 155 168 173 174
Soloveitzik J.D.	94
Soubirous Bernadette	182
Spencer H.	206 210
Spinoza B.	6 9 14 16 22 30 31 44 52 54 55 59 63 77 83-85 91 101 104 108-110 115 116 119 124 128 130 135 138 140 143 147 153 155 157 159 167 171-176 188 199-201 203 204 208 209
Steinberg M.	80
Steinheim L.	55 80 115 188 195 205 206
Steinthal H.	80 115
Stitskin L.D.	105
Strauss D.F.	80
Strauss L.	169 172 174 180
Susman M.	80
Swift J.	173
Tell Wilhelm	152
Tertullian	71 85
Tillich P.	55
Tolstoy L.	23
Toynbee A.	210
Urbach S.	107 117
Voltaire F.M.	127 175
Weltsch F.	80 107 123
Wessely N.H.	201
Whitehead A.N.	91 136 215
Wiener M.	80
Wiesel E.	210
William of Occam	78
Wittgenstein L.	29 91 101
Wolff Ch.	84
Wolfson H.A.	105 135 145 147
Xenophanes	83
Zunz L.	87 88

INDEX OF SUBJECTS

Absolute	4 22 43 181 217
Absolute Spirit	43 63 79 204
Aesopian Language	38
Aesthetics	9 21-23 36 57-60 100 118 136 217
Agnostic, Agnosticism	72 77 86 155 188
"Agudat Israel"	214
Allegory, allegorical	119 122 152 166 167 183 185
"Allegory of the Cave"	27 30 167 173
Analytic Philosophy	5 7 58 61 98 120 151
Anthropomorphism	44 64 75 77 83 122 169 170 192
Antisemite, Antisemitism	98 122 143
Apologetic(s)	107 117 121 122 163 192 203
Apocrypha	211
Aporia	17 18
Arab Philosophy	27 78 100 135 148 159 187 199
Aramaic	38 145 165
Art	9 13 22 23 31 43 58 98 111 127 128 153 195
"Ash'arya"	78
Atheist, Atheism	64 70 80 81 145
Attribute(s) (of God)	47 64 83 84 123 192 203
"Aufhebung"	10 11 98
Autonomy	75-78 160 184
Belief	64 67-69 71 76 112 123 154 156 164 165 170 182 185 188 199 210
"Beth Hillel and Beth Shammai"	93
Bible	4 6 9 15 28 44 52 54 61 63 71 76 79 83 93 98 101 103 104 110 113 116 118 129 135 137 138 140-145 148 151 152 156 157 159-161 163 165-167 169 177 179-180 183 184 197 203 208 209 211
Cabbalah	38 110 175 199 200
Categorical Imperative	44 77
Catholicism	58 72 93 107 180
Chosen People	see Election of Israel
Christianity	15 23 44 51 76 80 83 86 92 103 104 122 124 159 160 168 191 199 205 207 213
"Cogito"	49 155
Cognition, Cognitivity	25 55 57-61 65 68 73 86 87 187 221

Commandment(s), religious, divine	15 23 45 49 51 55 58 75 77
	83 84 94 116 124 137 138 140
	142 143 160 163 164 185 192
	197 199 201 203 209 211
Confusion	151 155 156
Conservative (movement)	11 198
"Copernican Revolution"	75
Copula	59-61 63 65
Creator, Creation	15 28 44 47 49 57 60 65
	83-85 87 88 112 113 141 142
	145 171 182 183 185 188 191
	192
"Credo quia absurdum"	71
"Credo ut intelligam"	72
Criticism	6 17 31 37 39 136 142 155
	166 176 184 185 200 209
Deism	84 149 180
Deity	15 19 27 48 55 63 64 73 75
	83 108
Determinism	51 76 91 145 183
Diachronic	10 136 195
Dialectic	4 5 10 11 17 36 217 218
Diaspora	109 123 124 137 201 203-205
	207 209 212
Dispersion	see Diaspora
Divine Will	4 78 163 191
Divine truth	45 163 187
Divinity	43 44 48 64 83 192
Dogma(s), Dogmatism, Dogmatics	17 18 37 40 51 83 85 86 90
	152 159 164 187
Doubt	39 49 154 155
"Ecclesiastes"	18 141 144 160
Election of Israel	124 137 207-211 215
Emancipation	109 197 198 211 213 214
Enlightenment	4 44 55 76 84 85 88 123 149
	156 180 197 204 206
Epistemology	21-23 58-60 63 75 77 88 175
	203 217
Esoteric(s)	86 165-168 171 173-177

Essence (of God)	64 68 123 170 192 203
Ethics	21-23 25 31 36 58 65 77 83 92 100 112 136 137 143 145 148 160 161 165 175 181 203 210 217
Exile	23 104 111 137 197 201 204 211 212
Existentialism, Existentialist	25 31 39 78 80 99 120 121 129 149 205 214
Exoteric(s)	165 167 171 176
Faith	6 45 48 49 51 55-58 60 63-65 67-73 75 77 84-87 90-91 114 121 124 125 142 143 145 157 159 163 164 167-170 179-182 184 185 187 188 197 201 202209 214
Freedom	see Free Will
Free Will	44 47 76 77 83 123 125 145 152 183 188
Gnosticism	110
God, Godhead	3 4 16 18 21-23 28 31 32 43-45 47-49 51 53-55 57 58 60 63-65 68-70 72 73 75-80 83-91 104 105 113 113 116 122 124 128 129 138 139 141-145 154 157 160 164 166 168-171 173 180-186 188 191 199 200 202-204 207-210 214
God's Existence	48 49 55 69-73 75 77 80 83 84 90 123 184 185
Greek Philosophy	3 4 15 18 71 98-100 115 120 123 136 139 141-146 148 151 153 155 157 160 195 197 199 201
"Halakhah"	30 85 103 116 118 124 137 138 146 156 159 161 168 176 179
"Hasidej Ashkenaz"	121
Hasidism	99 100 110 117 120 206
"Haskalah"	see Enlightenment
Hasmoneans	180 204

Hebrew	9 13 15 30 63 67 85 98 105 107-111 113 117-120 126 146 165 176 184 212
Hellenism, Hellenistic	114 121 140 141 146 147 149 166 203
Hermeneutics	83 117 141 144 166 175
Heterodoxy	171 174
Heteronomy	75 78 160
Holocaust	31 210
Holy Writ(ings)	see Bible
Idea	4 10 11 38 43 84 89 93 105 115 128 140 166 214 217
Idealism	10 84 91 112 214
Idealism (Classical German)	120 149
Idolatry	22 23 58 144 160 170 204 205 211
"Ignorantiae asylum"	54 188
Immortality (Survival of the soul)	45 76 77 83
Intellect, Intelligence	13 18 19 22 25 28 29 142 156
"Intellectual Love of God"	16
Islam	58 86 93 123 148 159 191 197 233
Israel (People, Land of)	3 21 31 48 51 70 104 105 123 124 128 129 137-140 142 143 161 180 184 200 204 208-212
Israel (State of)	73 80 93 98 100 101 104 107 108 137 199 204 206 212 214
"Jacob's Ladder"	27 167 203
Jewish People	31 53 104 111 123 127 130 139 141 142 204 206 207 208 212 214
Jewish Religion	5 86 87 111 113-115 123 145 148 156 191 197 202 213
"Job"	142 144
Judaism	11 15 23 28 44 49 51 58 61 72 76 84-86 88 89 92-94 97 99 100 103-105 107-109 111-131 136 137 141 143-144 146 157 156 159 160 163 168 180 184 185 191 192 198-201 203-208 210 214
Kabbalah	see Cabbalah
Kalam	76 114 135 147 232

Karaite(s)	104 163 198 199
Knowledge	3 5 10 13 15 19 25-28 31 36 44 45 48 51 52 56 61 67-71 75 77 78 83 92 93 152-155 159 164 167 187 188
Knowledge of God	16 45 55 69 128 129 157 188
Language	23 57 97 98 108 109 140
Law (Divine)	3 28 75 84 111 116 125 140 156 166 169 184 200 202 208
Linguistic Philosophy	5 22 118 217
Linguistics	6 36 59 67 110 118
Logic	5 21 22 35 57 59 60 64 68 69 100 115 118 136 137 156 164 185 217
Logical Empiricism, Logical Positivism	14 25 39 58 98
Maccabees	see Hasmoneans
Man	29 31 47-49 64 72 73 76 77 80 83 105 112 113 128 138 141 147 155 160 182-186
Marxism, Marxist	99 120 213
Messiah, Messianism	71 207 213-215
Metaphysics, Metaphysical	21-23 43 84 138 155 171 176 185 187 192 212 217
Methodology	35-37 103 107 112 118 119 136 155 195 217
Middle Ages	43 47 54 55 71 72 75 83 86 87 90 94 105 110 114 118 121 129 141 145 148 157 159 161 191 197 198 202
Midrash	113 119 137 142 144-146 182 211
Miracle(s)	83 123 124 138 179 182-185 215
Mishna	118 139 145 180
Mission (of Israel)	205 207 208 210 211 215
Monotheism	79 89 139 142 144 146 179 191 205
Monotheism, Ethical	205 208
Morals, Morality	27 54 57-59 75 77 78 92 137 142 143 161 207
Moral Law	75-77
Mosaic Law	139 148
"Mu'tazala"	75
Mysticism	16 85 147 153 157 168
Myth	22 23 115 145 152 180 182
Mythology	48 91 98 145 151 152
Nature	4 15 19 21 51 113 116 182 187 191 208
Neo-Kantianism	120

Neo-Platonism	14 25 75 103 110 113 114 120 121 147 157 195 198
"Neturei Karta"	214
New Testament	76 98 182
Noema and Noesis	44
Old Testament	see Bible
Ontological proof	70 84
Ontology	21 23 65
Oral Law	see Talmud
Orthodoxy	11 81 179 180 198 201 202 213 214
Paganism	44 205
Pantheism	83 84 116 147
Phenomenology	44 107
Philosophy of History	22 23 127 203
Philosophy of Religion	22 23 43 47 79 86 90 111
Philosophy of Science	6 22 36 127 128 186 217
Political Philosophy	22 32 35 203
Practice, Praxis	25-27 31 32 89 90
Predestination	83 145
Pre-Socratics	25 30 83
Principle(s) of Faith	51 70 71 83 86 88 145 159 160 176
Prophet(s), Prophecy	28 43 47 63 83 88 93 107 112 113 117 123 138 141 146 163 165-167 179-181 183-185 188 191 200 208 213 214
Protestantism	59 72 180
"Proverbs"	141 160 165 167
Providence (Divine)	53 55 72 75 76 78 83 84 112 124 144 145 168 182 200 207 210
Rationalism	31 37 72 114 141 142 159 179 183
Reality	14 32 51-53 63 67 68 84 93 188
Reason	13 22 23 25 26 31 53 55 59 71-72 75-79 85-87 110 114 131 132 142 149 156 157 159 163 166 167 171 176 177 179 185 186 187 188 203 206
Reconstructionism	81 198
Redemption	83 211-214
Reform (movement)	11 79 198 201 213 214
Religion	18 22 27 31 32 43-45 47-49 51-59 64 71 75-80 84-87 90 92 93 104 111 112 114 115 121 130 137 156 161 163 169 171 174 180 182 184 187 191 192 197 199 201 209

Religious Language	57 59-61 63 65 69
Religiosity	44 45 71 111 114 164 168 169
Renaissance	13 23 31 52 110 124 147 157 174 175 197 200 201
Revelation	4 23 28 37 47 53 54 56 75-77 83-88 91 113 131 156 157 159 163 164 179-182 184-189 191 192 201-203 206
Reward and Punishment	44 77 183 184
(The) Sages	3 15 17 18 39 49 54 86 100 118 124 139 142-146 156 168 169 181 183 197 199 200 211
Samaritan(s)	104
Scepticism	see Skepticism
Scholastic(s), Scholasticism	54 69 72 85 87 118 148 159 164 187
Science(s)	6 10 13 14 18 25-27 29-31 35-37 47 51-54 55 87 88 89 112-114 128 136 146 151 153 159 164 166 169 181 185 186 187 195 214 224
Science of Judaism	92 93 114 136 203
Scripture	see Bible
Secular, Secularization	51 123 137 143 198 199 201 209 210 213
Septuagint	184
"Shulchan Arukh"	11 92
Skepticism	85 97 154 197
Socialism, Socialist	69 117 145 204 206
"Song of Songs"	141
Stoa, Stoic(ism)	120 147
Structuralism, Structuralist	166 175
Subject and Predicate	63-65
Synchronic	10 136
Talmud	3 11 30 39 44 52 61 85 93 105 113 116 118-120 124 135 137 142-145 151 156 161 164 170 179 182 185 197 200 204 211
Theism	87
Theology	21 43 47 48 51 54 56 65 72 79-81 83-92 94 123 127 144 159 167 179 180 185 189 191 201 203 205 215
Theology, Negative	64 75 85
Theology, Positive	75 85
Theory	25-27 30-32 47 89 90 112 167
Theory of Knowledge	see Epistemology
Tolerance	18 73 86 191 217

Torah	28 44 51 54 58 59 61 70 88
105 110 111 114 116 119 122
125 129 130 137 140 142-144
146 156 161 163-167 179 180
182 184 185 192 200 207 224
Tradition, traditional	11 48 89 92 113 116 119
120 121 140 151 152 159 160
162 170 179 181 182 185 192
210 213
Transcendental Idea	76 77
Truth(s)	3-5 11 16 18 19 25 43 44 49
51 54 55 58 59 61 63-65 68
83-85 87 88 94 105 131 135
146 154-157 163-165 172 175-176
179 181 187 188 191 200 217
Understanding	25-27 29 60 71 114 153
Universe	15 25 28-32 40 47 49 51 57
60 65 83-85 113 123 128 142
151 152 171 183 185 192
Value(s)	25-27 31 33 58 65 77 101 116
143 164 181
Value Judgment	60 65 221 224
Vienna Circle	6 98
Wisdom	3 4 5 13 15 26 27 28 29 31
51 52 54 63 75 105 141 146
153 160 165 171 197
Wonder	5 40 151-154 157
Young Hegelians	79
Zionism, Zionist	118 204-206 208 212-214

Einstein, Albert

ÜBER DEN FRIEDEN. WELTORDNUNG ODER WELTUNTERGANG?

665 S. inkl. 13 Fotographien und Faksimiles.
ISBN 3 261 01384 2   hardback US $ 17.20 / sFr. 27.50

Recommended prices - alterations reserved

Erste deutsche Originalausgabe
Herausgegeben von Otto Nathan und Heinz Norden
Vorwort von Bertrand Russell

Dieses Buch vereinigt alle Schriften, Reden und Briefe Albert Einsteins über Krieg und Frieden. Es enthält viele seit langem historisch gewordene Dokumente, wie den berühmten Briefwechsel, der zwischen Einstein und Freud über "Warum Krieg" kurz vor Hitlers Machtergreifung stattfand, und den Briefwechsel zwischen Einstein und Bertrand Russel kurz vor Einsteins Tod. Das Buch zeigt, wie einer der Grössten seiner Generation unablässig und mit seltener Hingabe für die totale Abschaffung des Krieges gekämpft hat. In gewissem Sinne ist das Buch eine Geschichte der Friedensbewegung vom Ausbruch des Ersten Weltkrieges bis zu Einsteins Tod im Jahre 1955, denn in dieser Zeitspanne gab es kaum eine Aktion für wirklichen Frieden in der Welt, an der Einstein nicht beteiligt war.

PETER LANG PUBLISHING, INC.
62 West 45th Street
USA - New York, NY 10036

Flusser, David

DIE RABBINISCHEN GLEICHNISSE UND DER GLEICHNISERZÄHLER JESU

Judaica et Christiana, Bd. 4
ISBN 3-261-04778-X   336 pp.   US $ 31.60

Recommended prices - alterations reserved

Der hochbegabte, auch in der christlichen Wissenschaft weltweit anerkannte jüdische Jesusforscher David Flusser legt eine neu akzentuierende und die christliche Forschung korrigierende Interpretation der Gleichnisse Jesu vor. Ausserdem verfasst er eine Geschichte der jüdischen und teilweise auch der griechischen Gattung der Gleichnisse. Auf Grund seiner immensen Kenntnis der rabbinischen Literatur ("... das Meer des Talmuds, das niemand durchschwimmen vermag ...") kann er christlichen Gleichnisforschern in vielen Fragen begründet widersprechen. Flussers Kritiken beinhalten keine gegenchristliche Nivellierungen Jesus.

Er bringt Jesu als meisterhaften Gleichniserzähler deutlich und eindrücklich ins Bild.

PETER LANG PUBLISHING, INC.
62 West 45th Street
USA - New York, NY 10036

Hirsch, Helmut

MARX UND MOSES
Karl Marx zur 'Judenfrage' und zu Juden

Judentum und Umwelt, Bd. 2
ISBN 3-8204-6041-1   181 S.   br. US $ 18.85 / sFr. 32.00

Recommended prices - alterations reserved

Der Autor widerlegt die extremen Positionen, wonach Karl Marx "ausgesprochener Antisemit" war (Edmund Silberner) oder "mit seiner genialen Fragestellung den Kern des Problems traf" (Otto Heller), indem er mittels einer breiteren, entwicklungsgeschichtlichen Analyse der einschlägigen Publikationen und brieflichen Aeusserungen beweist, dass Marxens Haltung gegenüber den "Stammesgenossen" - wie es auf anderen Gebieten bei ihm auch der Fall ist - recht komplex und zum mindesten ambivalent war.

Aus dem Inhalt: Amerikanische Aspekte - Auseinandersetzung mit Bauer - Bruch mit Ruge - Wie es wahrscheinlich geworden - Die Kölner Petition - Die Trierer Petition u.a. Dokumente.

PETER LANG PUBLISHING, INC.
62 West 45th Street
USA - New York, NY 10036

Laifer, Miryam

EDMOND JABÈS:
Un Judaisme Après Dieu

American University Studies: Series 2, Romance Language and Literature, Vol. 39
ISBN 0-8204-0283-4   151 p.   relié $ 33.70/sFr. 59.00

Recommended prices - alterations reserved

Ce livre est une étude du Judaisme dans l'oeuvre d'Edmond Jabès. Le Judaisme lie tous les différents thèmes des livres d'Edmond Jabès ensemble: le désert, l'amour, l'Holocauste, les échos mystiques et l'écriture. Jabès utilise la permutation des vocables jusqu'à leur éclatement comme les Kabbalistes dans leur recherche de la connaissance de Dieu. Pour Jabès le Judaisme ets une interrogation sans fin qui prend place dans le livre à travers les questions, les aphorismes et les commentaires.

Contenu: Judaisme à travers le désert, l'amour, l'Holocaust, les Échos Mystiques et l'écriture.

... a work of comprehensive range and scope... rigorous and acute in its argumentation and analysis (Wendell S. Dietrich, Brown University).

PETER LANG PUBLISHING, INC.
62 West 45th Street
USA - New York, NY 10036

Oberparleiter, Hermann

MARTIN BUBER UND DIE PHILOSOPHIE
Die Auseinandersetzung Martin Bubers mit der wissenschaftlichen Philosophie

Judentum und Umwelt, Bd. 7
ISBN 0-8204-7938-4   117 S.   br. US $ 17.20 / sFr. 27.00

Recommended prices - alterations reserved

Martin Bubers zentrales Problem ist das Problem der Lehre. Alle Lehre ist Vermittlung, das Leben aber ist unmittelbar. Dies ist der Widerspruch, in dem sich Bubers Denken befindet. Da nun der Weg der Lehre nicht anders sein kann als der Weg des Lebens, so muss das Prinzip der Wirklichkeit auch das Prinzip der Vermittlung sein, wenn das volle menschliche Leben vermittelt werden soll. Diese volle Vermittlungskraft traut Buber daher nicht dem Denken allein, sondern nur dem Leben selbst zu. Damit erlangt das Erlebnis für das Werden des Menschen eine grundsätzliche Bedeutung. Der Weg der Lehre ist also nicht der zur Ausübung einer Erkenntnis, sondern der zur Erfüllung in einem zentralen Menschenleben (Tao). Buber strebt darum eine umfassendere als nur die der bewusstseinsbildenden Vermittlung westlicher Bildung an.

Aus dem Inhalt: U.a. Philosophie und Wirklichkeit – Erkennen und Erleben – Die ursprüngliche Aufgabe der Philosophie – Reine lebendige und faktische objektivierte Vernunft.

PETER LANG PUBLISHING, INC.
62 West 45th Street
USA - New York, NY 10036

Seidel, Esther I.

«JÜDISCHE PHILOSOPHIE» IN NICHTJÜDISCHER UND JÜDISCHER PHILOSOPHIEGESCHICHTSSCHREIBUNG

Europäische Hochschulschriften: Reihe 20, Philosophie, Bd. 116
ISBN 3-8204-7746-2   223 S.   br. US $ 27.35 / sFr. 52.00

Recommended prices - alterations reserved

Durch einen Vergleich nicht-jüdischer und jüdischer Philosophiegeschichten werden unterschiedliche Behandlungsweisen und vielfältige inhaltliche Ausprägungen von «jüdischer Philosophie» vor dem Hintergrund der jeweils vertretenen philosophischen Haltung wie auch des religiösen Standpunkts der einzelnen Philosophiehistoriker aufgezeigt. Darüber hinaus werden Anregungen gegeben für mögliche Definitionen dessen, was «jüdische Philosophie» zu beinhalten hätte, und wie die künftige philosophiehistorische Forschung, jüdische wie nicht-jüdische, die gewonnenen unterschiedlichen Konzeptionen für Darstellung, Beurteilung und Einordnung in das Gesamt der Philosophiegeschichte berücksichtigen und fruchtbar machen könnte.

Aus dem Inhalt: U.a. «Jüdische Philosophie» in den Philosophiegeschichten Bruckers, der Kantianer, der Schleiermacher-Schule, bei Hegel und seinen Schülern - Aus jüdischer Sicht: im deutschen Sprachraum (Breslauer Schule, J. Guttmann), in den USA und in Israel.

PETER LANG PUBLISHING, INC.
62 West 45th Street
USA - New York, NY 10036